KEEPERS

WHAT VALUE DO TITLES HAVE *in a post-deferential age that seeks equality and fairness for all? If the incumbent expects a bended knee, then not much to a fast-changing world. But that very evolution creates its own utilitarian needs and thereby throws up a fresh demand for appointment titles and status to suit the time. Precedence of some sort exists in every part of the world. Sometimes it hinges on wealth, friendship or age, but the United Kingdom has chosen to keep history as a principal influence in this choice. This may be eccentric, it may seem wrong to many, but it has left an accretion of clues wrapped into each title that transports us back in time to tell us a story of our past. The core thread running through every title and appointment ever created in this, the world's broadest collection of surviving treasures, was the intent, at the time of creation, to make a better life for all.*

ALASTAIR BRUCE

KEEPERS

THE ANCIENT OFFICES OF BRITAIN

Alastair Bruce ✦ Julian Calder
Mark Cator

jcp

CONTENTS

The Sovereign is attended by Pages of Honour, wearing the monarch's scarlet livery and armed with a court sword, whenever the trains of robes or mantles need to be carried. This was originally a position of cadetship for those destined for powerful positions in the court.

This In-Pensioner sits with his memories in the panelled Long Wards that Sir Christopher Wren built in the Royal Hospital, Chelsea, to accommodate the king's old soldiers. On his chest are the medals that proclaim stories his generation seldom told of, concerning service in the First and Second World Wars. At their head gleams the Military Medal, which demanded courage that only his eyes hint at still. Once these Long Wards contained cramped berths with beds and straw mattresses. These conditions have improved greatly but the fraternity of these 17th-century communities still meets the needs of every military generation with memories of service to remember and affirm.

This is where the Queen works each day. Balmoral is also the place where she takes her annual holiday. In the year of the 60th anniversary of her coronation and comfortably in her eighties, there is no let up in the flow of papers demanding attention from the 16 realms of which she is Head of State and a Commonwealth of Nations once ruled by

her forebear, Queen Victoria. Her picture and that of her husband, Prince Albert, who designed this castle, look down from the walls of a room where they also once worked. Hers is the Kingdom and she 'keeps' this continuity in sacred trust: this book is dedicated by the three of us to the way she lives that trust by just quietly getting on with it.

INTRODUCTION

History has left its mark all around Britain. The story of these islands can be read in scars on the landscape, old buildings, institutions, books, pictures, and in a wealth of archive material. But it also lives today in the people who hold a collection of odd appointments, names and titles that were established hundreds of years ago. The desire to uncover and revive some of the historic clues that are vested in these reminders of the past was the impetus for this book.

Despite the rapid pace of modernization, Britain still has the broadest spectrum of extant appointments in the world. This is partly because there has been no conquest since 1066 and also because the monarchy continues, changing but constant. This book describes the holders of over 100 such posts. Many of them still play a role on the national stage, while others do little more than carry their strange titles.

Quite often the bearers of historic posts have no idea of their provenance. Time has worn out the purpose of most of these jobs, but in every case there was once a real need for them. Each tells a story, whether of post-Roman Britain, the evolution of our separate kingdoms, the union of the country or the growth of empire. Most of the appointments no longer carry any real power, but they have survived because there has been no pressing need to destroy them. No revolution has ever completely swept aside the old order; instead, succeeding events have concealed history.

Since the first two editions of Keepers of the Kingdom *were published in 1999 and 2002, some of the appointments have disappeared. This is a natural process, hastened by a change in the national mood, which was moving away from an enjoyment of seemingly anachronistic traditions. Few may mourn when old appointments are swept away, and fewer still may regret the constitutional changes that have reduced the powers of hereditary Lords. But none would applaud a similar destruction of architectural treasures that speak so eloquently of a shared past. By recording our culture's many ancient offices, this book seeks to preserve a fascinating aspect of our past, in case it disappears from view.*

In this Diamond Jubilee year of her coronation, the Queen has just got on with the job that was implied by the Coronation Oath in the aftermath of her father King George VI's death. She has brought further to the fore her heir and his eldest son. Just as she took on the role from her father, and he ultimately from his, so she has nurtured the office for those who will follow. Since the last edition, Prince William of Wales, now Duke of Cambridge, was created the 1,000th Knight Companion of the Most Noble Order of the Garter. He is included in this collection standing where his grandmother invested him with the Garter that he holds. This is to evoke the moment when the order is supposed to have been created in 1348, when Edward III created his son, the Black Prince, the first knight by an act of investiture. For the monarch's office, an implicit duty is to ensure the future is sure and, while the nation ceaselessly debates its attitudes to monarchy, there seems to be no real sign of laying it aside. Far from it: the example of this incumbent of office has brought forth a warm celebration for the 60th year.

Hidden behind some of the ancient titles and rituals that exist to this day are stories of ordinary people who did extraordinary things. The titles that arose from their actions offer clues as to how power was wrested from kings and placed in elected

[10]

representatives, leading to the parliamentary democracy we now enjoy.

Ancient titles survive because the monarchy continues. For example, Britain has a Chancellor of the Exchequer rather than a more prosaically named Finance Minister, but the responsibilities of the two are indistinguishable. The Lord High Admiral of the Wash, on the other hand, no longer has any duties: his title merely provides a clue to part of Britain's past, when it was his responsibility to keep the coastline safe from invasion. This task was already obsolete in the 16th century, when a properly organized navy assumed that duty, and these days satellite and electronic surveillance does the job. Typically, no one ever formally announced an end to the Admiral's role – there seemed no need.

Reactions to ancient titles in Britain today are mixed. The idea of men and women in ceremonial costume performing odd rituals sometimes provokes derision. It is some-times said that without titles the nation would rise above the burden of its class history, and that it would be better if archaic names, such as First Sea Lord, were dropped in favour of something more modern, such as Chief of Staff (Navy). Very sadly, our attempt to include in this edition the new appointment of Lord Speaker of the House of Lords, which was first adopted by election in 2006, was turned down. Perhaps some institutions or incumbents of great office still find the traditions of the nation distract from the core business of delivery. However, on the whole, most office holders seem comfortable to prosecute a profoundly reforming and modernizing zeal, within the framework of history's traditions, reassured that Britain's lofty past reminds us that change was ever part of the story.

Some argue that if power is under democratic control, there can be no harm in the survival of traditions that enable us to understand our past, particularly when they are self-funding. Britain possesses something that many other countries seem to covet. It is understood that preserving history within an evolving structure provides a valuable fingerprint, which has touched almost every one of us living in these islands. This print survives because the country has modernized without feeling the need to rid itself of its past: it may often dislike that past, even detest it, but confidence in the future is sometimes best measured by a country's ability to live at ease with its history.

The kingdoms that became Britain have wisely maintained their individual iden-tities, and their history remains available to all of us. The anecdotes associated with them and their sometimes bizarre appointments bear retelling: people enjoy a good story, and in the process may come to understand and respect little-known aspects of the past. Over the 60 years of the current Elizabethan Age few have attempted to share these stories. The holders of some appointments forget that their privilege involves a responsibility to explain and perhaps share the significance of their roles, and this has rightly earned the indignation of an excluded public. If the background to historic titles goes unexplained and people remain unaware of them, we will all eventually become alienated from our own historic inheritance.

This book clearly shows that the past can illuminate the present. Every ti-tle described in these pages reveals something of the nations and communities that currently form the United Kingdom of Great Britain and Northern Ireland, the Channel Islands and other Realms. Each title holder shares with us the history that they embody. Their stories belong to each and every one of us.

Britain's civilization developed from seeds that germinated in the disorder left by Rome's withdrawal at the onset of the 5th century. This disintegration of order and the tribal power struggles that followed were further stirred by the arrival of barbarian immigrants from the Continent.

Power was the key to forming unity from anarchy. The leaders who emerged were mostly proven warriors who held sway for as long as they were victorious. This changed in the four centuries that followed as brawn gave way to statecraft, and a structure of kingdoms developed known as the Heptarchy. Kings demonstrated power by patronage, forming a loyal administration founded on the understanding that what was given could be taken away. The Heptarchic kingdoms developed systems for passing power from generation to generation, in which laws of heredity were justified by religion, and patronage was distributed with rights of inheritance. Land was divided into areas, called hundreds, and the Saxon kings appointed 'reeves' (administrators of land for the owner) to enforce their rule. Among them were shire reeves (sheriffs), who enforced the law and gathered revenues.

From around 789, the Anglo-Saxon Chronicle records regular invasions of Viking warriors, who settled wherever they could land, particularly among the islands of Scotland and north-west England.

The Isle of Man was one such strategic location, providing easy raiding access to the wealthy shores of England and Ireland. The Vikings who settled in the north-east of England were kept at bay by payment of the Danegeld, a punitive tax.

With the end of the time of chaos went the beliefs of the ancients. However, pre-pagan rituals, such as Saturnalia, were adopted by Christian missionaries, including the first Archbishop of Canterbury, who converted the Saxon courts. This brought about the elevation of children at Christian festivals, such as the making of Boy Bishops. In Scotland, Ireland and Wales, Saints Columba, Patrick and David placed their indelible print upon subsequent offices.

The Heptarchy ultimately unified under the kings of Wessex and enshrined a democracy, albeit limited, in the Witenagemot, or council, that surrounded the king. St Dunstan, Archbishop of Canterbury, skilfully devised a coronation ceremony in 973 for Edgar, King of Wessex, that pleased both clerics and sheriffs. In the words of the Anglo-Saxon Chronicle, 'Here Edgar was (of Angles wielder!) with mickle pomp to king yhallowed in the old borough Acheman's-chester, but those that dwell there in other word Bath name it. There was bliss mickle on that happy day caused to all which sons of men name and call Pentecost-day. There was of priests a heap, of monks much crowd, I understand, of wise ones gathered.' The ceremony remains essentially the same to this day, placing the king's authority subject to God, which was granted only with the Witan's will. The Church thrived, as did the sheriffs.

The influence of feudal government touched everything. It was this, and the agrarian riches of England, that William, Duke of Normandy, won by conquest in 1066. The Conqueror ensured that the Witan approved his claim to the throne, and that Dunstan's ritual was used at his coronation to garner increased legitimacy for his conquest. He then used feudal power to dominate a defeated people. All land was his, and was managed by others subject to his will and terms. Successful Norman knights were rewarded with manors and acreage, and in return they became responsible for enforcing William's laws, gathering his dues and providing whatever services he might demand, generally to provide soldiers to defend the country and fight enemies abroad. This duty was called Sergeanty.

Government with reference to a council continued under Norman kings, though the Saxon magnates were soon 'cleansed' from the Witan, and Normans formed a new Curia Regis. The Byzantines had developed a feudal system of government distributing royal authority to Great Officers, and it was this that William I adopted. The Great Officers of State are still part of the constitutional arrangements in both England and Scotland.

The English Great Officers included the Lord High Steward, the Lord High Constable, the Lord High Chancellor, a secretary in Norman times, and the Marshal. The latter, originally right-hand man to the Constable in handling military matters, is now Earl Marshal and remains the architect for England's greatest State occasions. Then there is the Chamberlain, who looked after personal administration, and the Almoner, who passed on the monarch's obligatory largesse. All these roles survive, though it is only at coronations that the title holders are gathered together. They ensure that the monarch to be crowned is the selection of the country, according to law, and after the crowning they 'lift' the Sovereign into the Throne: the symbolic moment when possession is taken of the kingdom. The importance of the king's treasury grew and with it came the office of Lord Treasurer. The story of how this office evolved into the commissioned appointment of First Lord of the Treasury gives us a link from the deep past to the role of Prime Minister today.

Under the Normans, forests, which were common ground in Saxon times, became private playgrounds for the king and his nobles, and wardens were appointed for forests such as Savernake in Wiltshire and the New Forest in Hampshire to enforce unique Forest Laws. Norman knights expropriated farther territory; when the treaty with Wales expired, the small, mountainous principality was also ripe for conquest, and the king supported the Marcher Barons in their quest to seize power and wealth in new territory.

The Saxons and Normans in these first steps unified the land under one system of effective royal government. To develop and administer the country, they established appointments whose holders derived their authority and their titular names from the land itself. Agricultural revenue was organized so that it passed from the peasant farmer up through a chain of tenants to the king. Just as the Conqueror's feudalism used Great Officers to govern the kingdom, so a similar grouping of officers was employed at every level down to the manor: a system that was to be the norm for seven centuries.

The evolution of power from the hands of many leaders into those of a single king followed a predictable path. Supremacy was attained gradually by a combination of treaty, defeat and consent. The process depended upon loyalty, and rested upon the need for legitimate status and continuity. This right to wield power was considered ultimately to come, through religious ceremonies, from God; and the motto of the British monarch, 'Dieu et mon Droit', 'God and my right', still echoes this idea today.

GRAND BARD AND CORNISH GORSEDD
(GORSETH BJRTH KERNOW)

Many people in Britain are Celts to some degree. Irrespective of the number, we are surrounded by a rich Celtic culture and during the last century enthusiasts have revived the Bardic Orders to keep these traditions alive. ¶ Celtic words fill the English language and their place names can be found everywhere. In addition the art work, carving and craft inspired by these ancestors are great influences on contemporary design. Celts occupied the central and western parts of Europe and, though the facts are difficult to ascertain, evidence suggests that the Celtic migrants arrived from Spain, first in Ireland and then on mainland Britain, between the 6th and 5th century BC. ¶ Living now in a century of renewed ethnic awareness, it is worth reflecting on how much cultural integration happened in these islands before. In every case there is always a rich cultural seam to mine and evidence suggests a good mix occurs where art, literature and ideas are shared. Along with the ancient Britons, the Celts formed one of the founder races and they mixed over a thousand years with Romans, Angles, Jutes and Saxons. ¶ The Celts developed a great artistic identity. Their craftsmanship, ingenuity and adventurousness were matched by their literature, as if different humanities fed from each other. It was a race that celebrated learning and wisdom through a ritual celebration of both. The Bards, who were poets, led this process and they versed everything, including the legends of history. Unfortunately, the Anglo-Saxon and Norse invasions pushed the Celts to the far west of Britain, particularly to Wales: a country named by the invaders from a word which means 'foreign'. ¶ In 926 King Athelstan fixed the boundary of the 'West Welsh' as the River Tamar, and this remains the boundary of Cornwall. Use of Brythonic Cornish gradually dwindled and, while there is evidence that in Elizabeth I's reign it was still quite widely spoken, the Reformation struck a heavy blow because no effort was made to translate the new prayer book into the language. ¶ There had been no Bardic Order in Cornwall since the 12th century but, with support from the 'Mother Gorsedd' of Wales, the Gorsedd of the Bards of Cornwall was revived at the traditional site of Boscawen in Un, near Land's End, in 1928. It meets annually on the first Saturday in September, on sites throughout Cornwall, and is opened by the blowing of the *Corn Gwlas* (Horn of the Nation). The Bards wear simple blue robes with the Grand Bard adorned in a crown and plastron. Specially invited guests then compete in rhyme and performance for awards of both literary and musical merit. Their intention is to 'maintain the national Celtic spirit of Cornwall; to encourage the study of literature, art, music and history in Cornwall; to encourage the study and use of the Cornish language; to link Cornwall with the other Celtic countries; and to promote co-operation amongst those who work for the honour of Cornwall'. ¶ Ceremonies begin with the sounding of the symbolic horn, which calls to the four points of the compass. A specially selected Lady of Cornwall makes an offering of Fruits of the Earth and children dance to harp music before the Grand Bard receives new Bards into the Gorsedd. It is a pastiche which seeks to rediscover lost culture, and its system of customs has evolved to meet this need.

Among more than 200 ancient stone circles and monuments in Cornwall, which are older than the Egyptian pyramids, is the spiritual monument of Carn Brae, above Redruth. The Gorsedd's regalia is made from beaten copper with Celtic designs on a background of knotwork. The Grand Bard leads her followers as they watch the sun set.

BARON OF THE BACHUIL, KEEPER OF THE BACHUIL

The earliest missionaries faced great danger when they sought to convert Britain to Christianity. Many are the stories of their courage and frequent are those of their execution. In most parts of the land, pagan or ancient rites were performed by different tribes seeking the answers that eternally vex mankind. The conversion of what is now known as Scotland was greatly enhanced by incoming missionaries from Dalriada, an Irish kingdom that ultimately ceded itself into a kingdom by the same name in what is now Argyll. The name, Dalriada, declared that these determined immigrants and their religious devotion were the descendants of Riada. ¶ One of these missionaries was a monk, who was probably called Lugaidh, but this name evolved into Moluag, possibly because all his adherents claimed him in name as their own, hence 'my Luag'. He left Bangor in the north of Ireland and settled on the island of Lismore, in the middle of Loch Linnhe, on Scotland's west coast. In the north of the island, close to where there had been a settlement for generations, this saint established a community that gained influence and converts. ¶ It was a race that first brought St Moluag to Lismore in 569. He had competed against St Columba for ownership of the place. They were supposed to have been brothers but Columba's missionary zeal in Scotland, from the nearby island of Iona, is much better commemorated. Lismore was highly prized because it had been a sacred island to the western Picts and the burial place of their kings, and so the race had purpose for these two men, determined for their mission for Christianity to succeed. The two agreed that the first boat to reach the shore could claim the island. As the coracles came close, St Moluag supposedly chopped off his finger and threw it ashore in order to win. ¶ Inevitably, as time passed St Moluag was revered by the religious community that he established and so was the stick. It might have been his crozier but, as was often the practice, it gained importance in the following centuries as a relic. So important did it become that its guardianship also gained in status. What survives is a piece of blackthorn, just under three feet long, known as the Bachuil Mór, or Great Staff. ¶ When St Moluag died his descendants, know as 'Coarbs', became hereditary abbots of Lismore and thereby keepers of the Bachuil Mór. The title evolved from the original keepership into a feudal barony, probably in the 6th century under the kings of Dalriada, and it became known as the Baron of the Bachuil 'by the Grace of God', which the Scottish Parliament recognized in 1399. ¶ The guardianship of the Bachuil Mór passed from the religious community to those who led the defence and people of the island. It survived the iconoclasm of the Reformation, when its qualities as kindling might have proved more attractive than its ancient claims. But having survived centuries, today its protection rests with the Livingstone family, who still live on Lismore and hold the Barony of the Bachuil. ¶ The Bachuil Mór is rumoured to be able to protect men from the plague and assure safety at sea. Perhaps its most useful asset was that it could protect cattle from murrain. It is also supposed to have the power to find its way back to Lismore. Legend has it that one baron left it behind on the mainland; he realized his mistake as the boat landed back on Lismore when he heard a sound in the air of something rushing past. The object landed in the seaweed and, as he stopped to investigate, he saw it was the Bachuil Mór. The very presence of this simple stick had its effect on history. The great feudal lord of the area was the Earl of Argyll, but it was said that even he would bend his knee to the Baron of the Bachuil, who was the descendant of St Moluag and keeper of the holy crozier. In 1544 the Earl of Argyll, as Lord of Lorne, confirmed the privileges and title of the baron. In 2004 what is probably the oldest barony in Britain was reaffirmed in the Matriculation of Arms granted to Alastair Livingstone of Bachuil by Scotland's Lord Lyon King of Arms, on behalf of the Queen of Scots.

Kilted in Livingstone family tartan and standing on the north shore of the island of Lismore, which is where St Moluag landed after his journey from Ireland, the Baron of the Bachuil and Keeper of the Bachuil holds aloft the saint's Bachuil Mór.

SPEAKER OF TYNWALD

The world's oldest parliament in continuous use is on Tynwald Hill on the Isle of Man, off the north-west coast of England. On a plateau close to the town of Peel there is a small village called St John's. Here there is an open field with a church and, some distance to the west, a man-made mound. The provenance of the mound is not known: it could have been a burial site or a memorial to the Norse god Thor. It is made up of four large seat-sized steps with a flat top that is about six feet across. Whatever its origins, since the late 970s when Godred I was king, it has been a place of assembly where law is made and justice dispensed, while providing a forum for the Manx people to have their say. ¶ 'Tynwald' derives from a Norse word meaning 'parliament Weld', and the site's design is similar to that of a *thing-vollr* (law-hill), where Celtic chiefs were probably inaugurated according to the rite of tanistry, whereby power passed into a new chief when he stood over the burial site of former rulers. Tynwald consists of the Lord's Council (now called the Legislative Council), which was made up of officers appointed by the Lord of Mann, and the House of Keys, in which sat 'the worthiest men', there by dint of land owner-ship and family succession. Together with the Deemsters (judges of ancient origin) they offered advice to the Lord of Mann on the relevant law to assist him in making decisions or passing judgement. ¶ The Speaker is the principal officer of the lower chamber, the House of Keys, and is himself an elected Member of the House of Keys (MHK). He is chosen by fellow Members at the first sitting of the House after a General Election, in which all Isle of Man citizens over the age of 16 may vote. Since the origins of Tynwald the Speaker has acted as the spokesman of the House, but within its walls he is in con-trol of proceedings and has the last word on the interpretation of the House's Standing Orders, which govern the procedures that each of the three chambers must follow. The Speaker remains impartial, unless a motion reaches an impasse where there is an equal split of 'ayes' and 'noes', in which instance he votes to uphold the status quo. ¶ Every 5 July, Tynwald still assembles on the ancient hill, a gathering that brings the Manx community together. The year's legislation is read out by the Deemsters, and if any Act is not read out, it lapses immediately. Freemen look on while Coroners, Parish Captains, Members of the House of Keys and the Legislative Council gather to hear the prom-ulgation. ¶ There are three seats on the top level of Tynwald: the first is occupied by the Lieutenant-Governor representing the Lord of Mann (who, since 1765, has been the Sovereign); the second seat is the Lord Bishop's; and the third was added in 1990 for the President of Tynwald. This new appointment, decided by election, was created in response to the constitutional need both for a democratic representative of the people of Man and to separate the executive from the Sovereign's representative. Before the Sovereign became Lord of Mann, the Lordship was given in tenure. In token of his fe-alty he presented a cast (pair) of falcons at every monarch's coronation. ¶ The Vikings ruled Man until it was ceded to King Alexander III of Scotland in 1266. From 1405 until 1736 the Stanley family were Lords of Mann; for 29 years the Dukes of Atholl took over before the title was vested in the British Crown in 1765. None of these overlords chose to interfere with the Viking Parliament. The Manx respond to criticism of Tynwald by pointing out the stability it has given the island. As the records show, the names of its members have changed little over the centuries.

The Speaker of Tynwald's House of Keys stands on the earthen tiers of the Viking Parliament at St John's in the Isle of Man. This ancient tumulus is tiered for the Legislative Council and Members of the House of Keys to sit on at the annual July session.

HEREDITARY HIGH STEWARD OF THE LIBERTY OF ST EDMUND

The abbey town of Bury St Edmunds grew up around the legend of a local saint and national hero, Edmund. An early king of East Anglia, Edmund was a pious ruler, whose peaceful reign and virtuous life were cut short in 869 by marauding Danes. Although the English put up a valiant defence, they were outnumbered. Edmund was captured and, after refusing to renounce his faith or submit to his captors, was shot with arrows and beheaded. ¶ His life and death bore all the hallmarks of medieval sainthood - tried and tested virtue, martyrdom and miracles. Immediately after his death, his severed head, which had been tossed into a thicket, called out in Latin 'Here, here', until it was found and restored to its body. More miracles followed at his graveside: the sick were healed, the wronged righted and the evil punished. Before long, the saint's body was uprooted from the site of his martyrdom and ceremonially buried closer to the living in the nearby town of Beodricesworth, later named Saint Edmundsbury. ¶ News of the sainted king's worthy life and miraculous death spread through Christendom. His shrine drew the faithful from far and wide. Medieval pilgrims would often embark on tortuous and treacherous pilgrimage trails, seeking salvation, enlightenment and miracle cures. The main attraction at every pilgrimage site were holy relics – saintly remains – often just glimpsed through peepholes in a priceless reliquary. Far from being ghoulish trophies or sentimental keepsakes, relics were powerful talismans, charged with sacred charisma, with the saint's virtu, or holy power to work magic and change lives. ¶ Venerated pilgrimage sites like Bury went from strength to strength, attracting gifts from rich and poor. Donors gave sincerely, but also in a clear-sighted bid for salvation. Alms were part of holy currency – a good deed on Earth accrued interest in heaven. Religious donations also paid for the monks' devoted prayers – almost a guarantee of salvation. Small wonder, then, that the shrine of the sainted king should attract generous donations from great and royal patrons. King Cnut built a splendid Benedictine abbey in 1020, which in 1044 attracted another royal patron, Edward the Confessor, soon to be sainted himself. He helped house and support the brethren of the shrine by offering the royal manor of Mildenhall and a large liberty, or plot of freehold land. A generous gift, it covered eight and a half hundreds, or hides, so-called because 100 families were meant to live on one hide. ¶ The abbey grew in fame and fortune, inspiring reverence and patronage even from unlikely royal patrons, such as the Norman invader William I, who took a special interest in the abbey, partly due to his regard for the able Abbot Baldwin. Not only did William think to appoint a Steward to look after the liberty, he also paid for his services by providing the royal manors of Lidgate and Blunham. After the first Steward, named Ralph, the title passed through various hands, becoming hereditary with the De Windsors in 1115. The office passed to various distinguished local families – the Hastings in the 13th century and the Howards in the 16th. A powerful Roman Catholic family, the Howards fell from grace in 1688 when James II was ousted by his Protestant son-in-law, William of Orange. Having lost the power to hold office, the family was forced to sell to Thomas, Lord Jermyn. Passed down the line, the office finally came to rest with the Herveys, Marquesses of Bristol, who inherited in 1806. A local family, with deep roots in the area, the Herveys seem well placed to keep the ancient office and guard the hallowed ground of Bury's much-loved saint.

The Hereditary High Steward of the Liberty of St Edmund holds a cartulary, containing copies of grants made by various kings and popes to the Abbey of St Edmund, which is undated but probably comes from c. 1350-1375. He stands beside two of the four crossing piers that once supported the tower of the abbey begun in 1080 by Abbot Baldwin, at Bury St Edmunds in Suffolk. This is where St Edmund's body was enshrined; the fame and wealth this earned for the monastery led to special privileges from the Crown, including a 'liberty', or jurisdiction, over which his family has held stewardship for nearly two centuries, even though the ancient responsibilities have long since ceased.

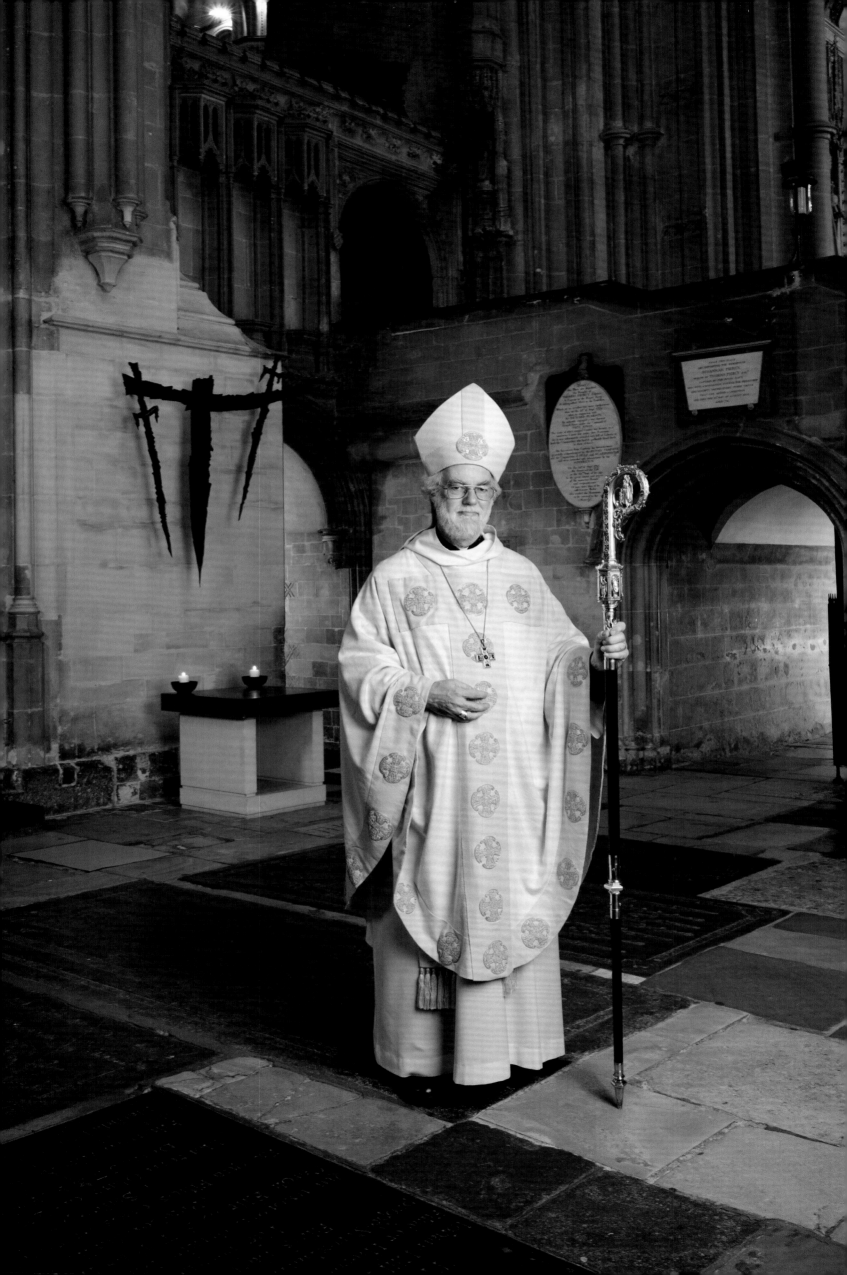

LORD ARCHBISHOP OF CANTERBURY AND PRIMATE OF ALL ENGLAND

In 597, around the time that the history of the Anglo-Saxon people was starting to take shape, St Augustine, with about 40 monks, arrived at Thanet in the south-east of England on a mission dispatched by Pope Gregory the Great. They faced a dangerous task, but at the court of Aethelbert of Kent the king's Frankish wife Bertha was a Christian and she made the monk from Rome welcome at the church of St Martin outside Canterbury. ¶ The mission was successful and, that same year, Augustine baptized the king and many of his people. In 601 a grateful Pope sent Augustine the Pallium, a simple scarf woven from lambs' wool that symbolized the Pascal lamb carried on the shoulders of the spiritual shepherd. It was also the symbol of his authority to act as Metropolitan over all the Christian churches in Britain. Augustine set up his cathedra, or episcopal seat, in Canterbury as the first Archbishop. A marble cathedra, probably 13th-century, still stands in the cathedral behind the high altar, and has been used to enthrone an uninterrupted line of successors to Augustine. ¶ One of the most famous incumbents of the see was Thomas Becket. As a clerk in the household of Archbishop Theobald he was groomed for high office. In 1154 he was appointed Chancellor to assist the young King Henry II. Immediately they built a strong friendship. Thomas raised taxes for the king's wars in France and fought for him on the battlefield. Believing this loyalty was his forever, against the wishes of the cathedral monks Henry appointed Thomas to the See of Canterbury when it fell vacant in 1162, hoping that Thomas would work with him to reduce the Church's power and privileges. But the king was outmanoeuvred, as Thomas began to oppose him on a range of issues, including the demand to bring the Church courts under secular authority. ¶ The king issued the Constitutions of Clarendon, which sought to assert secular law over the clergy, and to supervise their relationship with Rome. In 1164 he also brought charges against Thomas over his conduct as Chancellor. Thomas fled to France, hoping to gain papal support, returning in November 1170 with the dispute still unreconciled. A month later four knights, believing they would earn the king's favour, murdered the troublesome Archbishop in his cathedral as he was on his way to vespers. ¶ The murder sanctified Thomas and strengthened the Church, in particular the see of Canterbury. Pope Alexander made Henry do penance at Becket's tomb. By the Accord of Winchester in 1172, whereas England's other Archbishop, of York, would be *Angliae Primas* (Primate of England), the Archbishop of Canterbury became *totius Angliae Primas* (Primate of All England). Following Henry VIII's break with Rome in the 1530s, the monarch took over the role of the Pope in England. The new Church was anxious for effective leadership in difficult times, and it was Thomas Cranmer, as Archbishop of Canterbury, who played an important part in its reforms. Elizabeth I and her early Stuart successors recognized the importance of an episcopacy whose hierarchy they could control, and this too confirmed Canterbury's supremacy. ¶ Today, membership of the worldwide Anglican Communion still requires acknowledgement of Canterbury's position as 'first among equals', although some Anglicans from outside Britain challenge this because they feel excluded from the possibility of filling St Augustine's cathedra. In 2001 a new bishop, of Lambeth, was appointed to advise on this worldwide responsibility. The Archbishop presides over the Lambeth Conference, an assembly of Anglican Communion bishops held every 10 years.

Standing where four knights murdered St Thomas Becket by the north door of Canterbury Cathedral, the 104th Lord Archbishop of Canterbury and Primate of All England holds his episcopal crozier and the chasuble and mitre from the vestments that commemorate St Augustine, which are embroidered with the Canterbury cross, based on a Saxon brooch made c.850. The altar and sculpture bring a sense of unease to a place now known as the Martyrdom.

LORD PARAMOUNT OF HOLDERNESS

In the 19th century archers of the Lord Paramount of Holderness gathered at Flamborough Head on Bridlington Bay in Yorkshire and, for the last time, fired golden coins into the North Sea. Legend has it that the Lord of the Manor had once observed this custom every year, in order symbolically to ward off the return of the Danes. As he fired an arrow carrying this payment into the sea, he is supposed to have uttered the words, 'If there be a King of Denmark, this is our sign of loyalty.' ¶ Such a ritual, if indeed it took place, demonstrates the fear the Viking raids instilled over centuries in the men and women who lived on England's east coast. By 867 the Danes had established their rule over a large area of north and east England that became known, to the retreating Saxons, as the Danelaw. The coins the arrows carried represented Danegeld, a tax levied by the Anglo-Saxon kings from 868 to buy off the Danes. The Danegeld was raised again by Alfred the Great in 871 and regularized some 100 years later by Ethelred II, known as 'the Unready'. ¶ By the time the Danish ruler Canute was elected king of England at Southampton in 1016, the Danegeld no longer seemed necessary. Until 1163, however, it continued to be levied periodically, to raise funds for military campaigns. Indeed, it was in order to collect this tax that William the Conqueror compiled the Domesday Book. The Danelaw ceased to exist soon after the Norman Conquest. However, the unique administrative system introduced by the Danes, which divided shires into thirds, or ridings, and replaced Saxon hundreds with wapentakes, survived until relatively recent times. Danish customs from this region also survive and the jury system arguably evolved from Danish practice. ¶ The first Lord of Holderness was a beneficiary of the Norman Conquest. In the north of England discontent with Norman rule erupted into rebellion. William resolutely put down this uprising and redistributed the region's Danelaw land to his friends. Among them was a Fleming named Drogo de la Beuvriere, who was married to William's niece. In 1071 Drogo was granted the lordship of the manor of Holderness, on the peninsula between the River Hull and Bridlington Bay. ¶ This rich prize was large enough to be subdivided into a number of lesser lordships, as a result of which the Lord of Holderness came to be described as Lord Paramount, in order to reflect his status of overlord. In return for the grant of this feu, William expected Drogo to provide him with 350 archers, mounted and on foot, whenever they were needed, and to supervise the gathering of taxes. Unfortunately Drogo was no model friend to his king. Not only did he kill his wife – possibly by accident – but he also embezzled money. Fearing the king's wrath, he escaped to the Continent before William realized what had happened. In 1086 the lordship was granted to the king's brother-in-law, Odo of Champagne. The title passed through various families until, in the 17th century, Charles II granted it to an ancestor of the Constable family, who still hold it. ¶ At its height Holderness was virtually a palatine, with its own courts, sheriff and coroner. The Lord Paramount was supreme within his demesne, receiving dues from all the lesser lordships. His courts had franchises over all shipwrecks, yielding a considerable income from the treacherous local seas, which are sprinkled liberally with the wreckage of vessels ancient and modern. With the motive of protecting such power, it is understandable that an early holder of the title might have instituted the superstitious custom of firing a coin of Danegeld into the sea – because no Lord Paramount would relish even the possibility of Viking longboats once more rounding Flamborough Head.

Below the cliffs of Flamborough Head and surrounded by three bowmen of the Burton Constable Company of Bowmen, the Lord Paramount of Holderness, with her son and heir, hands out gold coins to meet the obligation of the office.

LORD HIGH CHANCELLOR OF GREAT BRITAIN, KEEPER OF THE GREAT SEAL AND KEEPER OF THE ROYAL CONSCIENCE

In June 2003 Tony Blair abolished the office of Lord Chancellor in a press release, despite its place in history, dating back to the Norman kings, and its significant symbolic role in 'presiding' over Parliament for the Sovereign. This ended one of the subtle constitutional links between Parliament and the Head of State: something neither restored nor addressed in the replacement post of Lord Speaker of the House of Lords. Of course, 'abolition' proved impossible. Within days, the replacement Secretary of State for Justice had to resume the office of Lord Chancellor, in order for the House of Lords to convene. But this muddle only increased determination to see through change. At the heart of the plan was a sensible aspiration to stop one person being active in too many areas of the constitution. Unfortunately, rather than cleverly adapting where necessary and protecting history, the Executive acted in a manner equivalent to knocking down Canterbury Cathedral in order to erect a shopping mall. ¶ Powerful but illiterate Norman kings needed secretaries, and appointed a *Cancellarius*, or Chancellor, to the job. This was the name given by the courts of ancient Rome to a scribe who sat behind a trellis recording proceedings. From these humble beginnings, the post became the highest-ranking secular office in Britain, responsible for issues affecting the Executive, the Legislature and the Judiciary of which the Lord Chancellor is head. Monarchs have always appointed their Chancellors, though since executive power moved from the Crown to Cabinet government, this choice has been made on the advice of the Prime Minister, who then takes precedence beneath the Lord Chancellor. ¶ The advantage of literacy, a skill largely monopolized in medieval times by the Church, was that in a world of law driven by documents, reading and writing gave access to power. Saxon royalty legitimized its correspondence by using seals, a practice that William I continued. As these Great Seals were deposited with the Chancellor, every important document passed under his gaze. His scrutiny became a formalized responsibility when he was named Keeper of the Great Seal. When a new Chancellor is appointed, his powers do not become effective until the Sovereign hands over the Great Seal. The new one, first used in 2001, is still formed of two six-inch matrices, but no longer shows the monarch on horseback in impression. ¶ Few appointments can boast three saints called Thomas. Henry II appointed his mentor and friend, Thomas Becket, as Chancellor in 1155 – the first Englishman to achieve high office under Norman rule. The other two were Thomas de Cantilupe, who served Henry III, and Thomas More, who, when Speaker, was celebrated for standing up for the rights of the House of Commons to his predecessor, Cardinal Wolsey, the most powerful chancellor of them all. ¶ As Keeper of the Royal Conscience, the Chancellor assumes the Sovereign's responsibilities for those unable to help themselves. One commentator describes his duties thus: 'the general guardian of all infants, idiots and lunatics, and has the general superintendence of all charitable uses in the kingdom'. These responsibilities have now largely been farmed out to the courts. ¶ Today the Lord Chancellor remains the second most important Great Officer of State, after the Lord High Steward (an appointment with so much power that it is only appointed from sunrise to sunset on coronation day) but he is no longer much more than Secretary of State for Justice. That said, he still presents the Queen's Speech in the House of Lords at the beginning of each parliamentary session.

The Lord High Chancellor's symbol of office, the Great Seal of the Realm, rests beside him in the Salisbury Room of the House of Lords, as does a wax impression of the seal attached to Letters Patent. He is consequently Keeper of the Great Seal and traditionally carries it in the Lord Chancellor's Purse, which he holds in his left hand. Ministerial business is done using the red boxes that bear the name of his office.

DAME DE ROSEL AND BUTLER TO
THE DUKE OF NORMANDY

The ancient rules state that the Dame de Rosel, who lives in the north-eastern corner of Jersey, like all the Seigneurs before her must be ready at any time to ride into the sea, up to her stirrups, in order to meet the Duke of Normandy's boat. She must then carry the Duke ashore, so that the ducal feet remain dry. Throughout the visit she must be available, at close quarters, and serve as Butler. Finally, when the stay is over, she must ride back into the surf and convey her overlord back to his boat. ¶ This rule is a relic of the feudal system imposed so stringently following the Norman invasion. Fiefs, or areas of land, were granted to deserving knights, called Seigneurs, in return for services rendered to the overlord. Mostly these services amounted to providing the Duke with trained knights on demand, delivering revenue and maintaining order. Failure to fulfil these obligations would render the land forfeit. ¶ It was in 933 that the Channel Islands became part of Normandy. At that time, the barbarian northmen, or Normans, who had run amok through most of coastal Europe for four centuries, had only been recognized as legitimate settlers for 22 years. In a treaty between their chief, Rollo, and the king in France, Charles the Simple, the dukedom of Normandy was established. Following an unsuccessful invasion by the neighbouring Bretons, a primitive treaty annexed the Channel Islands to the new dukedom. The Dukes of Normandy became kings of England in 1066 and the duchy all but disappeared in the 13th century. But the British Sovereign still reigns over the Channel Islands and is affectionately referred to there as 'Our Duke'. Thus a close relationship exists between Britain and the Channel Islands, through the person of a shared monarch, with the islands remaining outside the United Kingdom. ¶ Ducal visits to the Channel Islands have always been rare and they still are, by modern standards. When they took place in medieval times, the journey was made by boat over the shortest navigable distance. This meant landing on the island's eastern shore, which faces the mainland. There are no deep harbours here; instead the coastline is made up of shallow tidal bays with beaches and occasional outcrops of rock. Such conditions are not without danger, so it was quite sensible to have support waiting on the shore to give assistance, especially as the boat needed to be kept off the rocks and far enough away so as not to beach itself in a falling tide. The Seigneur of Rosel's servants would have kept a constant vigil over his shoreline and the sight of a boat flying the ducal banner would probably have triggered the community into action. ¶ The name Rosel derives from the old French word *roseau*, meaning a 'reed', and was probably imported to Jersey by the first Norman settlers there. Ingram de Fourneaux was the first recorded Seigneur, and for one and a half centuries, it was held in fee by the Barentin family, after Henry III gave Drouet Barentin 10 livres of land and the manor in 1247. The Dame de Rosel's family, the Lemprières, came to the manor in 1376. This was when Raoul Lemprière was successful in petitioning Richard II for a special licence to leave Brittany and settle in Jersey. Most of the old feudal rules have been abolished, but a few rituals survive: when the Queen, as Duke, visits now, she arrives by plane, and at the bottom of the steps waits the Dame de Rosel who, as Butler, serves Duke Rollo's descendant.

For more than a thousand years the Seigneurs de Rosel have been ready to gallop into the sea, up to their horse's girth and stirrups, in order to carry the visiting Duke of Normandy ashore from the ducal boat. Traditionally, the vessel landed here, in Archirondel Bay, a favourite landing place for smugglers facing the shores of Normandy. The Dame de Rosel, pictured here wearing the red heraldic banner with three golden eagles, has inherited this feudal duty from her ancestors.

BOY BISHOP OF HEREFORD

The supreme sanctity and innocence of childhood is one of the central tenets of Christian philosophy. When Christ was asked by his disciples, 'Who is the greatest in the kingdom of heaven?' he called a child to his side and explained that unless they became like children they could not even enter its gates. Christ's birth was itself marred by the jealous rage of King Herod the Great, who ordered the massacre of all the young children in Bethlehem. Those murdered children became the Church's first martyrs, and the Feast of the Holy Innocents, as they were called, came to be celebrated soon after Christmas every year, on 28 December. ¶ On Holy Innocents' Day during the Middle Ages, the Church did much to elevate children symbolically, drawing precedent from the pagan rites embodied in the ancient Saturnalia of pre-Christian Rome. From the 13th century onwards it became customary for cathedral choristers to select one from their number to be appointed *Episcopus Puerorum* (Boy Bishop), also known as Bishop of the Choristers or Bishop of the Innocents. ¶ The Boy Bishop was nominated on 6 December, the Feast of St Nicholas. A period of theological preparation then took place until the Feast of the Holy Innocents, when the real Bishop handed over his pastoral staff to the child and installed him in the cathedra (bishop's throne). The Boy Bishop, assisted by two chorister Deacons, would preach a sermon, bless the people, then lead all the choristers around the cathedral close, singing carols to the priests for a reward of food or money. It is believed that this established the tradition of carol singers going from door to door. ¶ During the Reformation, this tradition of elevating the Innocent over his Episcopal master was thought to be demeaning to God and was therefore banned. Henry VIII's daughter, Mary I, removed the restriction, but it was reimposed during the reign of Elizabeth I. Only under Elizabeth II was it to be lifted on a more permanent basis. ¶ In December 1973 a Gift Service was held at Hereford Cathedral for the Church of England's Children's Society. To mark the event, the cathedral's staff reached back into history and revived the appointment of a Boy Bishop, thus turning the clock back to the years before Henry VIII's reign. ¶ The following year, John Eastaugh was appointed Lord Bishop of the diocese. Much taken with the idea of symbolically handing over his powers to a child, he proposed an annual appointment of Boy Bishop from among the cathedral's choristers, an idea that received support from the Dean and Chapter. Ten years later, ancient ceremonies last exercised in Tudor times were dusted down and the ritual took root. But it was in 1986, when the Royal Mail issued Christmas stamps depicting Hereford's Boy Bishop, that the appointment really came to the attention of the public, seemingly capturing the magic that marks Christmas while providing a colourful service full of symbolic meaning. ¶ The revival of this ancient tradition has added a new poignancy to Christmas at Hereford. At Evensong on the Feast of St Nicholas, a procession of candle-carrying choristers leads the Boy Bishop into the cathedral. The Lord Bishop hands over his crozier, relinquishing his authority to the child. To the words 'He hath put down the mighty from their seat: and hath exalted the humble and meek,' the Boy Bishop is installed in the Lord Bishop's throne, before blessing the people. Powerful and moving, the ceremony is a lesson in humility to all who witness it, and is a profound expression of the fragile nobility and wisdom of innocence.

The Episcopal robes, which have evolved from the symbols of Byzantium – mitre (a hat designed to symbolize the Holy Spirit's tongues of fire), crozier (a shepherd's crook for guiding believers), pectoral cross and cope – are given to the Boy Bishop in Hereford Cathedral during his brief incumbency. Sitting upon a small cathedra, or bishop's throne, the boy delivers his sermon on the Feast of St Nicholas. Behind is the tomb of a previous Lord Bishop.

VERDERERS AND AGISTERS
OF THE NEW FOREST

'Am I fascinated? Have I lost my senses? Where am I? Had I not a delightful wood here close to Winchester?' So asked the disoriented William the Conqueror, the keen hunter who had chased the Saxon kingdom into oblivion 20 years before. The words are supposed to have been said when the king discovered what Walkelin, his Bishop of Winchester, had done to the royal hunting forest of Hampage, just to the east of his capital city. Given permission to cut trees for three days to rebuild his cathedral, Walkelin took the king at his word and felled the entire wood. After such a surprise it is no wonder that one year later, the hunt-loving monarch was dead. The story goes on that, following the Conqueror's wishes, a New Forest was opened up for the pursuit of royal hunting in 1097. Whatever the real reason for its name, the vast acreage still enjoyed as a rural wilderness around Lyndhurst in Hampshire took up two pages in the Domesday Book. ¶ Forest Law came with the afforestation of the area. What had been a sparse wasteland on which Saxon monasteries eked out a living was cleared for the wild beasts of hart, hind and hare. Vigorous punishment was meted out to poachers or those stealing timber, an oppression of the hungry that became a source of great tension between the king and his people. To impose these penalties, the New Forest had its Attachment and Swainmote Court, where the Verderers' role was to record details of the offences. Their title derives from the French word *vert* ('green'), which had since Norman times meant any vegetation to feed or shelter deer. ¶ From early medieval times until the 1700s the Verderers' Court, which must be one of the oldest judicial bodies in the country, exercised the unique edicts of Forest Law upon the commoners of the New Forest. Forest Law finally ended with the Wild Creatures and Forest Laws Act in 1971, with the words, 'The forest law is hereby abrogated.' ¶ Another piece of legislation, the New Forest Act, was used to revise the Verderers' Court in 1877. After 150 years in disuetude, when the area had been exploited for timber for the Royal Navy's wooden ships, Parliament revived the institution to fulfil a very different brief. Deer were nearly exterminated in 1851, with pronounced effects upon the habitat, but the interests of a large area of common land owned by the Crown needed protection. To do the work, the Official Verderer, appointed by the Crown, was assisted by six Verderers elected by the registered Commoners. Today the court is made up of ten Verderers: the Official Verderer, five elected Verderers and four who each represent the Forestry Commission, the Minister of Agriculture, the Countryside Commission and Hampshire County Council. They are responsible for the health and welfare of the ponies, cattle, pigs and donkeys that the Commoners have rights to graze across the New Forest. They must also consider the various needs presented by Commoners and an increasing number of visitors, all of whom may attend any of the ten open meetings of the court and raise issues if they wish. ¶ Since the 12th century the Lord Warden of the Forest and the Verderers have been able to call upon the Agisters, who were mounted, to act as their agents in collecting all manner of fees and pannage from the Commoners who grazed their pigs on acorns in the autumn. Their chief task today is to tend to the animals legally at pasture. This is particularly important during long months of harsh weather. And it is no longer Norman kings who kill animals in the New Forest but speeding motorists. The five Agisters, all expert riders, are quickly on the scene tending to the injured animals and informing the owners.

The Verderers' Hall in Queen's House, Lyndhurst, is where the Verderers of the New Forest hold their Open Courts. The Official Verderer, standing, is the Sovereign's representative. Agisters are on call 24 hours a day, seven days a week, to respond to any problem involving livestock. Under the leadership of the Head Agister, they each have their own area of the forest and their own mark for 'tail marking' the ponies once a year.

PERSONS, UNLESS HAVING
BUSINESS BEFORE THE
COURT OF SWAINMOTE AND
ATTACHMENT, ARE TO KEEP
OUTSIDE THE BAR

KEEPERS OF THE CROWN LANDS OF
THE NEW FOREST

A mood for change swept out of Westminster after the General Election of 1997. The new Prime Minister, Tony Blair, led a reforming zeal that was supported by an enormous mandate, and the New Forest felt these winds of change. Within a few years of the New Labour Government taking office, plans were set to alter the way this wild terrain was managed and, after several extensive consultations, the New Forest, which was one of five forests described in the Domesday Book, became a National Park. ¶ This change secured for all people access and a sense of possession over the rich inheritance that had been nurtured for generations not only by the Crown's aristocratic guardians but also by the men who actually tended and kept the land and its wildlife. The latter have now become known by many as the Keepers of the Crown Lands and their work continues in the National Park today much as it always did. Almost all rural farmland in Britain is cared for by keepers, who manage wildlife, nurture game and help develop the environment for flora and fauna to thrive together. ¶ It is probable that when the Jutes settled in this area, having emigrated from what is now Denmark, they both cared for the land and exploited its resources with a similar instinct in order to survive and trade. At the same time, the West Saxon kings would hunt the land, while protecting the many hamlets that huddled around small churches. ¶ The Normans uprooted all this, razed the churches and many aspects of Anglo-Saxon life too. The new brush of conquest swept through the culture that had nurtured this environment because the new kings had clear aspirations for what this land was exclusively to provide. In the future it was specifically to deliver the sport they craved. The hardship that this self-interest caused to the uprooted population was not to be forgotten. Indeed, curses followed the eradication of livelihoods and the destruction of churches for the pursuit of royal sport. It led many to assume that this was why two of William the Conqueror's sons died in the forest, not least his heir William Rufus who was struck by an arrow while out hunting. ¶ In order to maintain the environment that best sustained the stock for hunting, the New Forest was subject to special administration under endless Royal Decrees and laws. Nothing was to harm the animals that one day might be the quarry for a day's sport. The New Forest was divided into bailiwicks, and documents from the reign of Henry VIII list the Keepers in these jurisdictions and the wood they were permitted to fell. To fell a tree without permission and thereby harm the habitat of the potential quarry was a capital offence. The bailiwicks include those of Burley, Brattamsley, Fritham, Inn and Godshill. ¶ The Keepers of the Crown Lands today face new environmental challenges, both enhanced but also threatened by the new sense of ownership that the status of National Park has placed upon the New Forest. The emphasis now placed on recreation over sanctuary has put ground-nesting birds at risk, for example. A close watch must be kept for damage caused by invading species such as muntjac, while Keepers have noticed the decline in the forest's songbird population likely caused by hen harriers. Each Keeper is encouraged to follow an individual specialist interest, such as reptiles or wetland habitats, and while some are university-educated, others come from generations of New Forest dwellers, inheriting a profound practical knowledge of their natural heritage. With instinctive skills and a deep perception for the needs of the land, acquired through nurture by the seasons, Keepers continue the tradition of their Jutish predecessors for wildlife and game husbandry.

The Keepers of the Crown Lands of the New Forest ensure enforcement of forest bye-laws. As Special Constables they have powers to deal with civil offences in addition to their responsibilities for the wildlife.

LORD WARDEN OF THE CINQUE PORTS AND
ADMIRAL OF THE CINQUE PORTS

When Winston Churchill was appointed Lord Warden of the Cinque Ports in 1941, in the dark days of the Second World War, Britain was facing invasion. As the country's resolute wartime Prime Minister, Churchill was a wise choice by King George VI for this most ancient appointment, established to coordinate the defence of England's vulnerable south-east coast. *The Times* commented, 'to this august tradition of Keeper of the Gates of England and Watcher of the English Seas, Mr Churchill now succeeds ... As the dauntless leader of the Nation in the moment of its greatest peril he can wear the symbolic dignity as no other man can do.' ¶ As the name suggests, the Cinque Ports originally formed a group of five – *cinq* in French, which in this case the English pronounce 'sink'. They were a creation of military logic whose foundation pre-dates any records, though the original five ports – Hastings, Romney, Hythe, Dover and Sandwich – are described in an extant Charter as existing as a federation in the reign of Edward the Confessor. Collectively these ports were known as the 'head'; by the 14th century Winchelsea and Rye had also joined them. Meanwhile over 30 other ports became 'limbs', each associated with a particular head port, and often at some distance. For example, Brightlingsea (north of the Thames, in Essex), Sarre (north Kent) and Fordwich (well inland, on the River Stour) were Sandwich Limbs – and each year their Mayor Deputies still pay token 'Ship Money' to the Mayor of Sandwich. ¶ There was no official navy during the medieval period, and the ships of the Cinque Ports effectively provided this service for the nation. According to a feudal agreement formalized in the 11th century, the Cinque Ports Confederation was expected to provide whatever ships and sailors the king needed for battle. Its vessels occasionally sailed towards enemy ships, lashed together so that the combatants could fight it out on the open decks. The Cinque Ports navy was so successful at controlling access to the south-east coast, and at generating revenue, that it became a law unto itself. Useful in war, it went on fighting in peace, in flagrant acts of piracy. By the 13th century it became imperative to place the confederation under formal authority. To achieve a strategic all-round defence, based at Dover, there had to be a coordinated policy under a single command, which lay with the Lord Warden, a post established in 1268, who acted as a virtual palatine governor within his considerable domain. ¶ Under a Royal Charter of 1278, a good feudal bargain was struck between the monarch and these towns. For their part, the Cinque Ports would generate harbour revenue for the national exchequer. They would also provide England's navy with ships and men to patrol the Channel and secure the kingdom from invasion, and to convey armies to the Continent. This was a massive commitment, which continued until the creation of a permanent navy in Tudor times. In return, the Crown gave a degree of independence and considerable judicial privileges. These included exemption from tax and tallage, along with such odd-sounding legal powers as 'soc and sac, tol and team, blodwit and fledwit, pillory, tumbril, infangentheof, outfangentheof, waives and strays, flotsam and jetsam and ligan' – in other words, extensive powers of local jurisdiction, of collecting taxes and tolls, the authority to try cases involving bloodshed, fugitives from justice and thieves, and the right to keep unclaimed goods, wreckage and salvage. The ports also acquired the right to hold a portmote, or parliament, to which came representative mayors from each of the original five and the two 'ancient towns' of Winchelsea and Rye. ¶ The last time the Cinque Ports were active as a naval power was during the defeat of the Spanish Armada, in 1588, when Dover provided a ship manned by several hundred men to serve alongside others commanded by Sir Francis Drake. ¶ As Admiral of the Cinque Ports, the Warden also exercised full maritime jurisdiction. The coastline faces out over what has become one of the busiest sea passages in the world, and some of the maritime laws of the ancient Cinque Ports still apply in this infamous sea lane. ¶ The nation's defence policy has long since ceased to rely upon the contribution of the Cinque Ports. Gradually the shape of the coast has changed, through erosion, flooding and the accumulation of

silt. All of the seven head ports but Dover are now silted up; some are even inland since the shore shifted position. Today the post of Lord Warden is only titular, but it is considered a distinguished honour and is conferred by the Sovereign for service to the Crown. There is an official residence at Walmer Castle, a fortress built by Henry VIII between Dover and Sandwich. ¶ The title has been borne by many great figures, including Churchill. It seemed doubly fitting that the Lord Warden appointed in 1978 was Queen Elizabeth, the Queen Mother, who, as a contemporary of Churchill, acted as a very involved Queen Consort to George VI throughout the Second World War.

Cannon placed on the battlements of Walmer Castle, near Deal in Kent, look out across the English Channel towards France. This was once part of England's most secure line of defence against attack from the Continent. It was one of the fortresses built by Henry VIII to bolster the ancient Cinque Ports. Today, it remains the official residence of the Lord Warden of the Cinque Ports, who is also Constable of Dover Castle and Admiral of the Cinque Ports. The Silver Oar, the symbol of her centuries-old jurisdiction, is engraved with her special cypher. She wears a brooch, showing the Lord Warden's Oar within a golden chain.

QUEEN'S CHAMPION, LORD OF THE MANOR OF SCRIVELSBY

The manor of Scrivelsby Court in Lincolnshire has been neither bought nor sold since it was given by William the Conqueror to his friend Robert Marmion after the Battle of Hastings in 1066. It remains in the hands of Marmion's descendants, but the house has changed a good deal. Nonetheless, it bears witness to one of the most romantic family stories in the kingdom. ¶ From here, at most coronations and in order to fulfil the terms of the Conqueror's grant, knights have ridden as Royal Champions to Westminster, ready to stand and die for their monarch. In the words of the grant, written in Edward III's reign: 'The manour of Scrivelsby is holden by Grand Sergeanty, to wit, by the service of finding on the day of Coronation, an armed knight who shall prove by his body, if need be, that the King is true and rightful heir to the kingdom.' ¶ Norman justice offered the bizarre appeal process of trial by combat, in which people could prove their innocence by felling a fully armed knight without appropriate weaponry. The Dukes of Normandy made use of specially selected knights to stand in and do combat on their behalf, especially to challenge anyone doubting their right to rule. Robert Marmion had been that knight in Normandy, and, in the heady days after the defeat of Harold, the Conqueror offered him Scrivelsby on this condition. It was a challenge and Marmion accepted. ¶ Surprisingly, no descendant of Marmion has ever been called to fight for his master. However, when the challenge was made at the coronation of George III in 1761, the crowd fell silent: rumours abounded that Bonnie Prince Charlie was in London and would do mortal combat with the Champion. ¶ The Marmions grew strong with the benefit of royal patronage and became powerful barons. Earl Philip Marmion was a staunch supporter of Henry III throughout his troubled reign, but his demise meant confusion for the inheritance of the Marmions. The Earl produced only daughters, so the inheritance had to be divided, the eldest taking Tamworth as her dowry, while the younger retained the estate of Scrivelsby. She married Sir Thomas de Ludlow, and their grand-daughter's marriage to Sir John Dymoke in 1350 brought the Champion's duties to the Dymoke family, which still holds them to this day. ¶ In return for putting their lives ceremonially on the line, Champions retained the estate of Scrivelsby and were given generous perquisites. They included a horse, 'the best but one' available from the royal stable; a fine saddle, armour and furniture for the horse; a complete suit of armour for the Champion himself, including a shield and lance; 20 yards of crimson satin; and the gold cup and cover with which the Sovereign drank his health. Strictly, these gifts were only his if combat ensued but, as no king ever wanted a poorly turned-out Champion, no expense was spared on his knightly panoply or the caparisoning of his horse. ¶ The last time a Dymoke was called on to answer a challenge to the king was in 1821, at the coronation banquet of George IV. The doors of Westminster Hall were opened and Dymoke, flanked by Great Officers of State, rode in to throw down his gauntlet. The Garter King of Arms read the challenge and this was repeated three times. The armour of Champion and horse worn on this occasion now stands as the principal feature in the restored St George's Hall at Windsor Castle. ¶ Coronation banquets no longer take place in Westminster Hall, so neither does the Champion's ceremonial entry. Instead, for the last four coronations the Champion has carried the Union Flag or Banner of England.

The gauntlet on the lawn at Scrivelsby Court in Lincolnshire was last thrown down in 1821 to challenge any would-be detractors of George IV. The Queen's Champion no longer has to ride in armour to coronations and risk mortal combat for the monarch in order to keep his land; instead he has the privilege of attending and carrying the Union Flag.

LORD BISHOP OF SODOR AND MAN

The Lord Bishop of Sodor and Man, who tends to the souls of this windswept semi-independent tax haven, still holds the last remaining Viking barony. It is not known when the first Bishop established the Cathedral of St Germain on the island. Legend suggests that St Patrick and other Celtic saints made visits in the 5th century and they probably established a bishopric on Man. However, little evidence of Celtic life, or Christian worship, survived the arrival of Scandinavian invaders. ¶ Viking raids caused havoc along the Scottish coast as the Norsemen established territorial holds in Shetland and Orkney, which they called the Nordreys, and in the Hebrides, Skye, Mull and other outlying islands, which became the Sudreys. Early in the 9th century Viking longboats beached on the shores of Man, which their men plundered and then settled. They established jurisdictions that evolved into eight feudal baronies, and the Barony of Jurby is the one still held by the Lord Bishop. This may be the oldest ex officio barony in the British Isles. It is certainly the provenance of his enduring right to be a member of Tynwald. The ancient Parliament maintains its historic importance, as the provenance for the island's jurisdiction and legislature. ¶ Not long after the raiders had first established their conquest on Man, Norway was converted to Christianity, in particular through its kings, Haakon the Good and St Olav, in the 10th and 11th centuries. Through the mission of these kings and the archbishopric that was finally established in Nidaros, now Trondheim, the lands ruled from Norway were gradually evangelized. In the Sudreys a cathedral and bishopric were established on Man in 1154. ¶ The combination of spiritual and temporal power gave the Bishops considerable sway. One medieval Bishop tested the guilt of witches by tying them to the keel of a boat that was rowed from Peel across the bay to St Patrick's Isle, which involved total submersion for a considerable time. It was a no-win situation for the accused: death by drowning proved innocence, while survival meant guilt, punishable by death. ¶ The Scottish-Norwegian War ended in 1266 with a treaty in which Norway ceded the Isle of Man to Scotland. Since 1079 the Sudreys had been organized into a demi-kingdom ruled from the Isle of Man. The settlement with Scotland came at a price, some 4,000 marks were to be paid to Norway and a further sum every year forever more. Despite this massive change, the bishopric maintained its alliegance to Trondheim, presumably because this suited Rome. ¶ Man was finally ceded to English suzerainty in 1334, since when it has been a Lordship. This was first held by the Earls of Derby before the Dukes of Atholl took it on in 1736, until they surrendered it to the Crown about a century later. The Isle of Man remains a Crown Dependency and not a part of the United Kingdom. Throughout, the right to nominate the Bishop rested with the Lord of Mann. ¶ It is not clear when the diocese assumed the name Sodor and Man, nor is it understood why this tautology took place. By the 17th century the interchangable names had been combined and the title has stuck, perhaps carrying something of its territorial independence into the annals of the Church of England. The diocese and its Bishop are in an interesting position because, now that they sit within the See of York and are subject to the Canon Law of the United Kingdom's established church, the Prime Minister is involved in nominating Bishops to the Queen, who is Lord of Mann, even though this office has no remit over the island whatsoever.

St Germain's Cathedral on St Patrick's Isle near Peel was once the seat of religious power in the Isle of Man. The island's Viking heritage is reflected in the Lord Bishop of Sodor and Man's title and in the ancient Viking barony he still holds.

MASTER OF ST CROSS, BROTHER OF THE ORDER OF NOBLE POVERTY AND BROTHER OF THE HOSPITAL OF ST CROSS

On the outskirts of Winchester is a thriving 12th-century welfare organization, perhaps Britain's first sheltered housing, certainly England's oldest almshouse. ¶ The colossal Norman tower of the Hospital of St Cross rises above the lazy River Itchen. When Henry de Blois walked this riverbank in c. 1133, he was not only Bishop of Winchester and Papal Legate, his half-brother was king and he was also one of the country's wealthiest men. But England was enduring 'the Anarchy', as the civil war between King Stephen and his cousin Matilda became known, and food was scarce. The legend goes that a milkmaid carrying a small child came into view, and, momentarily, he thought that they were a vision of the Madonna and Child. It is difficult to comprehend today what this would have meant to a believer in the 12th century. For de Blois, this was a portentous sign and demanded the attention of his God-fearing conscience. He was therefore attentive when she implored him to help her starving village. So, in the name of Sancta Crux (the Holy Cross), de Blois established the Hospital of St Cross to provide accommodation for 13 brethren, a number to match Christ and the 12 disciples. These brethren were referred to as the Poor in Christ and would live in the community, abide by strict rules and worship as a body for the soul of their founder and for their own souls to be worthy of the next life. Henry de Blois appointed a Master to administer the endowment of land and wealth to support this eternal promise and provided additional resources to feed up to 100 poor people each day. ¶ In the 12th century St Cross was administered by the Knights Hospitaller, which meant that during the preparations for the Crusades, the knights intent on protecting their place in Heaven would assemble at the Hospital and pray in its church. The brotherhood founded by de Blois therefore wears black gowns with silver crosses, which derive from the heraldic cross of the arms of the kingdom of Jerusalem, established during the Crusades. ¶ In 1445 a second brotherhood (the Brethren of Noble Poverty) was established. Its members wear dark red gowns and a silver badge engraved with the 15-tailed cardinal's hat of their founder, Cardinal Beaufort. He was another wealthy and royal Bishop of Winchester, closely connected with the Lancastrian Plantagenets, and he wanted to make provision for a different, surprising, set of needy people: impoverished noblemen, particularly those in his own family. ¶ The Master is no longer politically influential, and neither does wealth come with the appointment, but his domestic and pastoral responsibilities are little changed. Masters in the past administered payments from across the country, and when the village of Twyford failed to pay up, one Master arranged for all its inhabitants to be excommunicated. ¶ One very powerful, yet simple, symbol of kindness continues: the Wayfarer's Dole. It links today's visitors with the vision of Henry de Blois when he met the milkmaid and her child and it resonates with the virtues of Christian chivalry and charity. Perhaps the inspiration came from when, as a boy, de Blois entered the Cluniac Order, an offshoot of the Benedictines, so as to be educated at Cluny Abbey in Burgundy. Cluniac monks believed in supporting travellers, and so to this day, all visitors to St Cross can ask for the Wayfarer's Dole that de Blois instituted. This consists of a tiny mug of beer and a small piece of bread, given to anyone who asks for it. Recipients find welcome and shelter in the medieval quadrangle as they drink their bitter beer, and the brethren go peacefully about their business. Beyond the walls, the roar of the M3 motorway is audible. It beckons non-residents to move on, just as Jerusalem beckoned the Crusaders from this place of safety 800 years ago.

In the Brethren's Hall of the Hospital of St Cross, just outside Winchester, the Master of St Cross is the head of this Norman almshouse where two brotherhoods are housed. Representative Brothers, one from the Order of Noble Poverty (in red) and one from the Hospital of St Cross (in black), wear distinctive badges that have passed from brother to brother over the centuries.

SERGEANT AT MACE AND
HORNBLOWER OF RIPON

The borders between legend and fact become increasingly blurred as the centuries unfold. Saxon history may benefit from having been recorded in the Anglo-Saxon Chronicles, but little else remains of a period from which few parchments were adequately stored to survive the vicissitudes of fire and flood. In this vacuum, Ripon, in North Yorkshire, dates its antiquity from the gift of a Bugle Horn by Alfred the Great, King of Wessex, in 886. The meaning of 'bugle' has changed over the centuries, but in this instance (and originally) it meant 'wild oxen', the horns of these creatures being used to make the instruments. Although King Alfred's involvement is hard to prove, the Horn has survived. Like a witness whose testimony threatens to go either way, it could confirm or upset Ripon's claim to antiquity. ¶ As the Horn is now extremely delicate, three others have been added over the years to the Hornblower's collection. They share a demanding schedule, with one being blown each evening at nine o'clock at the four corners of the Market Place Obelisk and outside the Mayor's House. This signal commemorates the start of the Watch, an important responsibility undertaken by the Wakeman. ¶ A Charter issued by James I in 1604 enshrined the need for a Hornblower and, perhaps foreseeing the potential risks the Wakeman might face, also gave provision for a Sergeant at Mace and two Stave Bearers to provide close protection. ¶ The Charter specifically instructs the Wakeman, whose role has evolved into that of today's Mayor, that he 'shall cause a horn to be blown every night... at nine of the clock at the four corners of the cross... And if it happen any house or houses be broken... and any goods to be taken away... then according to old custom the Wakeman for the time being shall make good.' Having to compensate from his own pocket anyone robbed during the night was a powerful incentive to ensure the night patrols were thorough. ¶ It is worth remembering that civil obedience in the country at large during the 17th century was maintained by Sheriffs and other men-at-arms available for military duties. This system was seldom reliable, but for people living in the aftermath of the Reformation, the Charter made Ripon an attractive place. The promise of security at night and the benefit of insurance should the need arise helped the city develop. It was a reputation that helped attract a community, and it is a tradition that, despite the arrival of a nationwide police force, Ripon chooses to maintain. It may no longer do more than help the city and its police set their clocks, but it still attracts visitors who wish to feel part of an unbroken tradition. ¶ The original Charter Horn is now a venerated object, its original form almost completely hidden by the protection of velvet and silver clasps, and it hangs from a baldric, or belt, covered in the emblems of earlier Mayors. Nonetheless, it is carried before the Mayor when both are guarded by the Sergeant at Mace. Perhaps Ripon will take advantage of carbon-dating to discover how ancient its Horn really is. Few believe that the result would confirm an ox's death in 886. However, if it proved to be from that date, the 9th-century Charter and the legends surrounding one of England's oldest customs and appointments would take on renewed importance. In their wake further legends might take shape – perhaps even that Alfred the Great felled the animal himself. But history is no ally to Ripon here: it would seem that the king was busy fighting elsewhere that year.

The baldric worn by the Sergeant at Mace, who stands beside the obelisk in Ripon's Market Place, has 61 silver shields carrying the names of the city's Mayors from 1570. From it hangs the Charter Horn supposedly presented to the town by Alfred the Great. The Hornblower uses a more recent instrument, as the original is now extremely fragile.

BAILIE OF THE ABBEY COURT OF HOLYROOD AND THE MODERATOR OF THE HIGH CONSTABLES

A Bailie administered justice on behalf of a great landowner. A Constable was responsible for seeing that justice was enforced. The medieval Abbey of Holyrood, with the palace built adjacent to it, was a large estate from early times, and although at its head was a churchman, it still needed to be run efficiently. The Bailie and the Constables are the office holders whose positions have survived from at least the 16th century to the present. ¶ Scotland underwent considerable change in the reign of David I. As Malcolm III's sixth son he had been sent south for education at the English court, but he succeeded his brother, Alexander I, in 1124, and brought to Scotland many civilizing ideas. By his death David had introduced the philosophy of the Norman court, imposed a feudal system on the lowlands and laid the foundations for efficient justice. He also strengthened the Church with six new bishoprics, occupied by Anglo-Norman bishops committed to keeping the Church free from Roman intervention. ¶ On 14 September 1128, David was living at Edinburgh Castle and chose to go hunting, rather than attend Mass on the feast of the Holy Cross. Legend says he became separated from the rest of the hunt and was set upon by a white stag. Thrown from his horse, he wrestled with the beast but, when grabbing at its antlers, found nothing but a wooden cross in his hand. That night, he dreamt of a voice saying, 'Make a house for Canons devoted to the Cross.' ¶ In response, David founded the Augustinian monastery of the Holy Rood, or Holy Cross. Its foundation charter of around 1130 grants the Abbot the right to hold a court, where guilt could be tested through a trial of ordeal by fire, water or duel. ¶ Like all medieval churches, Holyrood provided Sanctuary to men escaping pursuit; having petitioned for protection, unless guilty of premeditated crime, fugitives were safe from their pursuers. Holyrood's Sanctuary became well known and records survive of those seeking protection. ¶ In 1342 David II, the son of Robert the Bruce, raised the status of Holyrood to that of a regality. This made the Abbot a powerful magnate, and the extra legal burden suggests that the office of Bailie may date from this time. The appointment definitely existed from 1535, when James V directed that all Sanctuaries should be supervised by Bailies. ¶ In 1531 Holyrood received its first recorded debtor into Sanctuary. As it was also increasingly used as a royal residence where Parliaments occasionally sat, the noble and great were juxtaposed with the destitute and dangerous. To control potential conflict, a police force was needed within the peculiar jurisdiction of the abbey. In 1504 comes the first recorded Constable, who was also in charge of the Queen's Wardrobe, and in 1709 William Robertson was appointed; he had to keep the peace, arrest criminals and run the prison, which frequently was in his own house. Starting with just one Constable, the number has fluctuated with needs, and now stands at 30. In 1821 these officials assumed the title High Constables, to differentiate them from police bodies forming in the city. Among their most important duties was maintaining order during the election of the 16 Scottish peers who served in the Parliament at Westminster. ¶ The Duke of Hamilton became hereditary Keeper of the Palace in 1646, and the Bailie is now appointed by the Duke. The Bailie is formally in command of the High Constables. Since 1812 they have elected a Moderator, or presiding officer. ¶ Imprisonment for debt ended Sanctuary in Holyrood in 1880. The High Constables are now a ceremonial body responsible for keeping order in and around the palace when the monarch is in residence.

When the roof of Holyrood Abbey was removed during its destruction the ancient appointments associated with its monastic privileges survived. The Bailie of Holyrood wears the stag's head symbol, which alludes to the mythical fight between David I and a white stag. His baton is encircled with ducal symbols relating to his superior, the Duke of Hamilton, who is hereditary Keeper of the Palace of Holyroodhouse. The Moderator of the High Constables carries similar symbolism on his uniform.

LADY MARCHER OF CEMAES AND
MAYOR OF NEWPORT

In 1087 William Rufus reneged on his father's treaty with Rhys ap Tewdwr, the King of Deheubarth. This treaty had held the English border with Wales in peace because it kept the land-hungry Norman barons in check. But with Rhys dead, peace gave way to land-grabbing violence. All along the Welsh border, from Chester down to the River Severn, the Normans advanced with small armies across the Marchiae Walliae (marches or boundaries of Wales). They deposed the Welsh rulers by sword or drove them into the hills. Their reward was land over which no English king had ever ruled, and consequently they owed no fealty to the Crown. Instead they held Jura Regalia (sovereign power), which was theirs by conquest. ¶ One of the furthermost outposts grabbed in this way was Cemaes, one of the seven *cantrefs* (hundreds) of Dyfed. Taking its name from the Welsh *camas*, meaning 'river bend' or 'sea inlet', it included the land around the town of Newport. The people here were well used to war and had endured Norse invasions before Norman ones. Wales itself endured a culture of domestic battles between rival princes. They had also heard tales of William I's recent progress, at the head of a vast army, to nearby St David's. ¶ A Norman named Martin de Tours supposedly landed at Fishguard. The natives bombarded his ships with boulders as they lay at anchor, forcing him farther east 'where the harbour was on the flat and safe from projectiles from above'. The King's Antiquary, John Leland, was sent to Wales in the 1530s to record the country's history: he wrote, 'one Martin de Turribus, a Norman, won the countrey of Kemmeys in Wales about the tyme of King William Conqueror, and that this Martinus foundid the abbey of S. Dogmael in Kemeis and that he lyith buried in the quier there'. ¶ This was an endless saga for Cemaes, caught in the fray between Anglo-Norman and Welsh interests that, with the nationalism of the great Princes of Gwynedd in conflict with Norman and Plantagenet aggrandisement, could never be compatible. Cemaes was merged into the County of Pembroke, for a long time the possession of English kings. ¶ It was not until 1536 that Henry VIII gave equal status to the Welsh under the Act of Union between England and Wales. The Act ended the independence of the Marcher Baronies, bringing them into the shires and creating new shires in the north. Cemaes was merged fully into Pembrokeshire, though the barony structure remained to administrate the community, as it did throughout England until councils took over. ¶ William Owen, 14th Lord Marcher of Cemaes, was born in 1469 and lived to be 105. As a young man he did well in his legal training at the Temple and met up with Lord Audley, who made him 'Clerk of the courts of Cemaes for the rest of his life'. Audley had recently had the barony returned to him, was not much interested in it and was thus happy to offer it in security against a loan from Owen. ¶ The Owen family still hold the Marcher Barony and considerable powers over its 22,000 acres. The Lady Marcher describes it as 'quite hard work in that we hold a Court Leet which meets three times a year in the Llwyngwair Arms pub, where it's met for hundreds of years. It deals with things like water, grazing, boundaries and travellers, and I always try to be there. Each member of the Court Leet still swears an oath of allegiance to me and the Queen, which dates from about 1400. Every November, I appoint the Mayor of Newport. The appointment is agreed between myself and the Court beforehand. At the Court Leet I place the chain of office round his neck and he gives me a red rose in fealty.'

The river bend and sea inlet that gave Cemaes its name is now overlooked by the town of Newport on the west coast of Wales. From its castle the Lady Marcher of Cemaes can keep an eye on the community's affairs and choose the Mayor of Newport from one of three names put forward by local people. She confirms her choice by giving the Mayoral Chain to her nominee. He gives her a red rose.

MASTER TREASURER OF THE HONOURABLE SOCIETY OF THE INNER TEMPLE

In 1119 a group of knights undertook to protect pilgrims travelling to and from the newly conquered Holy Land. They gathered others into a religious community, calling themselves the Poor Fellow Soldiers of Jesus Christ, and took oaths of chastity, obedience and poverty, while dedicating their swords to the Patriarch of Jerusalem. Twenty years earlier, the First Crusade had captured the Holy City and established the kingdom of Jerusalem. Its king, Baldwin II, gave the knights lodgings beside the mosque of al-Aksa, otherwise known as the Temple of Solomon, from which they took their name as the Knights Templar. They were one of the three great military orders associated with the Crusades. ¶ In the 12th century the Knights Templar in England established their base in an area of London now called the Temple. Here they constructed the Round Church on the model of the Holy Sepulchre in Jerusalem. It was consecrated by Patriarch Heraclius in 1185, probably in Henry II's presence. The international influence of the Knights Templar grew dramatically, and with it their wealth and their need of lawyers. By 1312, the Knights Templar fell from grace. They then became tenants of the Knights Hospitaller, who in turn came to an end with the Dissolution. As a result, in 1539, the Crown took back the freehold of the Temple, which finally became the lawyers' possession by grant of James I. However, several of its buildings were destroyed by the Great Fire of 1666. ¶ When in 1207 Canon (Church) Law prevented the clergy – who had hitherto provided all educated legal practitioners – from undertaking temporal business, laymen were required to practise law in the secular courts. Magna Carta stipulated that the king's courts must be at Westminster, so a suitable place was needed to house, teach and administer the growing number of lawyers: Inns of Court provided the answer. Lawyers were trained, fed and lodged there as reward for their service. Two were established in the Temple, called the Inner and Middle Temples, and records show that both associations were operational by 1388. ¶ The Inns of Court are incorporated companies, deriving their constitutions from precedent, in a manner similar to the Common Law they practise. The Benchers, sometimes known as the Masters, are the senior members of the company. Each year, they elect one of their number to be Master Treasurer and act as chairman of the governing body. Treasurers have held this position since the end of the 15th century. Both Temples are responsible for the ancient Round Church and its nave, an extension consecrated in the presence of Henry III in 1240. ¶ The Round Church is a reminder of the Templars' ancient traditions, and its tombs stand as monuments to some of their greatest exponents. The somnolent black figures represent Knights of the Temple of Solomon and supporters of the order. Among them is William Marshal, the 1st Earl of Pembroke, whose surname derives from having shared the title of Marshal of England. His life is a phenomenal record of chivalry. Having at first supported Henry II, he was pardoned by his errant son King Richard I, then swore fealty to the Lionheart's brother, King John, and finally acted as regent to Henry III. ¶ The principal ecclesiastic at the Round Church is called the Master of the Temple. He is appointed under Letters Patent from the Crown, which carry an implicit authority that all lawyers recognize. Similarly, the Knights Templar had no argument when Edward II's sheriffs arrived at the Temple to arrest their Master in England, William de la Mare, on 9 January 1308.

The Master Treasurer of the Inner Temple is elected to chair his fellow Masters, or Benchers, for a year, and leads a legal community that has occupied London's Temple since the Middle Ages. Much of the Temple's Round Church survived the air raids of the Second World War, though there was considerable damage. So also did the 13th-century figures on the tombs of Knights Templar, including that supposed to portray William Marshal, who served four kings, from Henry II to Henry III.

MASTER TREASURER AND
MASTER READER OF THE HONOURABLE SOCIETY
OF THE MIDDLE TEMPLE

As with the Inner Temple, the chief executive officer of the Middle Temple is called the Treasurer. It was the training of this Inn that nurtured Sir Thomas More's concise legal mind and over which he presided as Treasurer from 1512 to 1516. At this time the office was generally filled for long periods, but after 1596 annual elections among the Masters of the Society chose the *Summus Thesaurarius*, or High Treasurer. Surprisingly, having been elected to the Bench, the future Edward VII was elected Treasurer in 1882. In addition to the Treasurer there are two Readers, who serve for six months each, known as the Autumn and the Lent Readers. ¶ The Master Reader has always kept a supervisory eye on the teaching of law within the Society. When the Inns of Court were formed, monasteries provided the template for education. Medieval monastic scholars wrote or copied manuscripts, which became the source of legal learning. These documents were rare and, in order to share their contents widely, one monk was selected to read them at student gatherings. The Inns of Court followed this practice, appointing Readers to read out the statutes and legal philosophies that, until Caxton's printing presses made the written word more accessible, provided the only means of developing jurisprudence. The importance of the Reader's role gave him precedence over Benchers in Hall, even though he was often not a Bencher himself. ¶ Students are no longer expected to 'keep term' for two 'Grand Vacations' by attending a certain number of dinners in Hall. In recent times the practice of 'dining' has been reduced to 12 educational occasions or 'qualifying sessions'. The object of dining is to enable students to mix with barristers and Benchers and learn the ethics and ethos of the profession. Thus they benefit from the experience and wisdom latent within the Society they have joined. Originally dining would have begun in silence, while texts were read by the Reader. He then directed the mooting of legal points raised by the text for the mutual learning of all. This tradition is maintained, with the Reader giving a talk or reading on an appropriate subject of his choice. ¶ The building of Middle Temple Hall began in 1562 under the auspices of the Treasurer, William Plowden, and after eight years it was ready for a visit by Elizabeth I. The first performance of *Twelfth Night*, with Shakespeare himself involved, is said to have taken place in the Hall, and is recorded in the diary of John Manningham, a member of Hall who was in the audience. On All Saints and Candlemas it provided the setting for great celebrations. The Reader would welcome distinguished judges back into the Society and wait upon them at table before the Master of Revels took his place and hosted a masque, during which students demonstrated their dancing and singing in a debauched entertainment. ¶ The Hall was also where the Reader instructed from the Cupboard (the table, or board, in Hall where at mealtimes empty cups were placed). As part of the ceremony of the Call to the Utter Bar, which gives students the right to practise as barristers after 12 months of pupillage, each one is presented to the Master Treasurer by the Master Reader, who 'calls them to the Bar'. The newly called barrister signs the book, which waits symbolically on the Cupboard. In the past students sat before the Reader on rows of benches, with the most accomplished placed at the outer, or 'Utter', ends. Hence, when students have passed the examinations they are called by the Master Treasurer to the Degree of the Utter Bar. Whereas in Elizabeth I's time this heralded a further 10 years of study, the ritual is now only the first stage before which a barrister is entitled to practise in the courts.

The book of new Barristers at Law sits on the Cupboard, which was made from a hatch cover given by Sir Francis Drake from his ship *The Golden Hind*. The Master Treasurer of the Honourable Society of the Middle Temple, on the left, waits to congratulate new barristers, whose names are read out by the Master Reader.

PRIME MINISTER AND
FIRST LORD OF THE TREASURY

It is typical of the way that the British Constitution operates that, even though the well-known post of Prime Minister, which is the Head of Her Majesty's Government in the United Kingdom, has existed in practice since Robert Walpole took office in 1721, the title was only formally recognized by statute in 1937. Until this date, 'Prime Minister' was the term used to describe the role of the First Lord of the Treasury. ¶ The First Lord's appointment evolved from the title Lord Treasurer, or Lord High Treasurer, which was created to manage England's Treasury, when it was formally established by King Henry I in 1126. Naturally, the power over money that this gave its holder imbued the office with great influence and it grew to be the third Great Office of State. Lord Treasurers served all monarchs in differing ways, in order to ensure the royal purse was full. When George I arrived from Hanover to claim his throne in 1714, advisors keen to protect the monarch from over-mighty Officers of State advised him to place the office of Lord Treasurer in commission. This replaced the Lord High Treasurer with a committee of Lords Commissioners of the Treasury, whose chairman was the First Lord of the Treasury. In order to supervise issues of cost pertaining to the king's business in Parliament, the First Lord sat on the Treasury Bench in the Chamber of the House of Commons. ¶ In 1715 George I appointed Robert Walpole as First Lord of the Treasury, a Whig politician in the ascendant who had come to prominence under Queen Anne. Some years later, the influence of the post altered when the king's interest in chairing the executive Cabinet of his Government waned. In his absence, George I recalled Walpole as First Lord and, as the trusted guardian over expenditure, it was logical for the absent king to rely on him to preside over Cabinet in his absence. This was in 1721 and from this point the role of premier, or 'first among equals' for his role as a Minister of the Crown was no greater in rank than any of the other heads of department, grew around the First Lord's role and the incumbent was logically seen as the king's 'Prime Minister'. ¶ In 1735 Sir Robert Walpole was offered No.10 Downing Street by a grateful George II. Previous occupants included the Countess of Yarmouth, Lord Lansdowne and the Earl of Grantham. As the great politician was already a man of considerable wealth and property, he refused it for himself but accepted it as an official residence for the First Lord of the Treasury, and the brass letter box on the famous black front door still has this engraved. ¶ The catalyst for the growth of the position of Prime Minister had actually happened with the Glorious Revolution in 1688. When James II was effectively banished by Parliament and the crown offered to William III and Mary II, they accepted a diminished royal power, and Parliament was sovereign. Royal Prerogative powers endured but, with almost every succeeding reign, these gradually shifted from the monarch's whim to be exercised on the advice of the First Lord and Cabinet. ¶ The first time the title Prime Minister appeared in a formal document was when Benjamin Disraeli signed the final instrument of the Congress of Berlin in 1878, and this occurred, arguably, because another nation's secretariat staffed the document. ¶ Walpole was appointed at the whim of his monarch, but while First Lords are still appointed at the pleasure of the monarch, this is limited by the harsh reality of democracy and the ability of any individual to hold the confidence of the House of Commons as the Queen's Prime Minister.

The First Lord of the Treasury is Prime Minister and chairs the Cabinet of Her Majesty's Government here in the Cabinet Room of No.10 Downing Street, which has been the official residence of this appointment since George II gave the building to Sir Robert Walpole, whose portrait hangs above the fireplace. The present boat-shaped Cabinet table was introduced by Harold Macmillan so as to provide a clear view of all his Ministers, and the only chair with arms is that of the Prime Minister's, which is always set at an angle to the table when not in use. The Prime Minister's official papers are conveyed in locked red boxes.

The first century of Norman rule in England was a time of consolidation. After a brief period of calm following their arrival, the Norman kings began their subjugation of Wales, gained influence over the Scots, and, in 1169, invaded Ireland. The Domesday Book of 1086 recorded more than 13,000 settlements in England. The king and his 300 Rentiers, tenants-in-chief, ran the feudal system and lived off the revenues of estates; at the bottom of the scale came the Villani (villeins), who owned only allotments, and the Cottars, who held small landholdings. The feudal structure gave rise to powerful Rentiers, who increasingly challenged royal authority. Civil chaos often ensued, as the king, the large landowners and the Church struggled for ascendancy, and the ideological balance of power shifted away from the king during this period. The titles described in this chapter have been chosen with these three competing factions in mind. Some survive from the earliest Parliaments of the mid-13th century, and others are those granted to significant tenants-in-chief.

The tenants who enjoyed the riches of the great feudal estates were often tasked with important duties. Medieval kings in England and Scotland divided up their shores into admiralties, placing the security of the coastline under supervision. The invasion by Louis of France in 1216 had been a reminder of the country's vulnerability, and it was decided that every cliff, cove and port should be supervised. One family was charged with the security of the area around the Wash, and their descendants still farm the lands that originally came with this job.

The barons forced King John to sign Magna Carta in 1215, a Charter that pruned royal power and guaranteed certain rights to his subjects. The Master of the Rolls was responsible for maintaining this document, and all other legal records, and although his function and position have changed radically through the years, the pipe rolls that recorded all judgements remain an archive of the law to this day.

Henry III also had to accept some restrictions on his power. His commitment to invade Sicily placed a massive burden on the English exchequer. At this the country rebelled, lead by Simon de Montfort, and the king was forced to submit his powers to scrutiny by a form of representational Parliament at Westminster Abbey, rebuilt by Henry as a mausoleum for the lately canonized Edward the Confessor. The Parliament made the Abbey the focus of national life, and it was granted special privileges by the king. Among them was the right to grant Sanctuary to fugitives, administered by the High Bailiff and Searcher of the Sanctuary.

Robert the Bruce's Scots army won the wars of independence against Edward II on the field of Bannockburn in 1314. Afterwards, the Treaty of Arbroath was dispatched to Rome, and the Pope recognized Scotland's sovereignty. Bruce took Scotland's castles under centralized Scottish royal control, and responsibility for them was dispersed through feudal means to loyal lieutenants. Their duties became dressed with titles such as Governor, Constable or Keeper. Bruce also appointed the Chief of the Hay family, who held lands and influence on the east coast, as Lord High Constable. One of the responsibilities of the post was the monarch's personal safety, and the appointment was made hereditary.

After Edward III became king in 1327, overseas expansion became a political objec-

tive. He planned to claim the crown of France by inheritance through his mother, but he could not go to war without security at home. To achieve this he leant upon the discipline of knighthood, a royal honour that had been vested since Saxon times upon proven warriors. The Church had used these knighted warriors during the Crusades as the basis of its military organization, and had obliged them to take additional oaths that encouraged loyalty to the king. Edward gathered round him the most powerful of these knights, and, by reviving the legend of King Arthur and the knights of the Round Table, he created a quasi-religious order of chivalry, called the Garter, made up of people on whom he could depend.

The medieval sciences of genealogy and heraldry flourished due to these matters of war and land, as their administration called for proof of inheritance, birth and ownership. Vibrant heraldic symbolism was developed to differentiate knights in battle. Monarchs entrusted disputes about privilege, position and status to their Great Officers of State – Lord Lyon in Scotland and the Constable and Marshal in England; each was assisted by officers of arms, who held important military and diplomatic responsibilities.

As the years passed, the merchant cities of London and York thrived as they traded with Europe, and Livery Companies developed a unique structure. As wealth increased, successful speculators and merchants pressed for special privileges, and monarchs, benefiting from their successes, were quite willing to grant them their requests. The City of London's wealth-based democracy developed its own court, charged with security, justice and revenue raising, and this court reflected the Crown's own blueprint of officers. The wealth that came from Cornwall's tin also commanded special privileges, granted with the caveat that an officer appointed by the monarch controlled their activities. This prevented the development of any separatist tendencies within territory so close to France. To tie Cornwall still closer, Edward III granted it to his son as a duchy.

For another son, John of Gaunt, Edward III revived the palatine status of the County of Lancaster as a dukedom. This gave authority for devolved powers, so the Count Palatine could administer his own laws. It was not always easy to remove feudal grants from those elevated to such power, however, and Lancaster later became the base for a challenge to the king's power. Lancastrians happily gave their loyalty to their Count Palatine, and supported the cause of Gaunt's successors, who adopted the red rose as a symbol, through the Wars of the Roses.

The Church's influence grew through these years, because educated priests ran the complex apparatus of the State; but their influence was threatened by the Black Death, which reached England around 1348. The plague was caught by clerics ministering to the sick, leading to a shortage of literate people. To check this dearth, and to continue the education of the laity, especially the poor, two great benefactors established important foundations: William of Wykeham founded Winchester College, and a century later Henry VI endowed Eton and King's College, Cambridge.

The Wars of the Roses, and aristocratic factionalism, destroyed much of the structure that had been carefully amassed around the Crown. It was only with the end of this civil war, in 1485, that a powerful monarch like Henry VII was finally able to regain the initiative and recreate a strong kingdom.

[57]

SERJEANT-AT-ARMS FOR THE HOUSE OF COMMONS

The links between the Crown and the House of Commons are many but, because of this kingdom's history and the critical importance of how and where power was vested, the relationship has been complicated. One appointment that stands between both, with its provenance in the Crown but its evolution intrinsically linked with that of the Commons, is the House's Serjeant-at-Arms. It is appointed by the Sovereign and carries implicit powers that stem from the monarch but it is chosen by the House of Commons and gains further status from the increasing power of that House. ¶ Serjeanty was a form of service that described duty given under the feudal system. When Richard the Lionheart set out on the Crusades in the 12th century, he was guarded by a close band of knights bonded to his personal security and called his Serjeants-at-Arms. They were expected to be armed and in armour to protect the king's tent, arrest traitors and do whatever the king needed. The great builder of castles, Edward I, appointed Serjeants-at-Arms to protect him in these fortresses in 1279. Wherever the king was, his court moved too. The king's council was a part of this court and so, as it developed, was the Parliament. Inevitably, the members of these embryonic Parliaments found fault with the monarch's wisdom, which often brought them into disagreement with the Serjeants-at-Arms. In the end, as the king's own men, there was only one who was able to hold their power in check. ¶ The House of Commons first met separately from the rest of Parliament in 1341 but only gained its own Serjeant-at-Arms in 1415. Nicholas Maudit was the choice of the chamber and his name and recommendation was sent as petition to the king. Approval established a precedent that is, broadly, maintained today, with the House of Commons establishing its own process for selection but then sending the selected candidate's name to the palace for the monarch to appoint. The Queen appoints her Serjeant to attend upon the Speaker during a Parliament but on her when there is none during the period of Dissolution. ¶ The mace is the symbol of office for Serjeants-at-Arms. This is no longer the rugged instrument of war it once was. The hefty metal club, often complete with ridges and spikes designed to pierce helmets and crack skulls, has been replaced by a splendid adorned symbol of gilt. Over time the warlike end has become emblematic, while the symbolic end now dominates the design. The mace has, in fact, been upended. The old warhead is now little more than a grip, while the old base of the shaft, which originally had the monarch's mark as a form of identification, is now at the head and has grown into fine heraldic metalwork, surmounted by the twin arches of the crown that hold a monde, or globe and cross. The mace is not only the symbol of the Serjeant-at-Arm's appointment, it has evolved the far more significant symbolism of the chamber itself. Convention and practice now dictate that the House of Commons mace incorporates the legitimacy of its assembly and stands for the House's ancient rights and privileges. Before debate can start, it must be placed on the table before the Speaker, or for committee, just beneath its surface. ¶ The Serjeant-at-Arms has considerable powers within the House of Commons. He has powers of arrest and is, in some senses, the guarantor, under the Crown, of the privileges of the House of Commons. A recent incident during the term of office of the first female Serjeant saw the Metropolitan Police enter the parliamentary estate in pursuit of a case. Many Members of Parliament protested that this was an infringement of their privilege, a reminder that representatives in a democracy who need to speak their truth are always vulnerable. The Serjeant-at-Arms is still vital in both that protection but also the security of the House of Commons, in the name of the Sovereign.

Framed by the statues of Churchill and Lloyd George, two wartime Prime Ministers, the entrance to the Chamber of the House of Commons bears the wounds of the Blitz on this home of democracy. The Serjeant-at-Arms carries the mace, and messengers stand close at hand, with one waiting at the Bar of the House. The lobby in the foreground was described in *Erskine May* as 'the political centre of the British Empire'.

BEARER OF THE DOG WHIPPER'S ROD

In the Bible, the first Book of Samuel describes the Philistine Goliath's abuse of the approaching child David. He is unaware that the boy walking towards him is about to defeat him in mortal combat and chides, 'Am I a dog that you comest to me with staves?' Perhaps this scripture gave clerics an idea. ¶ The British have a reputation for their love of dogs, which frequently appear carved into old buildings or on tombs, lying supine at the feet of country squires. Their ferocious aspect appears to growl from heraldic achievements or with them supported in their paws and almost every painting of the countryside includes one, either working to man's will or just acting as his beloved companion. In the stark conditions of life in the Middle Ages, dogs lived in close proximity with their masters, whether this was in the Great Halls of castles or in mud-floored hovels. The other great strand of life in this devout land of Christianity was regular worship, and into its comparatively robust stone churches came the believers, divided by almost everything other than their faith and their shared love for dogs. ¶ Therefore the churches filled with dogs. To these animals, such community was nectar. Unaware of the socially manufactured class or status of their owners, for dogs the daily offices of the Christian faith provided distraction and sometimes even a fight. Through this other kingdom of God's creatures, the venerable processions of priests and prelates made their way to sacred altars in vestments to celebrate Mass. In order to maintain the liturgical dignity of worship it was necessary to engage someone in canine control. This is the provenance of the Dog Whipper at Exeter Cathedral. ¶ Exeter was chosen by Bishop Leofric as a safe place for his cathedral in 1050. Dedicated to St Peter, it was rebuilt twice in the following three centuries, first by Bishop William in 1107, who was William I's nephew, and then, keeping much of this as a foundation, between 1258 and 1400 the building took its present shape. High in the wall of the nave aisle on the north side are two small windows. This is reputed to have been allocated as the lodgings for the Bearer of the Dog Whipper's Rod in 1823, when the Broadgate outside was pulled down. It is a small space reached up a winding stone stair, but from here the view of the church's layout is pretty well unsurpassed. He would have been able to spot any canine disorder or identify potential trouble before taking up the rod and ensuring the smooth running of the ecclesiastical procession. ¶ The earliest known reference to a Dog Whipper in Exeter Cathedral is 1685 but the post existed long before, perhaps even stretching back to the foundation of the cathedral. Bishop William of Wykeham in the 14th century directed churches in his diocese of Winchester to do something about removing dogs because of the disturbance and noise in 'divine service'. An undefined incident appears in the records of Exeter for 1758, when William Abbot is fitted for a coat as Dog Whipper because, on 4 November that year, his predecessor, William Bury, is dismissed for malpractices. No large wooden tongs survive in the cathedral, which were the favoured tool for Dog Whippers elsewhere for getting some dogs out from under pews without the risk of bites. ¶ Exeter Cathedral sees no good reason to abolish something that implies an insight into the cathedral's past. Today the Dog Whipper's Rod, which dates from 1839, is carried by whichever verger is appointed to lead the procession. Processions in England generally have the most junior at the front, so a more junior member of the cathedral's vestry is allocated to the task. Today dogs seldom enter churches: owners instinctively leave them attached by lead to a post outside the door either wagging their tails at passers-by or howling with umbrage and indignation.

The cathedral procession to Eucharist is led by the Bearer of the Dog Whipper's Rod, once a vital post to keep dogs out of the way. His role was considered sufficiently important that rooms overlooking the nave were allocated to the officer, the two lit windows of which can be seen on the left, under the arch and above its own doorway.

JUSTICES OF THE PEACE AND
CLERK TO THE JUSTICES

Trial by Ordeal was a gruesome test of guilt popular in the Middle Ages. It required the accused to lift an object from a deep pan of boiling water, or take hold of a red hot iron nugget and carry it for three paces; if the shocking wounds on the hand of the abused healed in three days, it showed that the goodness of God was working within, which was proof enough of innocence. From this furnace of justice, England has evolved its judiciary. ¶ Just as squabbling children are corrected by adults, so the human instinct is framed to presume that leaders will both set the rules and impose justice. The Court Moots of the Anglo-Saxons had operated like this within communities to keep law and hear grievances, but feudalism, which arrived with the Norman Conquest, imposed its will through a framework of baronial officers. Meanwhile, the greatest crimes were judged by the king at court. This was unsustainable and judges, who were generally priests, emerged to sit in the monarch's place. It is for this reason that judges still sit beneath the monarch's coat of arms, in a place still referred to as 'court'. ¶ In 1195, perhaps returning to the old Court Moots, the Crusader king Richard established 'keepers of the peace' from learned members of the community to hold and administer law around the country. In 1327, when Edward II was ruthlessly deposed by his wife in favour of their son Edward III, only to face a horrid murder in Berkeley Castle, an ironic Act was passed to appoint 'good and lawful men' in every county to 'guard the peace'. Well they might in the hiatus that followed this regicide. Then, in 1361, when the plague reasserted itself, the Justices of the Peace Act was passed that established the appointment that all modern lay-magistrates still hold. While by no means democratic, this enabled a number of the community to sit in judgement over others. In addition, they had powers to quell riots, impose proclamations and deploy force if necessary to maintain peace. ¶ Synonymous with 'Justice of the Peace' is the term magistrate, from the Latin for 'master' and referring to a public officer who administered justice. In ancient Rome, a *Magistratus* occupied, for his lifetime, an office that he probably gained from another and would one day pass on, but which remained, no matter who held it, bonded to an unaltering duty; in this case the maintenance of law and order. ¶ Ada Summers' appointment as Mayor of Stalybridge in 1919 was significant because she became a magistrate by dint of that office, even though women were still prevented from serving as Justices of the Peace. At a time when women's rights were being keenly fought for, this forced the issue and justice was done the following year, when the opportunity to serve the community in this way was opened to all. ¶ There are two types of magistrate in England and Wales: Justices of the Peace, or lay magistrates, who are volunteers; and district judges, formerly known as stipendiary magistrates. They can sit in pairs, though this is impractical if they disagree, so the Bench is generally made up of three, with the senior one present acting as Chairman, or Chair, and a Clerk to advise on matter of law. The term Bench is also a collective term for all the magistrates in a certain area. ¶ In the past, Justices of the Peace came from the well-heeled of the shires, with cities often struggling to find people willing to undertake the unpaid responsibilities. Recent Lord Chancellors have worked hard to open this up to be more democratic and reflective of the communities they serve. The intent of medieval kings was to secure the nation by holding the shires in check by the men who knew their community. That intent remains the aspiration but success depends on volunteers.

Local magistrates sat in the old Victorian courtroom in Norwich Guildhall until 1977, where prisoners first occupied the crypts in 1412. All three Justices of the Peace, or members of the Bench, have equal decision-making powers but only the Chairman speaks in court and presides over proceedings. A qualified legal adviser, known as Clerk to the Justices, sits with the Bench in the courtroom and is available to them at all times during the court sitting. Justices of the Peace, often referred to as 'the great unpaid', form the core of the judiciary, hearing the majority of all criminal cases.

EARL MARSHAL OF ENGLAND, KINGS OF ARMS, HERALDS OF ARMS AND PURSUIVANTS OF ARMS IN ORDINARY AND EXTRAORDINARY

Heraldry, with its strident colours, romantic beasts and strange language, provides one of the brightest illustrations for European history. Since the Middle Ages its semiology has been used to celebrate, identify and associate figures and families from the nation's story with buildings, documents and possessions. By enforcing complex rules, it provides a simple system of devices that convey considerable detail to the trained eye. The distinguishing symbols mirror similar systems adopted by tribes and nations throughout the world, each seeking a means to mark the individual out from his peers. Great importance was associated with the study of heraldic sciences and it was once seen as a prerequisite to advancement. ¶ In Europe the rapid development of heraldry created a need for regulation and control; in England this became the responsibility of a College, or body of colleagues, consisting of three ranks: Pursuivants, who were mere attendants or followers; Heralds, whose name derives from a root meaning 'controller of an army'; and Kings, who held administrative sway over vast areas with the right to grant armorial bearings in the monarch's name. Collectively they are still called the Officers of Arms. ¶ The earliest Heralds, referred to in the 12th century, were little more than criers who announced jousts at tournaments. However, as order came to the chivalric world and knights adopted symbols and observed rituals, the Heralds became guardians of the new language, and by 1350 they were responsible for arranging royal events, negotiating with foreign rulers and delivering proclamations. ¶ All the Officers' appointments have names that reflect either the territorial responsibility they held or some symbol closely associated with the Crown. At their head are the three Kings, chief of whom is Garter King of Arms, created in 1415, who has added responsibility for running the Order of the Garter. Oldest among the other two is Norroy, short for north king, which dates from 1276. Since 1943 Ulster has been added to his realm. Until then the division between his English responsibilities was the River Trent: he took the north and Clarenceaux (after the Earl of Clare's lands) took land to the south. At one time each King was crowned and anointed with wine pressed from grapes native to the region concerned. ¶ The Heralds are Chester, Lancaster, Windsor, Richmond, York and Somerset, all founded in the 14th and 15th centuries. The Pursuivants, founded in the latter, include Bluemantle, named after the Order of the Garter's robe, and Rouge Croix, Rouge Dragon and Portcullis, all appointed by the Tudor Henrys. ¶ From 1530 to 1700 Officers of Arms made visitations to their provinces and audited the heraldry people used. They supervised ceremonies, particularly funerals, and stopped social climbers from outranking themselves with too much undeserved display. Transgressions were heard at the Court of Chivalry, which is still extant at the College of Arms in London, although it has not sat since 1954. ¶ Anyone can go to the College to have their genealogy researched, check whether armorial bearings already exist in their families and, if not, petition for a Grant of Arms. The Heralds check against documents dating back to the 15th century. Few are prevented from adding their names to the armigerous, as those with arms are known, and displaying their bearings on anything from letterheads to pyjamas. ¶ There are up to 13 full time Officers in Ordinary, assisted by

Previous page: The Earl Marshal of England stands in front of the throne made for Queen Victoria, in the Robing Room of the Palace of Westminster. He wears the Parliamentary Robe of a Duke over the Court Dress of a Great Officer of State and holds the ebony-ended gold baton of the Earl Marshal's office. He is surrounded by the English Heralds. Tabards, or coats of arms, were worn over armour by kings. Henry V wore his at Agincourt in 1415 and Heralds wore the king's coat too to reflect his status in their work. The Corporation of Kings, Heralds and Pursuivants in Ordinary wear tabards of velvet, satin and damask respectively. The Extraordinaries reflect this, with only the lack of a tiny coronet on their wand marking them as junior to the College's Chapter.

part-timers when called upon, known as Officers Extraordinary. All of these Officers help the Earl Marshal of England in his hereditary responsibility as stage manager of State occasions, such as State funerals granted by Parliament or coronations. Just as they supervised early tournaments, the Heralds are now guardians of the way the State celebrates itself, evolving traditions to reflect changing needs. They are the professors of ceremonial provenance, the keepers of the national armoury and pedigree, and the three Kings wait to exercise the Sovereign's authority in granting new arms, just as they have done since the Middle Ages. The Earl Marshal also supervises the College of Arms and is one of the realm's Great Officers of State. Marshals were evident in the Byzantine and Frankish courts and so it was no surprise that the Norman kings established their own in 1135, to manage the horses and keep order. The office was first vested in the Dukes of Norfolk by Richard III in 1483 but this lasted only as long as the king. From 1485 the Norfolk association with the Earl Marshal's role was inter-mittent, due to the whims of loyalty and different monarchs. But it was established as an hereditary responsibility in 1672.

The Heralds lead Knights and Ladies of the Order of the Garter from the Upper Ward to St George's Chapel in Windsor Castle, wearing tabards and carrying their Wands of Office.

LORD LYON KING OF ARMS

Scotland's heraldry and ceremonial is run very differently from England, by the Lord Lyon King of Arms. He is a Great Officer of State and a judge, with his own Court of the Lord Lyon. Approved by the Sovereign, he answers to none other and has a unique control over the granting of armorial bearing of the recognition of Clan Chiefs. On the Queen's behalf, the Lord Lyon makes royal proclamations from the Mercat Cross in Edinburgh and it is in this way that news of Parliament's dissolution in Westminster is formally announced in Scotland. By tradition it is done three days after the Prime Minister gets the Queen's approval for a General Election, the time taken by a messenger to gallop 400 miles from London with the news. Emphasizing the significance of his role, Scots Law, which differs in so many ways from that practised in England and Wales, criminalizes as treason an assault on the Lord Lyon when carrying out the monarch's work. ¶ Heraldry is a relatively new concern for the Lord Lyon. His predecessors reached back into the ancient history of Scotland's monarchy when they filled the appointment as *Ard Seanachaidh*, or bard-recorder. It was necessary for a scholar to pronounce the king's genealogy, linking him with heroic ancestors for credibility back to Fergus Mor MacErch, who began the royal line in the 5th century. Thus, the emergence of heraldry in Europe dropped naturally into his lap. Lyon is said to have played a prominent part at Robert II's coronation and one source states that Robert the Bruce appointed a Lyon four years after Bannockburn, in 1318. ¶ The title evolves from the use of an heraldic lion by Scotland's kings on their arms. This may date from William 'the Lion', who reigned from 1165 to 1214 and established links with France. The lion first appeared on the seal of his son, Alexander II, who is depicted with it on his shield, and it has been used ever since. Lyons in the past even had their own coronation, having the crown, one of the three Honours of Scotland, placed momentarily upon their heads. ¶ Such detail has always been the substance of good heraldry and Lyon sits as a judge to oversee any abuse of heraldic law brought to his court by his Procurator Fiscal. His is the only court of chivalry in regular use and is totally integrated within the national legal system. Recent cases include the display of armorial ensigns by the Porsche motor company; as there was no acknowledged grant for the design in Scotland, he ruled that, while it would be churlish to demand that the radiator badges be removed, the company was prevented from displaying its shield on garages or publicity material. ¶ At his sole discretion grants for armorial bearings are made and, if evidence of inheritance is proved, the original grant may be altered for the grantee's descendants. He instructs the Lyon Clerk and Keeper of the Records to record these in the Public Register of All Arms and Bearings in Scotland. Proven family lines are likewise entered in the Public Register of All Genealogies and Birthbrieves. Among these are the Chiefly lines of the Highland Clans who bear patriarchal/matriarchal responsibility for families spread throughout the world. Lyon must be satisfied before a Chief has the right to hold sway. ¶ Scotland's State ceremonies are the Lord Lyon's responsibility and he advises the First Minister where necessary. The Scottish Parliament presents opportunities for the nation to celebrate both its history and new beginnings in fresh rituals that the Lord Lyon has the provenance to guide.

The Mercat Cross in Edinburgh, close to Scotland's old Parliament, is where all royal proclamations were once made and was often the scene of dissent. Since the Union of 1707, Lord Lyon King of Arms, as the Queen's representative, has delivered royal proclamations from this place, attended by his Officers of Arms in Ordinary and Extraordinary. The Cross is adorned with the arms of Edinburgh, Scotland and the quartered design of the three kingdoms, which the Lord Lyon also wears. Scotland's rampant lion takes precedence and is repeated twice.

HEREDITARY MASTER OF THE ROYAL HOUSEHOLD, HIGH JUSTICIAR OF ARGYLL, ADMIRAL OF THE WESTERN ISLES, HIGH SHERIFF OF ARGYLL AND KEEPER OF THE ROYAL CASTLES OF CARRICK, DUNOON, DUNSTAFFNAGE, SWEEN AND TARBERT

A son was born to James II, King of Scots, in 1455, providing security for the Scottish succession at a time when the fortunes of the Stuart dynasty were improving. To enhance this period of stability, a new peerage was established: one of these new peers was Colin Campbell of Lochawe, who was created the 1st Earl of Argyll in 1457. He already had plenty of titles, including Keeper of the Royal Castles of Carrick and Dunoon, and by 1470 this list of responsibilities extended to include Dunstaffnage Castle. ¶ Just as James II's government of Scotland appeared to be in strong royal hands, disaster struck. In 1460 James attacked Roxburgh Castle to remove the occupying English Lancastrians, but when a cannon exploded beside him he was killed. His death placed James III on the throne, aged nine, and the boy's mother became Regent. Among his other guardians was the new Earl of Argyll and it was not long before this position of loyalty was rewarded. In 1464 Argyll was appointed Master of the Royal Household before becoming Lord Chancellor as well. His son too held the post of Master until he died in the battle against the English at Flodden in 1513. In 1528 the 3rd Earl was made hereditary Master of the Royal Household and it has been held by each Argyll since. ¶ The 3rd Earl also became Lieutenant of the Borders and Warden of the Marches, thereby protecting Scotland from attack from any direction. In addition, he became Heritable High Sheriff of Argyll and by 1514 he was signing his name as High Justiciar. This title too was made hereditary and thereby placed the Argylls in a position to profit from the judicial system, a benefit largely surrendered to Charles I, on condition Argyll could retain Justiciarship over Argyll itself and the Western Isles. By Act of Parliament in 1633 the king, who promoted the Earl to Marquess, thereby consented to two hereditary appointments: High Justiciar of Argyll and Admiral of the Western Isles. However, since 1747, when heritable jurisdictions were abolished, this latter was reduced to a mere symbol. ¶ The Marquess tried to serve too many masters. He declared loyalty to Charles I but led the Covenanters, a popular movement against the king's interests in Scotland. After the king's execution, Argyll actually crowned Charles II, at Scone, only to turn his coat by assisting in the proclamation of Oliver Cromwell as Protector soon after. Little wonder that, after the Restoration in 1660, Charles II saw him tried for High Treason and hanged. His son, the 9th Earl, also stood for the Protestant faith and was sent for execution by James VII, against whom he had led the Scottish contribution to Monmouth's Rebellion. Loyalty to Crown, on the one hand, and Faith, on the other, presented a challenge to any family in the following centuries. The Argylls managed to do both and keep their appointments, and in 1701 the 10th Earl was raised to the rank of Duke. His son and successor was one of the first two officers promoted to the rank of Field Marshal in the British Army, a rank also held by the 5th Duke. ¶ The duties of the Hereditary Master of the Royal Household are now just ceremonial, but the Royal Navy, in particular HMS *Argyll*, still fires a salute to the Admiral of the Western Isles.

Beside the Brannie Burn, in Glenshira, Argyll, the Master of the Royal Household carries the red velvet rod of office. This is sprinkled with thistles and topped with the Sovereign's crest of a lion wearing the Honours Three: the crown, sword and sceptre of Scotland. In his left hand the Master clasps the High Justiciar's symbolic sword. On his jacket can be seen silver salmon-shaped buttons – ancient symbols of the highest status whose origins are lost in the mists of pre-Christian mythology.

HEREDITARY CAPTAIN OF DUNSTAFFNAGE

The 13th-century fortress at Dunstaffnage was once a vital strategic defence guarding Scotland's vulnerable western approaches. Within its impregnable-looking walls is the residence of the Hereditary Captain, a descendant of the first person appointed to the post in 1490. ¶ Before Ewen MacDougall, the Lord of Lorne, built this castle around 1250 to keep Norse raiders at bay, legend has it that a series of strongholds stood on this promontory. Local folklore suggests that one built by the mythical King Ewin existed here before Julius Caesar arrived in Britain. It has long been said that the Stone of Destiny, used at the coronation of Scots monarchs and removed for that reason by Edward I to Westminster, originally rested here, until Kenneth mac Alpin, the king whose marriage to a Pictish princess united Scotland, moved it to Scone. When the Queen was recently advised to return it to Scotland, there was speculation that it might return to Dunstaffnage. ¶ Such was the strategic and historical significance of Dunstaffnage, and the importance of the Lordship of Lorne it governed, that when its occupant MacDougall foolishly resisted Robert the Bruce in 1309, the king attacked, took possession and appointed Arthur Campbell as Constable of the fortress. Constable evolved into Keeper, an appointment that the Argyll family retain. In the 15th century the Earl of Argyll subcontracted responsibility for the castle to his cousin, creating the new title of Captain. ¶ This was no free gift. While it brought a reasonable acreage and income, and later included a golden key as a ceremonial symbol of office, it involved clear responsibilities. A Charter signed by the 9th Earl to his kinsman, the 10th Captain, in 1667 outlines them: 'holding our said Castell of Dunstaffnies and ever keeping and holding therein six able and decent men with armour and arms sufficient for warr and keeping of the said Castell'. In addition, the Captain had to provide the Earl with free access and lodging if required, and pass on certain rental payments. His family became known as Clann Aonghais an Duin (Children of Angus the Dun) – a reminder of the provenance of the word 'clan'. ¶ Scottish clans were bitterly divided by religion during the Reformation – a situation that polarized when some supported the Jacobite claimant to the throne against George I, the Hanoverian king, in 1714. Clans and their septs, or junior branches, were forced to take sides in the civil war that followed. In each case there was self-interest involved. Over some 50 years passions rose and once again Dunstaffnage was found to be strategically useful. The Captain was holding the castle for George I when the Old Pretender (the son of James II) planned to land there and claim the throne in 1715. Weather and circumstances saved Dunstaffnage from becoming the focus of the uprising's first assault. ¶ In 1746 the Captain had to fulfil his duty of garrisoning the fortress in the build-up to the Battle of Culloden, when every available redcoat was scouring the shores for Bonnie Prince Charlie. Later that year its dungeon received the bold and romantic Flora Macdonald, who risked so much to row the Prince to safety on Skye. ¶ When Argyll claimed the Captaincy back from the Children of Angus the Dun, the case went before a judge, who upheld the Captain's position as heritable Captain but underlined Argyll's superiority as Keeper. He also ruled that, to keep the title and the land, the Captain was required to spend three nights a year in the fortress. Since the fire in 1810 this has meant passing some Spartan nights in a bare, unfurnished building.

To maintain his livelihood and fulfil the ancient responsibilities given to his ancestor, the Hereditary Captain of Dunstaffnage meets his obligation of spending a night locked within the ancient walls of Dunstaffnage Castle on Scotland's west coast. With his key of office resting on the mantelpiece, this descendant of the Dun wraps himself in Campbell tartan and fortifies himself with whisky against the cold and the castle's heavy-footed ghost. So attached is he to this ancient castle that he even spent the first night of his honeymoon here.

MASTER OF BRUCE

The importance of inheritance touches most people, whether or not there are possessions to pass on. Throughout history, the instinct of parents has generally been to do
their best for their children, by passing on whatever there is, to enhance the future with
the best of the past. Each family has its own story and genealogy and, in some countries,
you can find links with a fascinating past through names that have endured. Scotland,
with its clans and family identities, has been one of the more successful European nations
at linking people with their history, helped by its recently revived romantic traditions.
This is especially true for the Masters of Scotland, as they wait to inherit a responsibility
and provide a living link with that past. ¶ A small village called Brix, near Cherbourg,
gave its name to a great House of Scottish kings. In the 11th century Adam, a younger
son of the Norman Count de Brix, crossed the Channel to support the daughter of his
duke, Richard the Fearless. This was Queen Emma, who was married to two kings of
England: the Saxon king Aethelred and Canute. In due course, Adam was raised high in
the nobility, and, being Norman, survived the aftermath of conquest in 1066. His successors gained a foothold in the north of England. Then the family, in the name of Robert de
Bruce, as Brix had evolved, moved into Scotland and gained the earldom of Carrick and
the lordship of Annandale. The lack of an heir to the throne in Scotland, when the Maid
of Norway died in 1290, led to the wars of independence and after a considerable struggle
a new king, Robert 'the Bruce', emerged to lead the Scots to victory from English over-
lordship at the Battle of Bannockburn in 1314. ¶ A generation later the Bruce male line
ran out and the kingdom passed to Robert II, the first of the House of Stuart and the son
of Robert the Bruce's daughter, Marjorie. This line of kingship continues to the House
of Windsor. The last Bruce king, David II, foresaw the end of his House and so passed
the sword his father had carried in battle to a kinsman in order to keep it with the Bruces.
Custody has passed through the Chiefs of the House of Bruce, who are now the Earls of
Elgin and Kincardine. In any generation, the grandson of an Earl, by dint of his father's
Courtesy Title as Lord Bruce of Kinloss and Torry, carries the romantic title Master of
Bruce, since the heir to a Scottish peerage carries the substantive title of Master of that
peerage. This legal status gave the eldest son the right to sit in Scotland's Parliament,
if his father was absent. 'Scottish peerage' refers to those created in Scotland prior to
the 1707 Act of Union, when the Great British peerages, and then in 1801 the United
Kingdom peerages, took their place. At the same time, the Scots Parliament ceased and
Westminster became the Parliament for the newly united country. The Masters, or
heirs, of the many Scottish peerages were the future of the family's power and status.
The title Master generally implied a cadet awaiting inheritance and the implicit responsibilities that came with it, which brought with it the dash and energy associated with
youth. ¶ Under the English tradition, peers with more than one title, of different ranks,
gave the eldest son the second title 'by courtesy'. This practice was gradually adopted in
Scotland, especially after the Act of Union when many Scots Lords were granted Great
British peerages as well. The latter were popular because, under the Act of Union, only
16 peers from the old Scots peerage could sit at Westminster: so, gaining another title
with these implicit powers increased a family's influence. The restriction on Scots peers
was removed in 1963 but in 1999 hereditary peers lost the right to sit in Parliament, save a
small number elected by the rest to serve. The remaining Masters are limited to the peerages that survive from pre-Union Scotland. Each holds the unique privilege of carrying
forward both their own title but also the baton of their family's story.

Seated under Dunfermline Abbey's Victorian pulpit, the Master of Bruce touches the representation
of Robert the Bruce's sword in the brass above his tomb with the tip of his ancestor's battle sword.
The ancient symbol of this great King of Scots seals the link between a new generation and a noble
history. Wearing his Bruce tartan kilt, family tweed jacket and holding a bonnet with the family's
buckled crest, there is opportunity here to lead something from the past into the future.

DUKE

The first Duke in Britain was the *Dux Britanniarum*, a Roman commander serving his emperor in the 4th century. *Dux* was a Latin word for 'leader' or 'general' and it was a title first given by Hadrian to commanders of major expeditions or garrisons. The Merovingians used Dukes, as civil and military magnates, to administer groups of lesser barons, and the Carolingians continued this. However, the decay of the Frankish monarchy's power in the 10th century gave these Dukes an opportunity both to consolidate their independent power and to make themselves hereditary; among these was the dukedom of Aquitaine, a valuable asset that came into the English crown with Henry II's marriage to the dukedom's heiress, Eleanor. ¶ Meanwhile, the Teutonic warlords created a post equivalent to the Duke, *Heretogas*, which in modern German is *Herzog*. Their tradition was democratic: the strongest and best warlord became the leader and remained so until he failed to deliver victory. The Saxons who invaded England were led by an Heretogas, as were the Scandinavian Northmannus, or Normans, who adopted the Frankish title as Dukes of Normandy. ¶ However, the domestic appointment of Dukes did not begin until 1337. Edward III made Cornwall into a duchy for his son the Black Prince. And in Scotland too, Robert III gave the duchy of Rothesay to his eldest son 61 years later. Non-royals were not given this quasi-princely rank until 1448, when the de la Poles were made Dukes of Suffolk. But the Dukes were rather exposed by their elevation to later jealous monarchs, and fared badly under the Tudors, being wiped out completely when Elizabeth I attainted the Duke of Norfolk. But Charles II spread his patronage widely after the Restoration, to reward the nobility he depended upon. It also provided an excellent way of keeping his mistresses in bed; of his 14 illegitimate children, six were made dukes. ¶ As the curtain descends on a legislative role for the hereditary peerage, there are 24 dukedoms in existence. Among them, two are Irish creations and six are Scots. Few now bother to attend the House of Lords and some believe their rights have lasted too long already. Instead, their work is devoted to maintaining what remains of the great or small estates that sycophancy, whiggery, coal, sheep, canals, illegitimate royal birth or feudal power granted to their ancestors. ¶ Standing on the ramparts of Alnwick Castle in Northumberland, this Duke is at the heart of a vast agricultural landholding, which started as an administrative feudal responsibility. It was given by William the Conqueror to his friend 'William the Whiskers' from the village of Perci. Thus, the Percy family took a hold in the north that they have kept for generations. ¶ Demonstrating the power of property in Britain's pre-industrial land-based economy, Alnwick Castle proves that while blood may be thicker than water, land is thicker than blood. The Duke of Northumberland today has barely any link whatsoever with his hirsute Percy 'ancestor'. His forebears were Smithsons, who changed their name to Percy, and the dukedom says less about the family that fought ferocious battles around these walls and more about the 1st Duke's ambition. But the title grew into itself and now it has a status that successive incumbents have fuelled by their effort: today it enjoys a brand of 21st-century respect that borders on fealty, with the castle known to legions of fans as Hogwarts in the first two *Harry Potter* blockbusters.

Under feudal law, land gave Tenants-in-Chief of the Crown the right to sit in Parliament. William the Conqueror granted the dangerous border lands around Northumberland to his friend 'William the Whiskers' from Perci, who represented this landed interest in court. Percys have continued ever since sitting as Dukes of Northumberland from 1766 and living behind the ancient ramparts of Alnwick Castle. A Duke wears four bars of gold and ermine on the 'temporal' side of his parliamentary robe.

GOVERNOR OF THE COMPANY OF MERCHANT ADVENTURERS OF YORK

The River Ouse, which flows south-eastwards into the River Humber and the North Sea, provided York with all the geographical advantages necessary to become a major trading centre. Successively a Roman, Anglian and Viking trading town, it became a bishopric in the 620s. A century later the early Church also established one of its two English archbishoprics here in 735. Before the Norman Conquest, York had grown to become a significant merchant city trading with the Baltic region. However, the Conquest led to several local rebellions, which were brutally suppressed by William the Conqueror, though the damage was short-lived and the city was flourishing again as a major trading port by the early 12th century. ¶ York's location was too important for the Normans to ignore for long and gradually the city, its population and its trading patterns were re-established. A system of guilds developed, starting with the Weavers, who received their Charter in 1163: a sign that wool in its raw state was already being superseded by woven cloth as the principal export. Some years later, in 1212, the city was given powers to regulate itself. This meant that all traders wishing to do business in the 13th century first had to become freemen of the city, thereby establishing allegiance to the burgesses and agreeing to observe the rules of commerce. By this time, York merchants were trading further than the Baltic region and Spain. ¶ The merchants built their hall in the 14th century, close to the quay on the bank of the Ouse, and it provided a meeting point, a centre for religious worship and for distributing charity and a place for doing business. The fraternity staged religious plays at the Feast of Corpus Christi and funded a hospital for the unfortunate. In 1430 Henry VI granted a Royal Charter to the Mistery of the Mercers of York, 'mistery' being the medieval word for 'handicraft'. In this document, the role of Governor is first referred to, and apart from some Masters during the 15th and 16th centuries, the appointment of Governor has always led the Company through its evolution. ¶ By the 16th century, competition from the Hanseatic League reduced York's revenues and it became more difficult to compete against London. The merchants' fortunes only revived with the Charter they bought from Queen Elizabeth in 1581. This incorporated their fraternity into the Society of Merchant Adventurers with a Governor who was directed to regulate its monopoly over business, which ensured a growth in wealth sufficient to fund trading all over Europe, from Russia and the Baltic to the Mediterranean. Business was interrupted by the Civil War, which placed York between the warring factions, and the Hall became variously a barracks and a storage for munitions. ¶ The monopoly survived until the 18th and 19th centuries, when it became increasingly difficult to restrain traders under the terms of an Elizabethan Charter. The Municipal Corporations Act of 1835 ended all guild restrictions and there was little that the new generation of industrial Governors could do but to evolve the Company's role to meet new requirements if it was to survive and remain relevant. This they did successfully, providing a conduit for members to lobby Parliament, establishing a short-lived stock exchange and returning to the original role of providing a social focus for the commercial community of York. The city's new industries, particularly confectionery, have provided resources and many of the recent Governors, each of whom supervises the continuing charitable work of the ancient foundation and seeks to sponsor and encourage new crafts and small traders in the city.

The Upper Chamber of the Merchant Adventurers Hall, in York, is where the Company still meet, as their predecessors have done since 1357, when the Hall was begun. The Governor of the Company of Merchant Adventurers of York, wearing aldermanic robes, holds the Royal Charter that was granted by Elizabeth I in 1581. It bears the Great Seal, which gave privileges and powers through which the Company flourished for many centuries. The Company's coat of arms, with white roses of York, was only granted in 1969. The Governor's Chair was made by 'Mousey Thompson' of Kilburn in North Yorkshire in the early 20th century, and it has his small mouse carved into its design.

LORD WARDEN OF THE STANNARIES, RIDER AND MASTER FORESTER OF THE FOREST AND CHASE OF DARTMOOR, KEEPER OF THE PRINCE'S PRIVY SEAL AND VICE CHAIRMAN OF THE PRINCE'S COUNCIL

Cornwall's wealth lies underground – at least that was once the case. Its deposits of tin provided the county with a status sufficient to establish its own coinage, courts and parliament. It even provided sufficient temptation for the Romans to set sail from Gaul and conquer England. ¶ The mines, now abandoned, once generated considerable income for the Crown and gave Cornishmen a strong negotiating hand, which brought them immunity from taxation, a unique royal status and a special governor. ¶ The wealth that the miners produced gave them self-confidence and a sense of independence that eventually disturbed the faraway English king into action. In 1198 Richard the Lionheart sent William de Wrotham to end this independence. He was given special powers and the title Lord Warden of the Stannaries (*stannum* is Latin for 'tin'). He imposed order and codified the ancient stannary laws in a peculiar jurisdiction for Cornwall. This legitimized the Stannary Parliament, which Lord Wardens had power to convoke and preside over. In Truro 24 Cornish stannators met four times a year, while the Devonshire stannators met at Crockern Tor on Dartmoor. Everything other than issues concerning life, limb and land fell within the remit of these parliaments, and their decisions were upheld through the Stannary Courts. ¶ In 1337 Edward III further recognized Cornwall's unique status and wealth by creating a duchy, consisting of much of the county and some other lands, and then conferring it on his seven-year-old son, the Black Prince. This was England's first dukedom, a possession intended to provide the heir with an independent source of revenue, which the Lord Warden was directed to run. This situation has not changed – the duchy still provides income for Prince Charles as Duke of Cornwall, although its possessions and income have altered out of all recognition. ¶ Henry III had granted the Forest of Dartmoor to his younger brother in 1239, along with the earldom of Cornwall, and thus it became part of Edward III's new duchy. At the same time, the Lord Warden was charged with responsibility for Dartmoor's extensive forest and chase, famous for its dwarf oaks: in particular he supervised the Venville tenure by which people held fishing or grazing rights on the land. ¶ The Lord Warden's principal duties remained the governance of the independent-minded medieval miners, who endured hideous conditions and great danger. Among the privileges they could apply to him for was the right to Tin-Bound – stake out territory and work it just as Gold Rush prospectors did in the USA several centuries later. Cornwall provided opportunities for fortunes to be made – not least for the Lord Wardens. ¶ Miners were excused the obligation of fighting for the king abroad. However, their skills could be summoned to burrow beneath the defences of a besieged castle. Whenever stanners were called up, they served only under the Lord Warden's command. ¶ Previous Lord Wardens include Sir Walter Raleigh, appointed by Elizabeth I to administer the duchy with no duke, and Prince Albert, who turned the estate into a model of efficiency. ¶ The Lord Warden now supervises 129,000 acres spread across the south-west and elsewhere, along with residential property in London and a portfolio of other investments. One of the few reminders of Cornwall's once-flourishing tin industry is in the Latin roots of the Lord Warden's title.

An abandoned tin mine on Bodmin Moor is a reminder of not only a once-thriving industry but also the centuries-old link to the Lord Warden of the Stannaries. As Common Law does not favour the 'doctrine of desuetude' (which causes statutes to lapse or become unenforceable by long habit of non-enforcement or passing of time), together with the Duke of Cornwall, the Lord Warden still has the right to convene a Stannary Parliament and veto United Kingdom legislation.

LORD OF THE MANOR OF ALCESTER

Alcester has maintained its ancient Court Leet for more than seven centuries, an enduring example of the feudal system by which England was regulated. Originally every feudal manor was run like this one. Alcester's Court Leet no longer performs the functions that once kept it busy all year; its duties have now been taken on by local government and related agencies. However, the regular gatherings in Alcester's Town Hall give a good insight into life before councils and into the way great estates were run, from the arrival of feudalism until quite recently. The officers created at a local level echoed the Great Officers of State in function: it was merely the more limited scale of their operations that distinguished them. ¶ The manorial system reached its prime in the 13th century, at about the time Alcester began keeping records of High and Low Bailiffs. The first appointee was called Roger the Bailiff. ¶ At the centre of this simple feudal system of interdependence would have been a manor house and church with the homes of other inhabitants clustered around. The Lord of the Manor divided out the ground to his tenants, either for rent or in return for military service. Each field was divided into manageable strips a pole (5 1/2 yards) or yard in width, known as virgate or yard-land, which extended to contain an acre of land. In that way the Lord, himself the proprietor of land given by the Crown in return for certain duties, was able to meet his obligations upwards while granting a livelihood to those below. This social structure

implied a complex balance of mutual responsibility according to wealth and position. In simple terms, everyone owed service and deference to their superiors, ultimately to the king, who owed his deference only to God. In return, the benefits of security and justice trickled back down. When this operated in balance, the feudal system worked very well. Sadly, greed, self-interest and other human failings often damaged it. ¶ The Steward was responsible for both accounts and the courts, and represented the Lord of the Manor. The Bailiff collected the rents and services, as many still do for the councils that took over from the manors. The Constable kept order, thus, when Robert Peel established the police force, he gave the name constable to the lowest police officer and divided policing into constabularies. ¶ The other appointments varied from manor to manor according to what was grown and sold there. Bread, meat, fish, ale and leather formed the ancient economy of Alcester, and today, when they meet, each appointee carries a symbol of office linked to the job title. ¶ The Court Leet no longer has any official responsibilities, but now raises money for local good causes.

The Lord of the Manor of Alcester (seated) is surrounded by one of the few remaining Courts Leet, forerunners of town councils. From left to right: Bread Weigher, two Fish and Flesh Tasters, two Ale Tasters, Marshal to the Court, Constable, High Bailiff, Surveyor of the Highways, Hayward, Steward of the Manor, Immediate Past High Bailiff, Searcher and Sealer of Leather, Brook Looker, Chapelayne to the Court, Town Crier and Beadle and Low Bailiff.

MASTER OF THE HORSE

Effective means of travel are essential to the maintenance of power, as monarchs have always been aware. Harold II, for instance, marched his infantry from Stamford Bridge to Hastings when he heard of the Norman invasion. William, Duke of Normandy, on the other hand, moved his army and horses by ship, thus keeping them fresher for battle. The outcome is seared into the national memory. ¶ Ever since man learnt how to break a horse's will to his own, there have been few more reliable forms of transport. Horses have carried knights into battle, conveyed messengers from one court to another and enabled monarchs to survey their territory. Indeed, the Normans ruled England from horse-back. This was reflected in the increasing prominence given by kings to their Marshals and Keepers of Stables. During successful campaigns in Scotland and Wales, Edward I's Keeper supplied his king's insatiable demands for new horses through a network of studs both north and south of the River Trent, the traditional dividing line between the north and south of England. ¶ Edward III's claim to the French throne was the catalyst for a war that lasted 100 years. John Brocas, a Gascon noble who had survived two royal coups and the murder of Edward II, was sent to Gascony to procure a local supply of horses. By turning procurement into an efficient military operation, he secured victory for the English at Crécy and later at the siege of Calais. The grateful king knighted Brocas and created him Master of the Horse. ¶ At Agincourt, Henry V placed even greater de-mands on his Master, John Waterton. He had to find horses for the long autumnal march through France and the battle at Harfleur, while also maintaining the garrison's horses on the Scottish border prior to departure. Waterton retired soon after the battle. His three successors had all seen action with Henry V at Agincourt, serving among the 'happy few' on St Crispin's Day. ¶ Following victory on Bosworth Field, Henry VII appointed Thomas Brandon as Master of the Horse. His instructions were to run an efficient, frugal stable but to ensure that it could meet the demands of Tudor pageantry , since display of royal splendour was a vital art of statecraft. ¶ Henry VIII's Master at the Field of the Cloth of Gold was Sir Henry Guildford, chosen partly because his horsemanship would not rival the king's. He followed immediately behind Henry, leading the king's second charger, as was the custom. The job well done coincided with a wealthier court, so the Master became better paid and more powerful. ¶ The Earl of Essex, one of Elizabeth I's ill-fated suitors, acted as her Master for 14 years. He was given many other lucrative ap-pointments besides but he still managed to reorganize the Queen's studs. He was one of five Masters to die on the scaffold. ¶ Others too have managed to combine demanding jobs with their duties as Master: John Claypole served Cromwell, and the 4th Duke of Devonshire was Prime Minister. The Master of the Horse was a powerful political ap-pointment and, until 1782, proffered the holder Cabinet rank, membership of the Privy Council and a peerage. Thereafter it was a Government appointment, changing with each ministry, until 1924, when it became permanent. ¶ The Master now has nothing to do with the acquisition of new horses for the army or running the Royal Mews for the monarch. His role is purely ceremonial – to accompany the Queen on his white charger whenever horses are involved. ¶ For the moment, the post of Master is held by a peer, but soon it may seem more relevant to appoint the Crown Equerry to the role, thus reu-niting a once-considerable rank with real responsibility.

In Windsor Great Park, with the castle to the right of the trees, the Master of the Horse rides his charger, St Patrick. The golden cords hanging from his right shoulder are called aiguillettes and sym-bolize the ropes he once used to tether the monarch's horse – perhaps while hunting here. The Master, who originally procured horses for royal travel and battle, now has a reduced role. He keeps close to the monarch when horses are about – usually on ceremonial occasions, such as the Queen's Birthday Parade , also known as Trooping the Colour.

Few professions generate more paperwork than the law. The archive produced by lawyers over more than 1,000 years is huge and it all needs to be stored. The individual appointed to do so needs to understand the history of law in this country and the wealth of material involved. ¶ The legal structure imposed on England by the Romans held sway for three centuries. When the Saxon kings of Wessex superseded the Romans, they introduced what we know today as English Common Law. This is not embodied in legislation but derives from the precedent of common custom and judicial decisions that derive from legislation. ¶ Following his victory over Harold II, William the Conqueror shrewdly chose to respect the country's existing laws and waited for the Witenamegot (high council) to 'elect' him as king – a vote he was unlikely to lose. ¶ English Common Law applied to the whole country and was quite distinct from any laws imposed at local level by barons. Its emphasis on precedent allowed earlier judgements to be introduced as evidence in legal arguments, so it was essential for all judgements to be recorded by scribes and stored for future reference. ¶ A reference in *The History of England's Chancery* states that parchment rolls containing the most important judgements and decisions were being stored in Chancery as early as 1199. By the time John de Kirkby was appointed *Custos Rotulorum* (Keeper of the Rolls) in 1265, it was a full-time job to keep them in order. ¶ Reflecting the growing importance of this archive, the status of its custodian increased during the early 14th century. By the end of Edward I's reign, the title Master of the Rolls was in use and its holder was allocated funds for a household. At this time the Master was both a senior judge and an administrator, responsible for running the courts and a group of other judges. ¶ In 1377 Edward III recognized the importance of the post by granting the Master a splendid residence called the House for Converted Jews, just off Chancery Lane. Perhaps because of the gradual accumulation of vellum rolls, this residence became an office and then an archive. Its site is now occupied by a vast Victorian building where, until recently, all significant documents of State, apart from Acts of Parliament, were stored along with the ancient rolls. Among them are the Coronation Rolls, the only contract that sovereigns sign, obliging them to rule according to law, as Henry I promised in 1100. This collection came to be known and administered as the Public Record Office, with the Master of the Rolls as its custodian. ¶ In the 18th century the Master of the Rolls was second in judicial power only to the Lord High Chancellor. Indeed, sometimes the Master sat as Vice Chancellor. For 50 years in the 19th century he had his own Rolls Court, but needs have changed, and now the Master presides over the Court of Appeal, dealing with civil rather than criminal matters. ¶ The 1990s saw further change for the Master and his rolls. The constant need to assess information and store it more effectively meant upheaval for the Public Record Office. Most of the documents were moved to Kew, leaving the Master responsible only for the Chancery Records. His title survives, however, despite the alteration in his responsibilities. This is partly because continuity and precedent form the basis of England's system of justice and partly because he still has a latent responsibility for the rolls. Today the Master of the Rolls is the Head of Civil Justice, which is the second most senior judicial position in England and Wales after the Lord Chief Justice. Also, by virtue of the office, he or she is a judge of the Court of Appeal and President of its Civil Division.

Until their transfer to the Public Record Office at Kew, government records had been stored here in the Rolls Estate, which lies between Chancery Lane and Fetter Lane in London, since the Middle Ages. Historically, the Master of the Rolls was not a judge but the Keeper of the Parchment Rolls, or 'king's filing clerk', supervising storage in the Sovereign's Chancery.

SEARCHER OF THE SANCTUARY AND HIGH BAILIFF WITH THE HIGH STEWARD OF WESTMINSTER ABBEY

Westminster Abbey is England's pantheon. It has been inextricably linked with the country's fortunes since Edward the Confessor founded it in lieu of making a pilgrimage to Rome in the 11th century. Its monastery was dissolved by Henry VIII, and the collegiate body, governed by a Dean and Chapter, was founded by Elizabeth I in 1560. It is arguably the most prominent ecclesiastical building in the country, attracting visitors influential and disreputable alike. ¶ To deal with this wide range of people the Dean made some non-clerical appointments – the High Bailiff and the Searcher of the Sanctuary (now combined in a single appointment) along with the High Steward – who acted for the monastery when it was deemed either politic or dangerous for the clergy to do so directly. ¶ The High Bailiff was a policeman who kept order in the Abbey's bailiwick – a considerable task as the Abbey then owned most of the land that now constitutes the City of Westminster, including Buckingham Palace, the Houses of Parliament, Soho and the West End. Maintaining law and order was particularly important because the royal court attracted development and an increasing population. The only areas outside the High Bailiff's jurisdiction were the immediate precincts of the Abbey and the Sanctuary. ¶ For millennia there had been a belief that holy places offered both spiritual and physical refuge in their Sanctuary. King Aethelbert codified Christian Sanctuary at the start of the 7th century, and subsequent Canon Law allowed those accused of violent crime a period of grace within Sanctuary. In fact, many churches had a Peace-Stool beside the altar for seekers of Sanctuary. Edward the Confessor granted Westminster Abbey the right of Sanctuary, but many rogues and criminals abused the privilege. Dean Stanley wrote that 'The precincts of the Abbey were a vast cave of Adullam for all the distressed and discontented in the metropolis, who desired, according to the phrase of the time, to "take Westminster".' Indeed, so bad did the surrounding neighbourhood become that it was known as the 'Devil's Acre'. Among well-known fugitives who took Sanctuary were Elizabeth Woodville, the wife of Edward IV, who was escaping Richard III, and Henry VIII's court poet John Skelton, who hid there after his satirical verse about Cardinal Wolsey backfired. Sanctuary covered an area bounded by Tothill Street, Horseferry Road and the Thames. This area was later policed by the Searcher of the Sanctuary, who checked that all within the defined area had a legal right to remain. ¶ The High Steward had to be a man of gravitas and diplomacy able to negotiate on behalf of the Abbey with the State. This role became necessary after the Dissolution of the Monasteries and the establishment of the Abbey as a Royal Peculiar (a church owing allegiance directly to the Sovereign rather than to a bishop or archbishop). At one time, the Abbot had the right to sit in Parliament, but Deans were not accorded the same privilege. However, they are still entitled to sit on the steps of the Throne. The first High Steward to be appointed was Sir William Cecil in 1560: he became Elizabeth I's trusted counsellor, which allowed him to advance the Abbey's interests. ¶ As the City of Westminster grew in importance, the Abbey's influence was eclipsed. However, attempts by the City Council to let the Mayor take over the High Steward's role were resisted. The Dean and Chapter said 'it was of great importance to them that their Lay Arm, so to speak, should not be cut off'. The High Steward is still able to lobby on behalf of Westminster Abbey.

The cloisters of Westminster Abbey have witnessed the best and worst of England's troubled religious evolution. This church's position is unique in the national story and is protected by both the High Steward, who wears the red robe and acts as the Abbey's conduit to Parliament, and also the High Bailiff and Searcher of the Sanctuary, in blue, who keeps the policies of the Abbey and those seeking its Sanctuary safe.

QUEEN'S REMEMBRANCER

The Queen's Remembrancer, along with the Chancellor of the Exchequer, are the only two appointments that survive from the time of the medieval Court of the Exchequer. The first Remembrancer was Richard of Ilcester, appointed by Henry II in 1154 'to put the Lord Treasurer and the Barons of the Court of Exchequer in remembrance of such things as were to be called upon and dealt with for the benefit of the Crown'. ¶ The Remembrancer represents an authority that is impossible to ignore – the Court of the Exchequer, which has now evolved into HM Treasury and HM Revenue and Customs. Its power has been enforced since medieval times by the barons of the Court of the Exchequer, in particular by the Cursitor baron, and the Queen's Remembrancer now performs the duties of that baron. ¶ The Remembrancer still receives feudal debts on the Sovereign's account. Each year he receives two symbolic debts owed to the Crown by the City of London. The first 'quit rent' is a strange payment, made since 1211, a few years before King John signed Magna Carta. The payment is for a scrap of wasteland called the Moors near Bridgenorth in Shropshire, and is paid off by providing two knives, one sharp and one blunt. The first was used to cut 'tally' sticks out of hazel rods, and the other to etch the debts between two people. The sticks were split and handed to both parties to act as unalterable evidence of the debt owed. The second symbolic debt was first paid to the Exchequer of Henry III in 1235. This was for 'The Forge', a tenement near St Clement Danes, which can no longer be identified. The payment is settled with six horseshoes, of the size worn by warhorses, and 61 nails, each laid out on the chequered cloth of the Exchequer. ¶ The Remembrancer is also custodian of a seal of office that the Queen hands to the politician chosen to be Chancellor of the Exchequer. The appointee becomes Chancellor from the moment he receives it and remains so until the moment he delivers it back. If there is a resignation or a change of Government, the Queen's Remembrancer must hurry to No. 11 Downing Street so that this exchange can take place, because without it business in the Treasury and Exchequer Court cannot proceed. ¶ The title of Queen's Remembrancer is one of the most ancient appointments of the legal hierarchy, but represents much more than something that has passed. The office is still responsible for the preparation of the nomination of High Sheriffs; for suing in the Courts for all fines and sequestrations imposed by the House of Lords, the Court of Appeal and the High Court; for the enrolment of the appointment of Commissioners of Customs and Excise; and it is before the Queen's Remembrancer that the Lord Mayor of London makes his declaration on Lord Mayor's Day. In addition to this, since the Queen's Remembrancer Act of 1859, whoever holds the title has also presided over the annual scrutiny of the coinage of the realm. ¶ The Remembrancer's main job, however, is the onerous one of Senior Master of the Queen's Bench Division, which together with the Chancery Division and Family Division make up the three divisions of the High Court. The work of the Queen's Bench Division consists of commercial and maritime law, serious personal injury, breach of contract, defamation and professional negligence. The Divisional Court, the Admiralty Court, the Commercial Court and the Technology and Construction Court are all part of the Queen's Bench Division. The Senior Master hears relevant cases in their interlocutory stages as a judge in that Division. Since the Lord Chancellor renounced his judicial duties under the terms of the Constitutional Reform Act 2005, the office of the Queen's Rembrancer is now the oldest judicial post to remain in continual existence since the Middle Ages.

The word 'exchequer' comes from the chequered cloth that covered the table in the 12th-century Court of Exchequer and helped illiterate people understand their accounts visually when counters were moved from square to square. This cloth was recreated at a studio in London's Clerkenwell. The Queen's Remembrancer, usually a senior lawyer, has duties both real and symbolic, most of which relate to monies and services due to the Crown, including the odd payment of horseshoes, nails, and sharp and blunt knives. Atop his wig is a baron's tricorn hat, which symbolizes that the Court of the Exchequer was once filled with barons.

LORD HIGH ADMIRAL OF THE WASH

On the eastern shore of the Wash is the church of St Mary the Virgin at Old Hunstanton. Beside it, in January the village pond freezes over and there is no relief whatever from the cold when the heavy church door closes the visitor inside its voluminous interior. Idle gas-heaters and rattling window panes struggle unsuccessfully to keep the icy wind at bay. ¶ Wandering round the aisles, the evidence is clear that this is the pantheon of one family. It was built by them, nurtured by them, and their mortal remains have been laid to rest here for nearly 800 years. Beside the altar, under worn carvings of heraldic achievements, lies Henry le Strange, his plaque dated 1485; in the North Aisle an altar tomb, covered with an intricate brass, celebrates the life of Roger le Strange. Plaques everywhere refer to others in the line, including Henry L'Estrange Styleman le Strange, who restored this freezing building (or desecrated it, depending on your opinion of Victoriana). What these memorials do not record is that the le Stranges came to England long before any surviving memorial can attest: their arrival in this corner of Norfolk, where they governed the coast as Lord High Admirals, was for a vital purpose. ¶ Roland le Strange supposedly left Brittany during the first decade of the 12th century. The attraction for many who crossed the Channel at this time was adventure. Duke William of Normandy's son, Henry, had seized the throne. Seeking riches and land, many knights came to assist in his coup, anticipating the rewards that success might bring. Henry had two elder brothers. The eldest, Robert Curthose, was made Duke of Normandy on the Conqueror's death, while England's crown was given to the next son, William Rufus. The latter, however, was killed in a hunting accident in the New Forest. Henry was present at the death of his unfortunate brother and, perhaps not surprisingly, seized the opportunity to take the throne. Robert attempted to claim his birth-right but was promptly imprisoned for life. Many Norman knights founded their fortunes on the abundant gifts bestowed upon them by Henry I, in order to secure their loyalty. With this new wealth Roland also found himself a wife, the eventual heiress of Hunstanton. ¶ Proving the family's knightly worth in the campaigns against Wales, John le Strange became Supreme Commander of the Marches in the 13th century. And it was around this time that the Plantagenets reviewed the administration of England's vulnerable coastline, establishing admiralties vested in noble families as part of their feudal obligation. The Welsh wars had proved the le Stranges competent and they were given authority over the Wash. Surviving documents confirm little more than the existence of the title that went with the job, but these land-based admiralties were usually responsible for preventing smuggling, administering courts and controlling shipping. ¶ None of these responsibilities remain with the le Strange family: over the centuries, as monarchs and governments chose to administer things differently, each has been assumed by other authorities. Nothing now remains but the title and the land. ¶ The Lord High Admiral today is as peaceful and unassuming a man as you could meet; nowhere in his bearing can be seen the swaggering bravado of his medieval ancestors. The son of a vicar, it was through his mother that he inherited the Admiralty and, with the hall gone, he now lives in the village of Hunstanton. ¶ Nearby, a lighthouse stands sentinel above the cliff, its famous coloured layers making the rock face appear like the walls of Constantinople. From it can be seen the open wildness of the Wash, with the flat landscape of Lincolnshire acting like a slipway for the endless penetrating winds. The commanding view from this place clearly shows why the le Stranges chose Hunstanton to control this Admiralty.

Standing on the beach at Old Hunstanton in Norfolk, where the family have lived since the time of the Domesday Book, the Lord High Admiral of the Wash wears the uniform of an admiral of about 1800. The uniform has no connection with the appointment, and was worn for this book. He owns all the land from the high-tide mark to as far as he can throw a spear. This land-based Admiralty, responsible for supervising the security of the Wash, was given to the le Strange family in the 13th century.

LORD MAYOR OF LONDON, ESCHEATOR, CLERK OF THE MARKETS AND ADMIRAL OF THE PORT OF LONDON

Contrary to common belief, Dick Whittington was led by his cat neither to riches nor to the mayoralty of London, but his appearance in pantomimes resulted from legends born from his life of splendid wealth, all of which he bequeathed to charitable causes. His enduring, if reinvented, reputation as Lord Mayor put the appointment on the map. In truth, Richard Whittington was no poor boy made good but the third son of a Gloucestershire knight, a mercer by trade, and while still young, already successful enough to make substantial loans. In 1397 he began his first term as Lord Mayor, a post he filled four times, being Mayor of Calais as well. When he died in 1423, having loaned money to three kings (Richard II, Henry IV and Henry V), he left a fortune. Since he had neither wife nor child to inherit, all of it went to charity, being used to build a new prison at Newgate, almshouses for the Mercers' Company, repairs to St Bartholomew's Hospital and more. ¶ The City of London has a history of wealth and generous giving. The best merchants in the country based their businesses within the protection of the walled city, established as Londinium by the Romans in AD 43. It was later overlooked by the turrets of William the Conqueror's Tower of London, from whose ramparts William's successors saw the sort of wealth they could only dream of, being paraded by merchants who were organized into trading Guilds or Livery Companies. Because this business brought revenue to the Treasury, royal cupidity was kept in check. However, the relationship between kings – who had power but never enough money – and the City – whose power existed only because it had money – was a tricky one. ¶ In 1189 the first recorded Lord Mayor, Henry FitzAlwin, is described as Chief Magistrate of the City. In a Charter of 1215, King John directed that the citizens of London had the right to choose, every year, someone 'faithful, discreet and fit for the government of the City' to be their own Mayor, who was then to be presented to him and swear fealty. As a result, each new Mayor made the journey up the Thames from the City to the royal court at Westminster, a tradition that evolved into what is known today as the Lord Mayor's Show. Edward III, who reigned from 1327 to 1377, appointed the Lord Mayor to be Escheator for the City. This means that the mayoralty receives the possessions of all who die without wills, or whose estates are seized for treason; 200 years later, Edward VI extended this appointment to include neighbouring Southwark. ¶ The Lord Mayor is also Clerk of the Markets: its markets have always been the lifeblood of the City and they still are today, although the staples of life – such as sugar, coffee, meat, cloth and other tradeable items from across the globe – have given way to the financial services industry. Moreover, since London, like many other ports and coastal areas, needed an admiral to keep its waterways secure, the Lord Mayor became Admiral of the Port of London. ¶ The Lord Mayor's title should not be confused with the new appointment of Mayor of London, which came into effect in 2000, following devolution of certain powers by Government to the Greater London Authority. Whereas both are elected – the former being one of the first democratic appointments in England – the Lord Mayor has authority only within the original boundaries of the City of London. The medieval City walls

---

The Lord Mayor of London wears the Scarlet Gown, over which hangs a Collar of SS that dates back to the 1520s; it is probably the oldest still in use and may have belonged to Henry VIII's Chancellor, Sir (later Saint) Thomas More. It consists of 28 letters 'S' in gold, interlinked with enamelled Tudor roses and golden knots; from the Portcullis in the centre of the collar hangs the Jewel, or Diamond Badge, which holds a cameo of the City's arms in the centre. To his right are the three ceremonial officers of the Lord Mayor's household: the Swordbearer, the City Marshal and the Common Cryer and Sergeant-at-Arms of the City of London, who carries the Great Mace of Government. These officers help maintain the unique laws and customs that have emerged from a trade-off in money for privileges between the City and the Crown.

were surrounded by open countryside, but London has since grown to cover a vast urban area that embraces a population of many millions. The new Mayor is directly elected by this wider community to be an executive figurehead, leaving the Lord Mayor to pursue his role of promoting the City of London as the foremost financial centre in the world. ¶ To enable him to do this the Lord Mayor inherits a lavish infrastructure. His home, the Mansion House, is almost lost among today's towering banks, insurance companies and brokerage houses. Nonetheless, it still remains a dramatic edifice, with the ancient Guildhall nearby to provide an arena for display. Numerous dinners and banquets are given there, where guests include Heads of State and Prime Ministers. In addition, the City's Livery Companies – trade or social guilds which adopted a uniform, or livery – are engaged in a wide range of charitable activities, which provide a framework for supporting a complex range of schools, hospitals, homes, help groups and other national institutions. ¶ It is an appointment that garners traditions like a light attracts moths. The Lord Mayor's own Body Guard is formed from the Honourable Artillery Company under Henry VIII's Charter of 1537. But it was as recently as 1925 that sanction was given for a Company of Pikemen to provide a close escort for the Lord Mayor, and in 1955 the Queen issued a royal warrant to the fully formed Company of Pikemen and Musketeers, a 20th-century reinvention from the 17th century. ¶ It is the task of the Pageantmaster to plan the annual Lord Mayor's Show, which has evolved out of the old river processions that conveyed new Lord Mayors to the monarch at Westminster. (The term 'floats' is still used to describe decorated lorries for this reason.) Elaborate pageants developed after the Reformation, when City poets were paid to write plays that expressed the Mayor's message to Londoners and were performed in the streets. ¶ In the 20th century the need to make the event more professional, particularly for television, led to the appointment of a full-time post. The Pageantmaster is responsible for bringing more than 5,000 people together in 120 serials, which include bands, marchers, carriages, dancers and massive floats. He has to ensure that what is the largest annual procession in Britain performs exactly as he expects and precisely to time, without rehearsal. Starting in Princes Street beside the Bank of England, it takes the new Lord Mayor to the Royal Courts of Justice on the Strand, in order to comply with King John's Charter of 1215 to the City. Fireworks mark the end of the day that ushers a new Lord Mayor into Dick Whittington's shoes: the legacy of duties and charitable patronage is perpetuated.

The Lord Mayor of London stands in Guildhall Yard, in front of the City of London's Guildhall, which was built in 1411 as the centre of City government. The Mayor is surrounded by his Body Guard, provided by the Company of Pikemen and Musketeers, which was re-formed in the 20th century for ceremonial duties and is part of the Honourable Artillery Company. To the left, leaning against the Church of St Lawrence Jewry, is a Drumbeater with Musketeers. To the rear a detachment of Pikemen stand at the 'Have a Care' position; armed with pikes, they wear uniforms from the 17th century. To the right, holding the Leading Staff, is their Captain, who talks with his Lieutenant. Both officers wear armour and have lace in abundance according to rank. The Guildhall was struck in December 1940, during the Blitz, when this part of London was heavily bombed.

CITY REMEMBRANCER

The relationship between the Crown and the City of London seems untrammelled to-day. When the Sovereign visits the City for great events, such as the Queen's Diamond Jubilee Thanksgiving Service in St Paul's Cathedral, the seamless pageantry of welcome hides an ancient tension. Indeed, occasionally, a ceremony that eloquently hints at this is performed, when a symbolic barrier is raised to halt the approaching monarch at Temple Bar. The Lord Mayor then affirms the rights of his Sovereign by offering up the hilt of the Pearl Sword for the monarch to touch. This sword was given to the mayoralty by Elizabeth I and represents the Lord Mayor's authority. In the group surrounding the Lord Mayor at this moment of polite inquisition is the City Remembrancer, one of the City's Great Officers, whose appointment also stems from the reign of the first Queen Elizabeth. ¶ The reason for the historically tense relationship between the Crown and the City was money. Over the centuries, even by the time of the Tudors, monarchs in need of loans, particularly in order to mount expeditionary warfare, would seek it from the London merchants. These merchants wanted to trade with the assurance of security from risk. Angry and jealous kings represented the most potent risk and so, whenever the king needed money and was willing to negotiate for it, the City's government sought to deliver the loan against an assurance of certain liberties. ¶ By the reign of Elizabeth I the City saw the need for an appointment that would keep an eye on its records. This also suited the monarch who had ambitions for the office as a conduit for keeping an eye on the City. This office holder would evolve into the best-placed person to spot any dangers to the privileges secured. Thus in 1570 the City appointed a RecordKeeper, called Thomas Norton, a barrister and London Member of Parliament, who was possibly the perfect choice because he was very well connected, having been employed by Lord Protector Somerset under Edward VI. He was also married to the daughter of Thomas Cranmer, the founding Archbishop of Canterbury in the new reformed Church. ¶ As with most such appointments, this one evolved in a manner both unexpected and logical. It went from being Record Keeper to becoming Secretary to the Lord Mayor and adviser to the Court of Aldermen on 'public affairs' of Parliament. Inevitably, by 1581 this gave access to all the important papers of the City and particularly its correspondence with Parliament. Increasingly, he was asked to act on behalf of the Aldermen and the Lord Mayor in direct dealings with Parliament. This includedmaintaining a lawyer's eye on draft legislation, in order to protect the City's hard-earned privileges and, where possible, enhance these. He was an enthusiastic participant in the conspiratorial politics of the late 16th century, earning the nickname 'Rackmaster Norton'. He was replaced by Dr Giles Fletcher, who was sent by Elizabeth on a mission to Tsar Feodor. This diplomatic role is echoed in the duties of the Remembrancer today, which include organizing all the great City ceremonies, in particular State Banquets held in the Guildhall, and liaison with the London Diplomatic Corps. ¶ Direct royal involvement in the selection of the City Remembrancer ended in the 17th century. The Court of Aldermen appointed the office to be the City's Parliamentary Agent and he was deputed to present petitions in Parliament on behalf of the City. This privilege was one of many that had accrued through rights conferred by Magna Carta that had earlier been confirmed by the Conqueror, anxious to uphold the rights and privileges London had gained from the Saxon monarchs. Some view these privileges as contentious in a time when all are equal. But the importance of the City to the nation is still recognized. The United Kingdom's balance of payments is fortunate to have the income from a thriving financial marketplace. So when the City Remembrancer takes his place under the gallery in the House of Commons he stands on an ancient privilege.

The City Remembrancer stands at the Bar of the House, which is near his chair by the door at the back on the left of the picture. The Bar is marked by a white line but the end of the Bar itself is above, set in the furniture.

MASTER OF THE WORSHIPFUL COMPANY OF TALLOW CHANDLERS

Throughout the United Kingdom today, there are countless shops offering any number of scented candles in order to add a soft light and aroma to leisure. This is a far cry from the absolute necessity of candles as the source of light that existed until the relatively recent discovery of electricity. When Edward I was king, tallow was used to make them, which was expensive. It was made from rendering beef and mutton fat around a wick, so the aroma was very different from today and the smoky detritus in the atmosphere both dirty and greasy. But, like all necessities, it created a business for the manufacturers. ¶ The first known practitioner of tallow chandling that is recorded was Edward the Oynter in the 13th century but doubtless there had been many before. The City of London was already a thriving marketplace with merchants trading the goods and services of England around the known world. Inevitably, the call on tallow chandlers was considerable to provide the flickering light that these merchants needed to complete their orders, balance their accounts and prepare the money they owed in taxation. Records bear witness to the trade done, on what is now Cheapside, by Roger and Stephen le Chaundeler. They would have understood well the Livery Companies that surrounded them, which had evolved in the City of London in order to provide structure for the merchants. ¶ Livery Companies probably existed in some form since before the Norman Conquest in 1066. In Europe's principal trading ports, there were differing forms of trading fraternities, which evolved out of the need to unite for professional advantage. Many of these developed out of Guilds, which gained their name from the price that each person paid to gain the benefits of membership. Livery evolved from the French word for something that is given, in this case a uniform, badge or mutually valuable membership of an organization that ran according to certain rules and standards. Membership of a Livery that led a trade demonstrated that the member had undertaken to meet uniform standards to raise the status of their trading quality and reputation. ¶ The oldest City Livery is deemed to be the Weavers. There is a reference to a payment by the Guild of Weavers in the Pipe Roll of 1130, during the reign of Henry I, the son of the Conqueror. Its Royal Charter came half a century later, at the hands of the second king Henry. Oddly, the Weavers' position in the Order of Precedence, which was established among the 108 City Liveries in 1515, is 42nd. The first, or Great Twelve Livery Companies, were the wealthiest at the time and great import was placed in this ranking. So much so that a disagreement broke out between the Skinners and the Merchant Taylors as to which was rightfully ranked as sixth. The dispute was finally settled when they agreed to take it in turns. This allegedly gave rise to the expression 'at sixes and sevens', which means to be unsettled. The Worshipful Company of Tallow Chandlers sits at 21 in the Order of Precedence. ¶ Many of the City Livery Companies hold strong links with professions that still operate. However, the Industrial Revolution reduced the capacity for such bodies to hold sway over the management of standards and regulations. There are a few that still have the reputation to uphold universal standards: one of them is the Goldsmiths' Company, which still regulates some Assay marks and hosts the Trial of the Pyx, when the Royal Mint is placed on trial for the quality of the nation's coinage. In the dock is the Waster of the Mint, otherwise known as the Chancellor of the Exchequer. The Tallow Chandlers no longer have a thriving trade to influence but rather exist with the noble mission to raise charity.

The Master's neck jewel and seat in the Tallow Chandlers' Hall holds symbolic importance for the year that each Master of the Worshipful Company of Tallow Chandlers holds office. Both bear the Company's coat of arms, which was granted in 1603. The candlesticks naturally have significance for the Tallow Chandlers and incorporate doves and crowned angels from this heraldic achievement.

SENIOR GRECIAN OF CHRIST'S HOSPITAL

When Christ's Hospital was moved from the City of London to Sussex in 1902, the 'Grecians' Arch' went too, and the architect incorporated it into the new building. Over 1,000 scholars and children made the move, including the two years of sixth-formers, who, since the 17th century, have been called Grecians. One of them is now appointed from among his or her peers as Senior Grecian. ¶ The roots of the school and its traditions lie in the 16th century. Nicholas Ridley, the Bishop of London, was a scholar of great standing. He preached on charity to the teenage King Edward VI, known as 'God's Imp', and his influence on the boy was profound. Ridley, who had already assisted the Anglican reformer Thomas Cranmer in preparing the new articles of faith, was set upon using the impressionable young monarch to spur forward the Reformation. As a result of the sermon, Edward gathered together the Bishop, the Lord Mayor and the Aldermen of the City of London and proposed the foundation of a substantial charity to put Ridley's charitable ideas into effect. Edward himself gave an endowment, and the monarch still contributes today. ¶ With adequate funds gathered, three hospitals were established in 1552, each benefiting from the large legacy of vacant monastic buildings that Henry VIII had left behind. They were Bridewell for the 'Idell vagabondes', St Thomas's Hospital for the 'sore and sicke', which still operates on the south bank of the Thames opposite the Houses of Parliament, and Christ's Hospital, which was established to educate gifted children and originally occupied the buildings in Newgate Street from which the Grey Friars were evicted. The financial endowment was considerable, but within a month of Edward presenting the Charter in 1553, the sickly monarch was dead. England immediately became a hotbed of intrigue, as Bishop Ridley pragmatically proclaimed Lady Jane Grey the dead king's rightful heir. Her reign lasted for only 13 days, and she was succeeded by Edward VI's Roman Catholic sister, Mary, who burnt Ridley at the stake in 1555. ¶ Religious turmoil made the first years of Christ's Hospital difficult to say the least. Queen Mary wanted to restore the building to the Grey Friars, but large bribes and an impassioned appeal by Friar John on the Hospital's behalf saved the day: he said that 'he had rather be a Scullion in theire kytchin then Stewarde to the Kinge'. ¶ Despite the politics, the new school set about providing education for boys and girls with talent but no financial means to pay for decent schooling. The doors first opened to 400 children, some of whom were still infants. Most children stayed in education only until they were 12 or 13 years old, when the demands for clerks in the City drew most away to earn money for their pauper families. Those who remained were destined for Oxford and Cambridge, and their obligatory proficiency in ancient Greek led to their being called Grecians. Within the school they were revered as intellectuals with their heads in the clouds. ¶ In 1673 Charles II set up the Royal Mathematical School as a branch within the school, with the aim of training potential sailors in navigation and mathematics. The Royal Navy still pays the fees for pupils who are children of service personnel. ¶ The distinctive uniform, worn by all scholars, earned them another name – the 'Blue Coats'. It dates from the foundation of the school and was possibly based on the habit worn by the displaced Grey Friars but similar to that of a Tudor apprentice. The unmissable bright yellow socks were originally designed to keep vermin at bay; apparently, yellow is a colour loathed by rats.

A statue of Christ's Hospital's founder Edward VI rests on a plinth above the figures of four 'Old Blues', Coleridge, Lambe, Middleton and Maine. Standing on her own plinth the Senior Grecian watches on as the pupils march in to lunch accompanied by the school band. This tradition is performed each weekday at 12.50pm precisely.

CHORISTERS OF KING'S COLLEGE, CAMBRIDGE

On 21 May each year, a group gathers in the oratory of the Tower of London's Wakefield Tower for the Ceremony of the Lilies and Roses. On this day and reputedly at this place, Henry VI was murdered in 1471. 'Pure displeasure and melancholy' were blamed, but this was disingenuous because he died on the very night that Edward IV returned to regain his throne. It was a grim conclusion to Henry's troubled life. He had been a naive ruler, burying his head in the sands of pious abstinence and religious observance. Succeeding to the two kingdoms of England and France from his valiant father, Henry V, aged nine months, he was almost abandoned by his mother and left in the hands of Richard Earl of Warwick, the Kingmaker, who taught him 'nurture, literature, language and other manner of cunning'. Henry had a particular interest in education and founded Eton College and King's College, Cambridge, to provide a first-class grammar-school and university education for poor scholars. ¶ He used money accrued by his father's confiscation of the alien priories (mostly monastic offshoots of French religious foundations), supplemented with funds from his Lancastrian duchy, and founded a college at Eton in 1440. The following year, on Passion Sunday, in the hitherto unfashionable university of Cambridge, he laid the foundation stone of King's College. This was originally dedicated to St Nicholas but renamed 'Our College Royal of Our Lady and St Nicholas'. ¶ The Founder's Charter was illuminated in 1446, depicting Henry VI at prayer, joined by his combined Lords and Commons. Parliament is thus shown united, which it still was then, in offering praise to God, the Virgin and St Nicholas for the new college. By 1453, its constitutional detail had been established, with a choir of 10 men and 16 boys to sing the daily services in the chapel. The Charter initially provided for a rector and 12 scholars, reflecting Christ and his disciples. The boys were selected from the 70 King's Scholars at Eton and placed on a roll for admission to King's College. ¶ As if predicting the magnificent evolution of English sung liturgy, despite the coming Reformation, Henry VI had provided for boys' voices to help maintain the spirit of worship depicted in that first illustrated manuscript. The number of choristers has never changed. Whilst these are no longer 'poor and needy boys', any boy may audition. ¶ The chapel was not completed until the middle of the 16th century, though the choristers sang from Foundation. Henry VI's popularity was not sufficient to survive the loss of France or bickering among the nobles whom he foolishly favoured. The country fell into the civil wars of the Roses and little building work progressed. After holding a chapter of the Order of the Garter at King's on St George's Eve in 1506, Henry VII sent a chest of money to enable the work to be completed, both as a shrine to Henry VI and as a celebration of the new Tudor dynasty. Plans for the murdered monarch to be canonized were rejected by Rome; however, his memory was venerated in stone, not only with chapels at both his colleges but also at Westminster Abbey. ¶ The heraldic arms of the two colleges show symbols of both kingdoms that Henry inherited, but where Eton shows three lilies of the Virgin Mary, granted in 1449, King's College has three white roses, which some say is for St Nicholas. The group that gathers in the Tower of London on the anniversary of his death for the Ceremony of Lilies and Roses are members of both foundations. They lay bunches of the flowers shown on the armorial bearings of their respective colleges.

Henry VI cleared a large area of land on the Backs of the River Cam, in the centre of Cambridge, to provide a magnificent setting for his chapel at King's College. Sixteen Choristers were established to sing at the daily services. They still wear top hats, undergraduate gowns and 'Etons', which consist of 'bum-freezer' jackets and stiff collars, when they go to and from the chapel.

TOLLY-KEEPERS OF
WINCHESTER COLLEGE

The ships landing along the south coast of England in 1348 imported more than cargo; they carried rats that brought bubonic plague. Within a decade, the Black Death, as it became known, had killed off one third of the country's population, before heading north to slaughter the Scots. Clergy were among the worst afflicted because they ministered to the sick and caught the incurable illness in the process. ¶ William of Wykeham, a priest who held some of the most influential and profitable benefices available, including Lord Chancellor and Bishop of Winchester, witnessed the terrible effects of the plague and decided to amend the situation in the only way he knew how. He applied to the Pope for permission to found religious houses, where prayers could be said for him and his many patrons, and to establish within them colleges for the training of priests ready to replace those who fell in the plague. ¶ On 26 March 1388 the first stones of what is now known as Winchester College were laid. William had been educated in the city and born nearby, at Wickham, so this was an obvious place to establish the college. As decreed by Pope Urban VI in the bull granting William permission for this undertaking, the College still provides for 70 'poor and needy' scholars, many of whom are educated on the income derived from wealth bestowed by William. The school's social structure, laid down in early statute, requires that boys of all ages live and study together as familial units in Chambers, the elder scholars encouraging and overseeing the younger ones. ¶ For several centuries, a particular responsibility of the older boys was to provide light for the communal rooms. From among the 14 boys in their penultimate year, the senior boy in College, the Praefect of Hall, nominated seven as Custodes Candelarum (literally 'keepers of the candles'). In the arcane vocabulary of the school, the word for candle is 'tolly', a corruption of 'tallow', the mutton fat from which the candles were made. ¶ As the Headmaster explains, 'The Tolly-keepers are best described by what they are not. They are above juniors but not yet Praefects.' Under the Senior Tolly-keeper, the seven boys were responsible for keeping the school supplied with tollies from the chapel vestry. When electricity was installed, the tradition ceased, but it was never formally abolished. To the surprise of some, a modern generation of scholars has chosen to revive the practice. Nowadays, the Tolly-keepers carry candles into College Hall, where the boys have eaten since scholars were first admitted to the school in 1394. ¶ William of Wykeham's principal desire, that both Winchester and his theological establishment, New College, Oxford (known collectively as the Winton colleges), would exist for eternity in order to offer up prayers for his soul, was not achieved: centuries of religious turmoil saw to that. However, both foundations have survived to become centres of learning that achieve consistently high standards. William is sometimes called the 'father of the public school system', and perhaps it is no surprise, therefore, that Winchester College is now one of the largest and best-known public schools in Britain. After the Royal Commission of 1857, the tradition of accepting entrants by patronage and nomination was replaced by competitive examination for the whole school. The original College founded for poor and needy scholars remains an elite within an elite. Although many Wykehamists, as old boys are known, achieve notable careers, few follow the path of their founder into the Church.

Before the advent of electricity, William of Wykeham's College Hall in Winchester College and the 'toyes', or studies, in which the 70 scholars studied required plenty of candles. The Senior Tolly-keeper, carrying the snuffer, organized six other Tolly-Keepers in this logistical enterprise. Today, the exercise is purely ritual.

In 1485 most of the Great Office holders who had served Richard III were either killed or captured in the last great battle of the Wars of the Roses, fought between the houses of Lancaster and York on the field of Bosworth. Henry VII had proclaimed himself king the day before the fight, making traitors of the vanquished. With the power of kingship in his hands the first Tudor monarch of England set about re-establishing unified government and the monarchy, and ending aristocratic factionalism.

The Tudors were to reign over a period of considerable change. The European Renaissance reached England at this time, and the Reformation, which was a movement of revolt against Papal authority, also swept from Europe through England, Scotland and into Ireland.

Henry VII used his patronage to grant appointments on merit, not rank, though he sold some judicial appointments to the highest bidder, such as Master of the Rolls, and even put the Speakership of the Commons up for sale as he worked to fill the depleted Treasury. Pragmatically, he formed a Body Guard from the most loyal of his soldiers as his first priority: there were still Yorkist claimants threatening his security, even though most had been killed by Richard. Now the oldest military body in the world, the Yeomen of the Guard still provide close protection to the monarch within England.

The Lancastrian King Henry VII married Elizabeth of York to unify his kingdom: by giving their daughter, Margaret, in marriage to James IV of Scots they also hoped to prevent trouble from the north. The child of this union, James, was named Prince and Great Steward of Scotland and the Lord of the Isles, a tactic designed to unite the warring western and northern isles with the Crown after centuries of fighting. The Prince of Wales today still carries these titles.

The Scottish court was fundamentally similar to that of England and stood at the centre of a feudal structure, with its own Officers of State. Many of these were phased out after the Union with England in 1707, but some survived, including the Keeper of the Signet, responsible for sealing all the king's business.

When Henry VIII, son of Henry VII, defeated and killed his brother-in-law James IV on Flodden Field in 1513, his nephew James V came to the throne in Scotland, and, after years spent as the pawn of his nobles, came into his own with a vengeance. However, after two marriages to strengthen the Auld Alliance with France, James's heart was broken by the disastrous Scottish defeat at the Battle of Solway Moss, in 1542. He died leaving an infant daughter in the regency of his wife, Mary of Guise. The infant, Mary Queen of Scots, was to provide the final Catholic bastion against Scotland's imminent Reformation.

Through the secular and spiritual changes of the English Reformation, Henry VIII brought about a daring and revolutionary realignment of economic power in England. It changed the nature of his kingdom, isolating it within Europe so that it looked further afield for expansion. By dissolving the monasteries, after his conflict with the Roman Church, he filled still further the Treasury that his father had worked to restore. The countryside is decorated with monastic ruins that once witnessed the moral trials in which people decided upon a faith by which they would live or die.

After the Dissolution in 1540, Henry took on many responsibilities once fulfilled by the monasteries. One such service was that offered by the Carter family as Guide over Kent Sands on Morecambe Bay.

Perhaps the greatest misperception of the period, a time that gave rise to some of the more extraordinary and portentous appointments in this collection, is that Henry VIII was a Protestant. Far from it. Indeed, the mere suggestion would have added your name to the State Executioner's list in this time of despotic judicial murder. Henry's own book on the sacraments resulted in one of the Sovereign's titles that, in its timing, is perhaps the most ironic: Defender of the Faith.

The devotions of monarchs on military missions, or progressing with their court through the country, presented problems throughout the period of the Reformation. To ensure no service was missed, the Chapel Royal, a sort of travelling clergy, followed the monarch, with a choir to sing the liturgies. This body felt the strain of changing doctrine directly, as the pendulum of creed swung violently through the reigns of Henry VIII and his three children, Edward VI, Mary I and Elizabeth I. Court composers too walked a spiritual tightrope, writing music for the Children of the Chapel and Gentlemen-in-Ordinary to sing at Anne Boleyn's marriage, but also when Mary led the Church back to Rome and persecuted the Protestants, and then again when Elizabeth endured excommunication for returning the country to Protestantism.

The charitable foundations of Edward VI's Protestant reign, including St Thomas's Hospital for the sick and Christ's Hospital for educating the poor, were also caught up in religious rivalry. It was especially difficult for scholars, and the universities, to tread between each creed. In Oxford, the new Protestant status quo set by Elizabeth's implacable stand gave one of her supporters, Thomas Bodley, the opportunity to establish a library that now houses every book subsequently published in England. Playwrights and poets also had to adapt to the changing religious climate, and became key figures as the court's political apologists. This role was to grow in importance and led in 1668 to the appointment of a Poet Laureate.

The feudal system was increasingly strained in the face of modernization during the Renaissance in England. The Tudors, recognizing that feudal systems would not efficiently provide the militia they needed, pioneered a new method for summoning men to arms. They appointed officers, who became Lord-Lieutenants, in each county to assist the existing sheriffs in both finding and commanding a militia. However, feudalism still had its uses. In 1565 Elizabeth I granted the island of Sark, in the Channel Islands, themselves remnants of the duchy of Normandy, as a separate fiefdom that survives with its unique form of government to this day.

The pressures imposed on society by the Reformation were made more complicated in Ireland by the Plantation, a sponsored immigration, that would further strain relations in the coming centuries and where the missionary inheritance of St Patrick was claimed by both denominations. The Dissolution in England had displaced Church wealth and power, though the new Church of England was to be a fervent episcopal successor to Catholicism in the following century, championed by a new royal house. Towards the ending of Elizabeth's reign, the Scots king waited at Holyrood to inherit England's throne, his Protestant education poised to set the political agenda for an isolationist Britain bent on unity and colonization.

[109]

LORD OF THE ISLES, PRINCE AND GREAT STEWARD OF SCOTLAND, DUKE OF ROTHESAY, EARL OF CARRICK AND BARON OF RENFREW

In medieval times, the Great (or High) Steward of Scotland maintained the king's household and protected his interests in his absence. The post was first granted by David I in the 1130s to Walter Fitzalan, the younger son of a Norman baron who had befriended the king in England. David, the youngest son of Malcolm III and St Margaret of Scotland, had grown up at the Norman court in England where his sister, Matilda, was married to William I's youngest son, the future Henry I. It was a web of alliances between two distrusting neighbour countries that did not last. But, during his stay at court, David learned about the civilizing effects of both a strong Church and a feudal system of landholding. When he inherited the throne in 1124, he set about modernizing Scotland, with Walter's help, imposing the feudal system and encouraging the spread of a vigorous Church. On Walter's death, the title of High Steward passed to his descendants, who used the alternative spelling Stewart as a family name. ¶ In 1290 the Scottish throne was cast into turmoil by the death of the infant Queen Margaret of Scotland (the Maid of Norway), on her way to marry the son of Edward I of England. Edward I intervened, claiming to be Scotland's overlord, and so sparked the wars of independence. James Stewart, the 5th High Steward, championed the rival claim that put Robert the Bruce on the throne in 1306. In gratitude, Bruce gave his daughter in marriage to James's son Walter. This marriage was significant because, when the Bruce line had no heirs on the death of David II, Walter's son Robert (7th High Steward) inherited the throne as Robert II in 1371. As a result, the office of Great Steward gave its name to the Royal House of Stewart (spelled Stuart after about 1567). In 1469, by an Act of the Scottish Parliament, the hereditary office that was now vested in the king was conferred on 'the first-born prince of the King of Scots forever'. Since then, heirs to the throne of Scotland have been known as Prince and Great Steward of Scotland. ¶ Lord of the Isles, another ancient title inherited by the heirs, stems from an old Viking title *Ri Innse Gall* (King of the Isles), dating from the 9th century, when the Vikings ruled the Western Isles and the Isle of Man. In the early 12th century Olaf, King of Mann, claimed the title Lord of the Isles and in about 1140 the warlord Somerled married Olaf's daughter. As a result, Somerled later claimed the title, after gaining control of the whole area and invading the Isle of Man and deposing Olaf's son and successor in 1158. In 1164 Somerled was defeated and killed by Malcolm IV, thus subsequent descendants of Somerled, who became the Macdonalds, ruled the Isles as vassals of the King of Scots. ¶ John Macdonald (c. 1326–87) was the first to be actually described as 'Lord of the Isles'. During the conflict with England in the early 16th century, James IV of Scotland became so exasperated with the intrigues of John Macdonald, the 4th Lord of the Isles, that he stripped the title from him, and James V formally annexed it to the Crown in 1540. ¶ As heir to the throne of Scotland, the Heir Apparent to the Crown inherits three further Scottish titles: Duke of Rothesay, Earl of Carrick and Baron of Renfrew. When in Scotland, he is known as the Duke of Rothesay, a title created by Robert III in 1398. Robert the Bruce held the earldom of Carrick before he became king in 1306, and the Barony of Renfrew was named after land granted by David I to Walter Fitzalan.

The Lord of the Isles, Prince and Great Steward of Scotland wears the uniform of Deputy Colonel-in-Chief of the Highlanders (Seaforths, Camerons and Gordons) in the inner quadrangle of Holyrood Palace in Edinburgh. It was here that David I – who appointed the first High Steward – had his vision of a white stag with a holy rood (cross) between its antlers. The stag supposedly instructed him to build a monastery, later rebuilt as a royal palace by James IV. The star on his left breast is the insignia of the Order of the Thistle, Scotland's senior order of chivalry, which was reconstituted in 1687 – though some claim it evolved from an earlier Order of St Andrew, in 809.

LADY OF THE ISLES

The story behind what is arguably one of the nation's most romantic titles held by the Heir Apparent to Scotland's throne, and thereby carried by his consort, is set in the wild islands along Britain's north-west coastline. These isles, with their remote bays, rugged cliffs and rocky inlets, stand against the endless ferocity of the Atlantic Ocean and centuries ago they became the domain of seagoing Norsemen. They were warriors who navigated in open boats from the area of what is now Norway and Denmark to take possession of Scotland's unguarded archipelagoes. Although they did this in the name of their king, the conquerors of this sea-bound colony became plenipotentiary vice-regents. ¶ Raghnailt was the daughter of one of these warriors, who was called Olaf, King of Mann and the Isles. In 1140 she married another local Norse leader, called Somerled, who was ruler of the Kintyre peninsula. Their marriage would shape the future of the Scottish Isles, because when the great Olaf died and his son Godred succeeded, it was quickly clear that he had none of his father's gift for leadership and he became hopelessly ineffective and unpopular. News of this discontent reached his sister Raghnailt and, not unnaturally for this time, her husband, Somerled, considered his options for action. ¶ In 1156 Somerled led a fleet of 80 ships against Godred, and defeated him during the Battle of Epiphany, following which the two enemies partitioned the Isles between them. Godred kept the islands north of Ardnamurchan with Somerled gaining the rest. However, in 1158 Somerled returned to the Isle of Man with 53 warships and successfully vanquished Godred, who fled back to Norway, while Somerled assumed control of Mann and the Isles. By marriage and by descent from her father, Raghnailt was now Lady of Mann and the Isles. The union of Kintyre with these new lands created a united rule for the Vikings and Gaels living along the Scottish coast that reached Ross, the Hebrides, Knoydart, Ardnamurchan and Skye. In the centuries that followed, the governance of Mann was separated from what was to become recognized as the Lordship of the Isles. ¶ The Isles were geographically so self-contained and remote that, despite being variously subject to the rule of the kings of Norway, Ireland and Scotland, the reality was that none of those overlords could hold any active sway over the Lordship. The Isles were, in almost every respect, a separate independent fiefdom that contained the tension of a warrior race. But at all stages the rulers in the Isles were pragmatic about what best served their survival and continued self-governance. For instance, Angus Óg (Angus 'the Young'), who was ruler of the Isles at the start of the 14th century, gave shelter to Robert the Bruce after the Battle of Methven in 1306 and brought his troops to fight with Robert the Bruce at Bannockburn in 1314. The Scots victory secured long-wanted independence for the northern kingdom, which chimed with the pragmatic interests of those in the Isles. In gratitude, King Robert's son, David II, acknowledged Angus's loyalty in 1336 by formally establishing the title *Dominus Insularum*, or Lord of the Isles. ¶ In 1462 John Macdonald II was Lord of the Isles, but he made a strategic miscalculation. He entered a treaty with England's king to rise against the King of Scots. When this treason was exposed 30 years later, James IV of Scots stripped the Macdonalds of their lands, and the title of Lord of the Isles was given, thenceforward, to the eldest son of the Scottish monarch. Following the tradition of Raghnailt, whose husband bore the title of her late father and errant brother, the wife of the Heir Apparent still carries all her husband's titles, as consort, and is therefore Lady of the Isles.

When the title was removed from the Isles and vested in the eldest son of the Scots monarch, the geographic link was broken. Here the Lady of the Isles sits in the Stumpery of Birkhall, within the Balmoral estate in Royal Deeside, Aberdeenshire. She wears Lord of the Isles tartan and holds a cromach bearing her crowned cypher 'C', as consort to the Heir Apparent.

MESSENGER SERGEANT MAJOR AND WARDROBE KEEPER WITH THE CLERK OF THE CHEQUE AND ADJUTANT OF THE QUEEN'S BODY GUARD OF THE YEOMEN OF THE GUARD

Going to bed was a dangerous business for 15th-century monarchs. With potential assassins everywhere, the Yeomen of the Guard were drafted in to prepare the royal bedroom at night-time and then sleep at the door to keep it safe. Among the extant appointments still shared out among the men who line the Queen's ceremonial path are two that reflect this responsibility – the Yeoman Bedgoer and Yeoman Bedhanger. ¶ As monarchs were also at risk of poisoning, the Yeomen acted as food-tasters too. They carried dishes to the dining room from the kitchen and, as they set each one down, took a mouthful to prove it was safe. The Exon-in-Waiting (so called because he is a regular serviceman 'exempt' from his duties in order to serve in the Body Guard) still stands beside the Sovereign's chair at State banquets, just in case he is called on to taste again. ¶ The Queen's Body Guard of the Yeomen of the Guard was formed after the Battle of Bosworth Field in 1485, and is therefore the oldest military corps in Britain. Henry VII claimed his crown by right of conquest: indeed, it was supposedly lifted from a thorn hedge on the battlefield by Rhys ap Thomas, who placed it on Henry's head. The country, however, remained divided. To ensure his safety, Henry VII – inspired by the Scottish Guard kept by the French kings – organized 50 of his loyal archers into a company called the Yeomen of the Guard of Our Lord the King: they would protect him at his coronation and afterwards. Not since Richard II had a monarch felt it necessary to engage 'a furniture of daily soldiers' to be in constant attendance. ¶ In 1605 the Yeomen of the Guard had their finest hour. Getting wind of a plot to blow up the Houses of Parliament, they searched the cellars and uncovered Guy Fawkes among some powder kegs. Since then, it has become a time-honoured ritual for the Yeomen to search the cellars by lantern light before the State Opening of Parliament to ensure the Sovereign's safety. ¶ When Charles II established a standing army after the Restoration, he also put the Yeomen of the Guard on a proper footing with their own officers in recognition of their service during his exile; it also explains how the corps has given the Sovereign unbroken service since 1485. Nonetheless, it suffered the indignity of having to accept royal favourites, with no military experience, as commissioned officers. However, the corps again enjoyed prominence when it provided close protection for George II, the last British king to command an army in the field, at Dettingen in 1743. ¶ Members of the Guard retain the title of Yeoman because they are all warrant officers or non-commissioned officers drawn from the Army, the Royal Marines and the Royal Air Force. Each must have an exemplary service record and hold a Long Service and Good Conduct Medal. The corps also includes five commissioned officers. They command the force under the Captain, the Government's Deputy Chief Whip in the House of Lords. ¶ Many Tudor ranks remain, including Clerk to the Cheque, who originally arranged duties but is now Adjutant as well, and thus responsible for discipline. The Messenger Sergeant Major was trusted to deliver important messages and became the senior rank beneath the officers: today he is also Wardrobe Keeper, the Wardrobe being where Tudor monarchs kept their stores. ¶ The Yeomen of the Guard turn out for State functions, investitures and garden parties, as alert today for threats of terrorism as they were when they foiled the Gunpowder Plot.

The oldest military corps in Britain, the Yeomen of the Guard have been quartered in St James's Palace for centuries. Yeomen, Yeomen Bedgoers and Yeomen Bedhangers, with titles deriving from security tasks performed to protect sleeping Tudor monarchs, parade in Colour Court, while the Messenger Sergeant Major talks with the Clerk of the Cheque and Adjutant. The Yeomen last fought for Henry VIII in France.

STANDARD BEARER OF HER MAJESTY'S BODY GUARD OF THE HONOURABLE CORPS OF GENTLEMEN-AT-ARMS

Almost as soon as the throne was his, the young Henry VIII set about spending the riches his cautious father had put by and he revived the romantic but disastrous struggle for possession of the French crown. ¶ One of his earliest decisions was to establish a close body guard. Henry VII had assembled a body of archers but his son wanted 50 men from noble families, armed with spears and lances, to be close at hand if trouble should break out. They were called the Band of Gentlemen Pensioners, a name that might suit the venerable former officers who fill its ranks today but, in 1509, this was an elite lean fighting machine. Then, the word 'pensioner' had nothing to do with stipendiary payments to the elderly; it implied that the king paid for their pension, or board and lodging. They were trained and fit for battle, well drilled and disciplined. Their establishment further demonstrated the change from an army dependent upon feudal arrangements, and it was not long before this new Band was pitched into battle. ¶ The cause was revenge: the booty, two towns costly to defend. The Marquess of Dorset had been sent to France in 1512 with an expeditionary force, to join up with the Spaniards and give the French king, Louis XII, a bloody nose. Unfortunately, Spain double-crossed the English, leaving them stranded while a cosy Franco-Spanish truce was struck. Henry VIII was furious so, the next June, he landed at Calais at the head of an army of 4,000. In this retinue were his worthies, the Band of Gentlemen, under command of their first Captain, the Earl of Essex. The Band numbered 400 mounted men for this invasion. A painting depicting the Battle of the Spurs that ensued shows a Standard Bearer was appointed in preparation for war: along with two others, the Harbinger, who ensured the Men-at-Arms were victualled with lodgings, and the Clerk of the Cheque, who checked that no one was absent and all were paid. ¶ The next trip to France was for diplomatic display and to impress the great Renaissance monarch François I, at the Field of the Cloth of Gold in 1520. Apart from the very real task of defending Henry in a situation that could have gone sour, they pitted their strength against their French counterparts, the Noble Guarde du Corps. This ceremonial role endured and, whenever a State visitor arrives in Britain, the Queen is surrounded by heirs of the original Band of Gentlemen. ¶ The oldest surviving muster role is 1526 and shows Edward Billingham as the Standard Bearer. Standards were first seen in Edward I's reign but became popular under the Tudors. They are narrow and taper to a swallow tail to suit the field of battle when carried aloft on horseback. As foot soldiers generally have squared flags, the one carried by the Standard Bearer now is a reminder of when the Band were a mounted corps. ¶ The last time they served as a military body guard was for Charles I in the Civil War, though they were stood by during the Jacobite Rebellion of 1745 and the Chartist Riots of 1848. King Charles confirmed that the Band had 'the honour to be our nearest guard and to have their daily access into our presence chamber', a privilege still held today. Even now, the Captain is a member of the Government. At the Battle of Edgehill, in 1642, it was Sir Edmund Verney who was killed as Standard Bearer, his place being taken by Captain John Smith: but strangely neither was in the Band of Pensioners. ¶ Charles II restored the Band, which Cromwell had suspended, but only as a ceremonial guard, the military one being filled by the Life Guards. It became a Band of retired officers of merit, which William IV renamed the Honourable Corps of Gentlemen-at-Arms, and at all great occasions it is the Corps that stand closest to the Queen, as 'The Nearest Guard', with their Standard Bearer ready to lower the standard in salute.

The senior Officer of the Honourable Corps of Gentlemen-at-Arms is the Captain, a political appointee who is also the Government Chief Whip in the House of Lords. Here the Standard Bearer is flanked by two fellow Officers in Friary Court of St James's Palace. In the background is the Proclamation Gallery from where the accession of a new Sovereign is proclaimed by the Garter King of Arms.

QUEEN'S SWAN MARKER

It is still true that almost every swan living on the open waterways of Britain belongs to the Queen. Recent attempts to revoke this unique status have been overruled, and the Royal Household includes a post to maintain an historic tradition that retains a surprising relevance. ¶ Since the 13th century monarchs have employed someone, known variously as Swan Keeper, Swan Master or Swan Marker, to protect these royal birds, and each has been supported by a Swanherd of qualified helpers. In medieval times harsh punishments were meted out to those who did the 'bird royal' harm. Stealing a swan's egg, for example, earned a year and a day in prison, while killing a swan cost the perpetrator a small fortune in wheat: the swan was hung by the beak with its feet just touching the floor, then the criminal had to pour out sufficient grain to envelop the whole bird. In 1895 unlicensed killing was punished by seven weeks' hard labour. Nowadays, stealing a tame swan is still larceny, and the Malicious Damage Act makes it an offence either to maim or kill one. ¶ Many stories, romantic and otherwise, attach to swans, and their associations with royalty have brought them a prestige that has found its way into successive statutes. Edward IV, for example, restricted applications for ownership, of which there were many, to men with land exceeding a value of five marks. This did not, however, stem the flow of requests, which made it necessary to develop unique markings on the beak, called Cygninota, to distinguish one owner's swans from another's. ¶ By the reign of Elizabeth I there were over 900 markings recorded, and each July new cygnets were marked according to the nicks and scratches on their parents' beaks. Any without markings belonged to the Sovereign. Those that could not be attributed to particular parents were given to the monarch or whoever owned the grass where they were found feeding. This practice of marking the birds was called Swan Upping or Swan Hopping. ¶ When Edward IV was short of money, he applied to the City of London's Worshipful Company of Vintners for a loan. In return, a Charter of 1473 granted them the right to own some swans on the River Thames. A few years later the same privilege was granted to the Dyers' Company. Every July since then the Queen's Swan Marker is joined by the Markers belonging to the Vintners and Dyers, and their teams row along the Thames in six skiffs between Sunbury and Abingdon. As they pass Windsor Castle, the Queen's Swan Marker gives the toast, 'Her Majesty the Queen, Seigneur of the Swans'. In the 17th and 18th centuries, when great barges were still used for this ceremony, they provided an excuse for Swan Banquets, when the Swan Uppers feasted on roast cygnet. ¶ Times are very different now, and Swan Upping is a hard week's work for the oarsmen, who are all licensed Watermen and Lightermen. The week remains a traditional event, but one in which conservation and education are also emphasized. Increased leisure activity on England's waterways has contributed to the reduction of swan habitats in many areas, and also reduced the number of birds. Swan Upping provides the opportunity to monitor the welfare of the swan population on the Thames. The information gathered is passed to Oxford University, which surveys the health of the birds – something that has improved significantly since the lead weights once used for fishing have been banned. The Queen's Swan Marker also has a national responsibility, confirmed by statute, to advise on the birds' welfare.

The Queen's Swan Marker is rowed on a quiet stretch of the River Thames at Cookham in a traditional Thames rowing skiff adorned with flags bearing the badge of his office and the Queen's cypher. He wears the royal livery of scarlet and gold, and sports a swan feather behind the Crown badge on his cap. An outbreak of disease and damage to nests caused by flooding on the Thames have affected the swan population in recent years. The Swan Marker's role remains relevant in the light of such threats to the Queen's swans.

GENTLEMAN USHER OF THE BLACK ROD, SECRETARY TO THE LORD GREAT CHAMBERLAIN AND SERGEANT-AT-ARMS OF THE HOUSE OF LORDS

Pageantry was a regular part of life for the first 26 knights who wore the Garter emblem of Edward III's order of chivalry in 1348. The order met annually at Windsor Castle on 23 April, the feast of St George. As the knights processed towards the chapel dedicated to St George, they were led by an Usher (from the Latin *ussarius*, meaning 'doorkeeper'), who carried a black rod. When they were safely assembled, the door was closed and its security guarded by the Usher. ¶ The earliest reference to this doorkeeping role is found in Letters Patent from 1361, stating that Walter Whitehorse, 'usher of the free chapel in Wyndesore Castle', received 12 old pence a day for life. ¶ The Usher eventually became better known by the name of his staff of office, Black Rod, and moved as part of the court to attend the monarch wherever he might be. When a fire in 1512 forced Henry VIII to move from the Palace of Westminster to York House, Black Rod was left in the burnt-out remains and has stayed there ever since. Ten years later, he was given custody over 'all the doors where any councils are held, as well in Our High Court of Parliament, as in other places'. ¶ The role of Usher has not always been straight-forward. Henry Norris, Black Rod to Henry VIII, was also Groom of the Stole to Anne Boleyn. In her tragic fall from grace, he was implicated in the web of fanciful accusations that Thomas Cromwell concocted and was executed. Such a situation might not have arisen if he had travelled more with his monarch, as Sir William Compton later did. He fought with Henry VIII in France, and accompanied him to the Field of the Cloth of Gold. But he was still expected to keep up his Garter duties and arrest errant knights by tapping them on the shoulder using his black rod. If the knight were found guilty – almost a certainty in Tudor England – he would have to pay a then-hefty fine of £5. ¶ Following the Restoration of the monarchy in 1660, Sir Fleetwood Sheppard was appointed Black Rod. He was also steward to Charles II's mistress Nell Gwynn, and a bon viveur, who once invited the membership of the Commons into the king's cellar to drink a loyal toast. In 1698 Admiral Sir David Mitchell became the first in a continuing line of military men to be appointed to the role. This fulfils the edict of Henry VIII that Black Rod should be a 'Gentleman of Name and Arms'. ¶ As recently as 1971, the role of Sergeant-at-Arms, responsible for discipline in the Lords, was merged with that of Black Rod, and he became Secretary to the Lord Great Chamberlain. The latter role fits in well with his responsibilities as a senior administrator for the Lords, and the influence Black Rod now exercises is greater perhaps than at any previous time. Every year, however, he returns to his roots at Windsor to lead the members of the Order of the Garter into St George's Chapel. ¶ During the State Opening of Parliament, which is televised, Black Rod can be seen walking through the Palace of Westminster to the House of Commons, where, in time-honoured words, he conveys the Sovereign's command that the Members of Parliament leave their chamber and appear at the Bar of the Lords to hear the Queen's Speech. As he approaches the door, it is symbolically slammed as a reminder that the Commons fiercely guards its independence. Black Rod then gives three resounding knocks on the door with his staff of office. When it is opened, he utters the Queen's command that 'this honourable House… attend upon Her Majesty immediately in the House of Peers'.

The Gentleman Usher of the Black Rod, an officer of the Order of the Garter, is now responsible for keeping order in the House of Lords. His Black Rod has remit throughout this Palace. Here he stands in Westminster Hall close to where Sir Winston Churchill and several monarchs lay in state and Charles I was tried before Parliament. Under the hammerbeam roof of Richard II, where Henry VIII's tennis balls have been found, this doorkeeper is now the principal arbiter of order in the Parliament.

CLERK OF THE CLOSET

When England faced the jeopardy of Spain's religious fury in the 16th century, Queen Elizabeth knew that her profound belief in the Reformation was in the balance. Her own life had survived the vicissitudes of this battle over Christian doctrine. It had ravaged the conscience of all English believers, ever since an alternative doctrine had emerged and particularly since her father, Henry VIII, broke with the Pope in Rome in order to marry her mother, Anne Boleyn. This was the situation for most of her generation, many of whom had burned for their beliefs or faced the fury of the inquisition. The catalyst for this showdown with Spain came with the death of her half-sister, Queen Mary. At this point, Elizabeth succeeded to the throne and King Philip of Spain lost his unloved wife. However, he gained the righteous determination to stop Elizabeth's Protestantism in its tracks. With the blessing of the enraged Pope, he crafted the largest fleet yet mustered and filled it with soldiers. No wonder then, with so much to lose and the massive power of the Spanish Armada but a favourable wind away, that Elizabeth retired to her Closet for prayer. ¶ A 'closet' is a small secure place and Elizabeth's Closet was the most private room where she could safely attend to State papers and worship, or take Communion. In St James's Palace the Closet was the name given to the old balcony above the chapel. It has been replaced now but the ceiling above survives, painted for Henry VIII by Holbein. To this Closet, from the surviving tower nearby, supposedly came the messenger who had seen the approaching fires of the coastal beacons, warning that the Armada had arrived. ¶ It was the task of a trusted cleric to keep the monarch's Closet in good order, offer religious counsel and prayer as appropriate. It is unclear how services were managed and by whom in Elizabeth's court but, records of an appointment called Clerk of the Closet date back to the 1430s. Religion underpinned monarchy and kings were in awe of their need to give worship. So a Chapel Royal emerged, a travelling group of clerics and musicians dedicated to providing services when required. In 1349 John Wodeford is recorded as the head of Edward III's Chapel Royal, and the Clerk of the Closet would have been closely connected to the Chapel Royal from the outset. From the 1500s the influence of Clerks of the Closet was so great that bishops were generally selected, though this only became the norm from 1714, when Charles Trimnel, Bishop of Winchester, was appointed to guide George I. ¶ The Chapel Royal of St James's Palace is now where the corporate 'Chapel Royal' most frequently worships, though these days the Sovereign rarely attends. The Clerk of the Closet is no longer a regular spiritual counsellor to the monarch but still organizes the Rota of Waits, or roll of duty preachers. He also advises on which clergymen should be selected as Chaplains to the Queen to do this preaching. In keeping with the concept of the Closet itself, the Clerk still introduces new Church of England bishops to the monarch, when each comes to pay homage to the Supreme Governor of the Church. Also, the Clerk is still supposed to check any book, or tract, on religious matters before it is presented to the monarch, presumably to ensure the once-powerful head is not inclined away from the accepted dogma of the time. ¶ Whenever there is a need, a Deputy Clerk is on hand to support in this work, but there is now only one, where once there were three. Also the Clerk could rely on the Serjeant of the Vestry to have the necessary vestments, plate and books available and ready for any service requested in the Closet or chapel. The Sergeant's appointment was extant in 1499 and still keeps the chapel ready for all eventualities. Not least the annual Epiphany service, when, following the example of the Three Wise Men, the monarch sends her Gentlemen Ushers with gifts of gold, frankincense and myrrh for the Church.

The Closet of St James's Palace is prepared for Divine Service in the Chapel Royal using silver altar plate from the Royal Yacht *Britannia*. This private balcony is where sovereigns assembled with their most private advisers. In company with the Clerk of the Closet is the Deputy Clerk and the Keeper of the Closet, and in the body of the Tudor church stands the Serjeant of the Vestry.

LORD-LIEUTENANT AND CUSTOS ROTULORUM

Every county has had a Lord-Lieutenant since Henry VIII appointed the first in 1557. Originally responsible for maintaining local defence and civil order, the lieutenant (from the Latin *locum tenens*, meaning 'one holding a place for another') stood in for the Sovereign. ¶ There is a buzz in the air. A small crowd has gathered. Many of them have Union flags and the police watch vigilantly while the royal car approaches. Around the main gate are well-dressed people ready to greet their monarch, but in front of them all is the Lord-Lieutenant. This scene is played out all over the country by Lord-Lieutenants who are the first to welcome the monarch, her family or visiting Heads of State into their particular county. Dressed in a quasi-military uniform, complete with top-ranking officer's sword and braid on their cap, they echo the role Henry VIII originally envisaged for them as local militia commanders. There is no uniform for a female Lord-Lieutenant, but there is a badge to be worn on ceremonial occasions. Having greeted the royal visitor and, as it were, handed over the county, the Lord-Lieutenant follows the visit and is the last to bid farewell. On the visitor's departure, he is once again back at the top of the county's pecking order. ¶ The necessity for a lieutenant arose when 16th-century kings realized they could no longer rely on the feudal system to provide knights and fighting men in time of need. Instead, the money that manors paid in lieu of providing soldiers was centralized and used to found the beginnings of a standing army. The new Lord-Lieutenants were then expected to command the county militias, but their role altered as the army changed. However, they retained a special association with the Territorial Army, and took a leading role in the Home Guard, or 'Dad's Army', of the Second World War. ¶ Until recently, most Lord-Lieutenants were local landowners with large houses and grand titles. This suited the benevolent unpaid nature of their work, especially when their military role declined and only their position at the top of the county's social pyramid remained. There are still parts of the country where this style of lieutenancy is greatly valued and works well. Lord-Lieutenants support the broader life of the community within their county by supporting schools, charities and other good works. The people whom the Prime Minister today recommends to Buckingham Palace to become Lord-Lieutenants more closely reflect society at the start of the 21st century. Women are also appointed to the lieutenancy, but the title of Lord-Lieutenant is applied to whoever holds the position, regardless of gender. ¶ Some Lord-Lieutenants are also appointed to be *Custos Rotulorum* (Keeper of the Rolls), the most senior civil officer in the county. Historically, this position gave the holder power to appoint senior officials, but now he or she is the senior magistrate in the county and presides over the Lord Chancellor's advisory committee for the appointment of lay Justices of the Peace. ¶ Somerset was first recorded with the name of Sumaersaeton, the land of dwellers (*Saete*) dependent on Sumaerton (a summer-only settlement), in the Anglo-Saxon Chronicle of 1016. Since the Domesday Book was compiled, the shire has altered its boundaries, but the Lord-Lieutenant and *Custos Rotulorum* is still the Sovereign's representative over land that includes the Mendips and the Quantocks, Exmoor National Park, the Somerset Levels, Bath and North Somerset. The lush landscape supports beef, sheep and dairy farming, which produces the county's famous cheeses, most notably Cheddar.

The Quantocks cut through the county of Somerset. Here, on Beacon Hill, the Lord-Lieutenant of Somerset holds sway on the monarch's behalf. Traditionally the office retains the now unused role of *Custos Rotulorum*. No longer is the Lord-Lieutenant expected to rally and command the militia, but links with the reserve forces and cadets remain strong.

MASTER OF THE CORPORATION OF TRINITY
HOUSE OF DEPTFORD STROND

Since Tudor times, Trinity House has safeguarded Britain's busy river routes and rocky shores, guiding mariners safely through coastal waters with a coordinated system of beacons, buoys and other navigation aids. Today, the Corporation's responsibilities have vastly expanded to cover the coastal waters of England, Wales, the Channel Islands and Gibraltar. Its modern Lighthouse Service oversees 66 automatic lighthouses, 10 major floating navigational aids, including lightships and lightfloats, 52 radar beacons and 436 buoys. Trinity House also clears all dangerous wrecks, apart from HM ships. ¶ The Corporation started out as a small medieval guild of mariners and navigators, who were active on the Thames from at least the 15th century. The guild's fortunes changed radically when in 1513 Henry VIII decided to build the first Royal Dockyard at Deptford, upriver from the palace at Greenwich. The Comptroller of the Navy, Sir Thomas Spert, was put in charge of the project and recruited the expertise of Trinity House. When, a year later, the dockyard was opened, Henry VIII formally chartered the guild to make the Thames safe for mariners. The Royal Charter established a 'Guild or Fraternity of the most glorious and undividable Trinity and of St Clement in the Parish Church of Deptford Strond'. The new fraternity, with a Master, 11 Wardens and Assistants, could now legitimately demand fees for its navigation services in guiding or piloting boats to and from the sea. ¶ The fortunes of Trinity House slumped briefly during Edward IV's reign, when many semi-religious guilds were dissolved, although it survived by changing its name to 'Corporation'. Elizabeth I restored its lost privileges and the right to place beacons, marks and signs along the Thames. ¶ Initially, business expanded during the reign of James I, and, in 1604, the Corporation organized itself more efficiently into two classes: the Elder Brethren, who discharged operational duties, and the Younger Brethren, who assisted. After Charles I's execution, the Corporation was dissolved until 1660, when Charles II revived its fortunes. Its restored powers and responsibilities were codified in a new Royal Charter granted by Charles's brother, James II, and drafted by Samuel Pepys in 1685. Growing income from its expanding business led to almshouses at Deptford, as well as a new headquarters, first at Ratcliff, then at Water Lane, and finally, in 1796, on Tower Hill, where Trinity House is the Corporation's London base today. ¶ For Britain, the 19th century was a time of rapid expansion, and the speed of seagoing traffic demanded ever safer shipping routes. For the Corporation, also, responsibility and income increased, and in 1836, Trinity House was granted the right to set up a coordinated, nationwide navigation system. ¶ Throughout the Corporation's history, its Masters have played a central role in promoting change or encouraging new technology and business. Two classic examples are the first Master, Sir Thomas Spert, and the first royal Master, Prince Albert. Appointed in 1850, at the height of Britain's naval and colonial expansion, Albert actively promoted the efficiency of England's beacons, improving the safety of her busy shipping lanes. It was Albert, also, who arranged for the Corporation to manage the Thames ballast, increasing its revenue. Since Albert's death, with the exception of his successor Lord Palmerston, all Masters of Trinity House have been princes, some of whom have also been professional naval officers. ¶ Today, the Corporation continues to play a vital role in contemporary navigation. Trinity House also enjoys the unique privilege of guiding the Sovereign safely through home waters with its vessels.

The Master of the Corporation of Trinity House of Deptford Strond presides over a Corporation that runs lighthouses, beacons and buoys, marking ports and rocks around the coasts of England, Wales, the Channel Islands and Gibraltar. These are maintained from THV *Patricia*, a model of which is shown. Elizabeth I granted the coat of arms that decorates the entrance hall at Trinity House. The Master's uniform recalls the old Royal Navy frock coat pattern, with bands of gold lace round the cuff, similar to that worn by rear-admirals. Trinity's badge is on the cap, buttons and sword belt.

CHIEF YEOMAN WARDER OF HER MAJESTY'S ROYAL PALACE AND FORTRESS THE TOWER OF LONDON, MEMBER OF THE YEOMEN OF THE GUARD EXTRAORDINARY

Jangling keys and chill winds were the chief recollections of those jailed in the Tower of London. Today, those keys inspire a different thrill among visitors to this place of safety that was once the pit of Hell for the condemned. All around the modern visitor are the Yeoman Warders, men and women chosen from those completing careers in the Armed Forces, with strong voices and plenty of charisma. Groups follow their lead and watch agog as they stand beside the place where two of Henry VIII's wives were beheaded and listen to the Warder tell all the gruesome details. These Warders are a continuous link with the first guard placed upon this fortress after the Battle of Bosworth Field by a very insecure new king, Henry VII. ¶ Answerable ultimately to the Constable of the Tower and more regularly to the Resident Governor, the Chief Yeoman Warder organizes the other Warders. His title has evolved from Yeoman Porter, the original appointment responsible for the security of the Tower and its prisoners. Two other specific appointments hold resonance with old responsibilities. The Yeoman Gaoler, who carries an axe on ceremonial occasions but was never an executioner, was responsible for ensuring that prisoners escorted for trial at Westminster returned; while the Yeoman Ravenmaster tends to the ravens held captive inside the walls because it is said the monarchy will fall if they leave. The Chief Yeoman Warder still takes the lead in the daily Ceremony of the Keys. With his Yeoman Watchman and escorted by soldiers from the Queen's Tower Guard, he secures the gates. In the pageantry of today, it is hard to imagine the very real risks their forebears might have faced, particularly when London was less illuminated and often overcome by fog. For this reason, the route is challenged and the Chief Yeoman Warder must explain that he carries 'the Queen's keys', which immediately gives him both safe passage and the keys receive a salute. ¶ There has been a guard on the Tower since William first stationed troops here after 1066. It was a vital place of safety for the monarch and strategically close enough to keep an eye on the source of revenue that the City merchants could attract. So safe was the structure that it became both the guardian of the regalia and also the principal prison of the realm. In 1337 Edward III laid down rules about the security of the Tower, and parts of the oath he set are still used by new Warders. ¶ The Chief Yeoman Warder's forebears once held Edward Seymour captive in the Tower. Desperate to get free, he offered anything if he could escape. When he was released in 1549, the Warders made their request clear. They wanted to be part of the Royal Body Guard, called the Yeomen of the Guard. Now Seymour was the new king's Protector, he granted the wish, which is why the Chief Yeoman Warder today wears a similar uniform to and is sworn in as an Extraordinary member of the Guard. In the 18th century Warders bought their appointments but when the Duke of Wellington became Constable in 1826 he stopped this practice, instead selecting sergeants from the army with fine service records. This was widened to include Royal Marines and Royal Air Force Warrant Officers. Recently the first Royal Naval Warders have been appointed and women too. They must still have unblemished records and live in the Tower. This way their understanding of the keys and the biting winds that famous prisoners such as Sir Thomas More complained of have been experienced first hand. The Tower remains the nation's top tourist draw and the Chief Yeoman Warder knows that his Warders help to keep it so.

In the heart of the Bell Tower of the Tower of London is the cell where Sir Thomas More wrestled with his conscience to the point that earned him canonization. Here the Chief Yeoman Warder stands with his rank on his arm and holding the Queen's keys with which this fortress is ceremonially locked each night.

QUEEN'S GUIDE OVER KENT SANDS

So fast is the incoming tide at Morecambe Bay on England's north-west coast that it can outpace a galloping horse. The ever-shifting sandbanks created by the waves are dotted with quicksand, but even those who avoid these pitfalls can be ambushed by the sea's rapid return. ¶ Good fortune, however, shines on a few, and these supposedly included the Roman governor Agricola, who successfully crossed Morecambe Bay with an army when heading north, and Robert the Bruce, who probably crossed when leading his marauding invasion south. Many travellers risked crossing the broad sands and the unpredictable River Kent to shorten their journey, but the risk was high. Indeed, the Abbot of Furness Abbey petitioned the king in 1326 to investigate the great loss of life on the sands. ¶ It is not known when the first Guide was appointed to show travellers across the Bay, but the first recorded is Edmonstone in 1501. He was given a 10-acre tenement at Cartmel and described as the Carter upon Kent Sands. His successor was paid by the Prior of the foundation at Cartmel, an outpost of Furness Abbey. With the Dissolution of the Monasteries, Furness, the largest Cistercian foundation in the country, was surrendered, with all its wealth, land and outposts, in 1537. In 1540 everything was transferred to the Duchy of Lancaster, including responsibility for paying the Guide. ¶ One year after the abbey was surrendered, Richard Carter was given the job, probably taking his family name from the appointment. He and his descendants drove a cart across

the Bay for an annual payment of 10 marks until 1865, but it was dangerous work and led to the death of one Guide in 1672. His son wrote to the Duchy asking for a pay rise. He described the expense of keeping two horses and reminded them that his father had died saving two people from drowning. He explained the hardships of wind, rain and fog while seeking fresh fording places over the constantly changing river. The plea earned him a few extra pounds in wages. ¶ The Guide still lives at Cartmel, on Guide's Farm, surrounded by laurel to protect it from the bitter winds and to provide 'brobs' that indicate safe routes across the Bay. Using his stick to test the sand, the Guide finds a safe path, every now and then pushing a brob into the sand, where it will stay as a marker until the tide has covered it many times. ¶ Today's Guide still helps travellers across the Bay, and takes large parties for a day on the sands to identify the different types, such as caff, slape, slutch and quicksand, which constantly change. ¶ The appointment is now funded by the Queen from her Duchy of Lancaster, and there is still a need for it. Some people still set off alone, and learn the hard way that Kent Sands remain as dangerous as ever.

'Brobs' of laurel, from the bushes around Guide's Farm, are placed at intervals to mark a safe route over the constantly moving sands in Morecambe Bay. These remain in place for several tides, but the practice has endured for at least five centuries. The Queen's Guide uses his eyes, feet and stick to find a safe crossing and has warned for generations against walking on the sand at low tide. When the tide comes in it can do so at the speed of a galloping horse. No unwise walker can escape.

ABBOT OF ST BENET-AT-HOLME

In summer, the Norfolk Broads become a teeming mass of sailing boats and pleasure craft, but away from these crowds, the open and often-empty countryside is punctuated by churches built to celebrate faith in God and the wealth of their benefactors. ¶ Standing on what was once a holme (island) in the marshes alongside the River Bure in Norfolk is a crumbling, grey stone wall surrounding a dilapidated building. Its incarnation as a windmill is its most recent one, and dates from the 18th century. These ruins are, in fact, all that remain of the only monastery that Henry VIII left untouched: indeed, he enhanced the influence of its Abbot by enshrining his office in legislation. ¶ The Dissolution resulted in the dismantling of a monastic tradition that had lasted for about seven centuries, and also saw the destruction of some of the most magnificent buildings in the kingdom. Their traditions of learning and devotion counted for nothing with Henry: it was their wealth, influence and power that he coveted. ¶ When the representative of Henry VIII's Vicar General arrived at this monastery, the countryside was already filled with displaced monks, while burning monasteries illuminated the skyline. Abbot Rugge of St Benet's, awaiting the fateful knock, had no resource but prayer to protect his small community. The Reformation in Europe, together with the consequences of Henry's decision to wed Anne Boleyn, fundamentally disrupted society and severed England's links with Rome. Resistance to the new order was hopeless. ¶ Fortunately for Abbot Rugge, the Vicar General had recently been a guest of the Bishop of Norwich, and witnessed a life of considerable opulence. By comparison, either through bad management or good fortune, the Abbey of St Benet was worth virtually nothing. Its Benedictine inmates were living in poverty, and their pious example of religious life gave Thomas Cromwell, mastermind of the Dissolution, an idea. Instead of dissolving St Benet's, he persuaded the king to depose the Bishop of Norwich. The wealth of Norwich was taken into the royal coffers, and Abbot Rugge suddenly found himself enthroned in the vacated bishop's cathedra. St Benet's thus won the distinction of being the only abbey that Henry VIII did not dissolve, and by an extraordinary Act of Parliament in 1536 it was protected in perpetuity. ¶ Unfortunately, this turned out to be just a handful of years. Bishop Rugge failed in his obligations to his former abbey, and gradually its buildings decayed and neighbouring farmers removed its stones. By the 19th century, all that remained was the ancient gatehouse, which had been transformed into a drainage mill, its sails obscuring the old monastery. ¶ Over the years, the See of Norwich was filled by successive bishops who sat in Parliament and saw no advantage in continuing to use their monastic title, so it fell into disuse. However, the 20th and 21st centuries have seen a change. Anomalies of history are now enjoyed, and there has been a will to revive old customs. Accordingly, the terms of Henry VIII's Act of Parliament have once again been put into effect: a vicar from a local parish now acts as Prior of St Benet-at-Holme, and he has 12 lay monks to assist him in his work. Since 1939 Bishops of Norwich have proudly assumed the title Abbot of St Benet's again, and each August Bank Holiday for the last 74 years, boats have brought a flood of pilgrims to join the Abbot for an open-air service. Thus, a unique title, granted by the king responsible for destroying so much, has kept St Benet's alive long after destruction. After a long abeyance, it has never been healthier than it is now.

Henry VIII united the abbacy with the bishopric of Norwich and therefore the Bishop of Norwich has remained Abbot of St-Benet-at-Holme to this day. The abbey was founded in the 9th century by the hermit Suneman, and under lands granted by King Canute in 1020 the cell grew into the monastery of St Benet-at-Holme. At one time the abbey was one of the wealthiest Benedictine establishments in the country, controlling not only all the peat diggings that became the Norfolk Broads but also large areas of farming.

LORD CLERK REGISTER AND KEEPER
OF THE SIGNET

The oldest surviving Office of State in Scotland is the Lord Clerk Register. The Act of Union in 1707 made many other appointments redundant because they no longer had a legislative or executive function once the Parliament at Westminster had taken over. However, the post of Lord Clerk Register survives as a link with Scotland's independent past, although most of its remaining functions were removed by Act of Parliament in 1879. He still retains a strong symbolic role as one of the guardian commissioners for keeping Scotland's ancient crown jewels, the Honours Three. ¶ Combined with his primary role, the Lord Clerk is also Keeper of the Signet. This more junior appointment dates from the time when the king's authority was communicated through the land by writs or warrants, written and read by barely literate people. In order to authenticate these documents, a system of seals was developed, and those matters that related specifically to the monarch, or were private to him, were sealed with the king's own Signet ring. The oldest surviving impression of the monarch's private Signet dates from 1342, but Robert the Bruce is known to have used one even earlier. ¶ As the volume of paperwork increased, the king appointed a Secretary to deal with it, and when the burden of work became greater still, the Secretary hired clerks to assist in the preparation of writs. These new clerks were first described as Writaries to the Signet, and their influence increased as fast as the workload. As the king did not have the time to seal everything that needed his Signet, he placed the ring in the care of his Secretary, who became known as Keeper of the Signet. ¶ In 1532 James V overhauled his legal administration and established the College of Justice. The Writaries to the Signet were established as part of the new court system, advising applicants for justice on how to proceed. Further legislation that year established regulations by which the growing number of Writaries was to be bound. In 1594 Sir Robert Cockburn of Clerkington, who was Lord Secretary to the King and Keeper of the Signet, commissioned John Layng to be Deputy Keeper of the Signet. In this role he had authority over 18 Writaries, but Cockburn retained responsibility for the Signet. ¶ The nature of civil writs in Scotland was such that, to achieve validity in law, they had to be seen by the monarch, and his sight of them was evidenced by the impression of his Signet on the writ. By the end of James V's reign, legal documents needed to be sealed with four Signets. Today only one is required. Among the documentation needing to be sealed by the Signet are those involving the Supreme Court, summonses from the Lords of Council and Session, letters of diligence and execution, and letters staying or prohibiting diligence. Each document is scrutinized by the Signet Officer to ensure it is 'right and proper' to go before the courts. Then it will 'pass the Signet', when the press is wound down and the document is impressed with the seal of the Signet. ¶ The ancient appointment of King's Secretary, which evolved into Lord Secretary, was abolished in 1746, following a shake-up of Scottish institutions after the Battle of Culloden, which concluded the Jacobite Rebellion. However, the office of Keeper of the Signet survived, and in 1817 it was given to the Lord Clerk Register. The combined titles have historic significance: that of the Lord Clerk Register retains ancient links with the original Great Officers of Scotland before Union in 1707, while the Keeper of the Signet reminds us of the evolution of royal law from the 14th century to the present day.

The Sovereign's seal or Signet is held within an elaborate screw press that is kept in Edinburgh's Petition Office. The bulk and weight of this device convey something of the seal's authority not least to initiate an action in the Court of Session. The Lord Clerk Register and Keeper of the Signet is a symbolic guardian of an object that still proves vital.

POET LAUREATE

The Greeks started the custom of crowning poets with laurels – the highest accolade in ancient Greece, as sacred to Apollo, the god of poetry and music. The fashion caught on in Rome, where not only poets and orators, but warriors, senators and emperors were honoured with glory laurels. ¶ With the collapse of the Roman Empire, the custom lapsed, but the spark of epic poetry was kept alight during the Dark Ages by wandering poets who sang their songs of gods and heroes around the courts of Europe. With the revival of classical culture in the late Middle Ages, Latin poetry and laurels came back into favour, initially at medieval universities, where classical scholars, such as John Skelton, were laureated in Roman fashion, and dubbed 'Poet Laureate'. The custom caught on at Renaissance courts, where favourite court poets were commonly known as 'Poet Laureate' as a mark of regard. It was the job of court poets to sing royal praises and entertain the court. The successful were promised, and sometimes paid, a fee. Tudor court poet Bernard Andreas received an annuity of 10 marks for drumming up Latin verse for Henry VII. The rate went up under the Stuarts. Ben Jonson, whose lyrical masques entertained the Jacobean court for much of his life, enjoyed a life pension of 100 marks and a 'terse of canary wyne'. Although Andreas, Ben Jonson and his successor, William Davenport, were called 'Poet Laureate', the title was not formalized until Charles II appointed John Dryden in 1670. ¶ An inspired choice, Dryden was a gifted narrator and political satirist, whose *Absalom and Achitophel* brilliantly satirized the king's political opponents. Although often labelled a turncoat, Dryden served his Stuart masters well, despite a brief spell under Cromwell. On Charles II's death, Dryden also served James II faithfully, even converting to his Catholic faith. When James was ousted by his Protestant rival, William of Orange, Dryden stuck to his guns and his new-found faith, refusing to swear the oath of allegiance. For standing by his principles, rather than his monarch, he was stripped of office, which passed to the Protestant Thomas Shadwell. The new Laureate did not rest on his laurels, but set to task with industry, if not always ability, setting in motion the onerous custom of royal birthday odes. Shadwell was the first in a long run of poets who seemed picked for political loyalty rather than poetic flair, and whose lack of literary success gave the office a very bad name. Other political choices followed in quick succession: Colley Cibber, derided by his peers; William Whitehead, denounced as even worse than Cibber; Henry Pye, described by Walter Scott as a man respectable in everything but his poetry. ¶ Pye drew contempt for a series of glowing birthday odes to ill-respected Hanoverian princes, which made the practice risible. He was also responsible for requesting that the gift of wine be suspended in lieu of cash. However, Sir John Betjeman requested that this be reinstated, when he was appointed in 1972; feeling that there was nothing to be lost in the pleasure of a drink and it might even free up the muse. ¶ The honour is now given to one selected from all on the recommendation of the Prime Minister, and the Crown makes no formal expectations. New appointments still trigger debate, just as they always have done. After the titan Alfred, Lord Tennyson died, no candidate was regarded as adequate. There are still some who deride the appointment but each holder carries the office in a unique direction while maintaining a tradition that reaches back through Dryden, Shakespeare and Chaucer to the Greek ideals and the god Apollo.

One of the attractions for visitors to London's Westminster Abbey is Poets' Corner. This church was founded by Edward the Confessor in 1065, and rebuilt by Henry III in the 13th century as a coronation church to rival that of Reims in France. It is regarded as the nation's pantheon and part of the south transept has been given over to monuments commemorating the great names of English literature. Here Chaucer was buried and Shakespeare is honoured, in a busy clutter of lettered stones bearing poets' names that capture the momentary recognition of passers-by. Among the names are those of Poets Laureate, such as the first official title holder, Dryden, and Tennyson. Sitting among the memorials the Poet Laureate observes the world, its people and its time, and maybe contemplates a history when minstrels and versifiers were an important part of the Sovereign's retinue.

MR HOUISON CRAUFURD WHO WASHES THE
SOVEREIGN'S HANDS

Legend has it that a 16th-century king of Scotland was saved from death by a yeoman farmer, unaware of the rescued man's identity. The rescue and the farmer's reward were described by Sir Walter Scott in *Tales of a Grandfather* and resulted in a custom unrivalled for its symbolism and charm. ¶ Cramond Bridge, between Edinburgh and the Forth Road Bridge, is an unremarkable place today, but it was here, in the reign of King James V of Scotland, that a farmer named John Howieson came upon a group of ruffians mugging a well-dressed gentleman. Fearing that they might murder the man, the farmer, with flail in hand, went to his aid. Unknown to him, the man was James V, who regularly travelled in disguise in order to learn what was happening in his kingdom. ¶ After a short struggle, the muggers fled and John Howieson took the injured man back to his cottage and washed his wounds. He then accompanied him back towards Edinburgh in case the muggers struck again. The gentleman had introduced himself as the Goodman (tenant) of Ballengiech and holder of a lowly court appointment. Howieson told him that he was working on the king's farm at Braehead. The gentleman asked what was the one thing he would most like to own and, in the words of Scott's story, 'honest John confessed he should think himself the happiest man in Scotland were he but proprietor of the farm on which he wroght as a labourer'. When they parted, the gentleman invited Howieson to look over the royal apartments at Holyrood Palace the following Sunday. ¶ The farmer kept the appointment in his best clothes and the Goodman of Ballengiech showed him around, 'amused with his wonder and his remarks'. When asked if he would like to see the king, Howieson excitedly agreed and was told that when they came into the royal presence, the king would be the only one wearing a hat. On entering a hall packed with courtiers, Howieson nervously searched for his hatted monarch. After looking everywhere, he turned to his escort and said, 'It must be either you or me, for all but us two are bareheaded.' The truth of this remark suddenly struck home, and the farmer knelt before James V, who gave Howieson the farm at Braehead that he wanted, but gave it away on condition that Howieson and his successors should be ready to present a ewer and basin for the monarch to wash his hands, either at Holyrood Palace or when passing by Cramond Bridge. ¶ In 1822 George IV set out on the 'King's Jaunt' to Scotland. It was a significant visit, the first since the 1745 rebellion when much of Scotland's culture had been outlawed. For the first time in nearly 100 years the king, wearing a kilt, gave permission for bagpipes to be played. The rebirth of Scottish culture was helped along by Walter Scott's romantic retellings of history, including the rediscovery of the Honours Three, the country's crown, sceptre and sword, which were found wrapped in sheets behind the panelling of Edinburgh Castle's throne room. ¶ To make the monarchy relevant to Scotland once again, the hitherto 'absentee' Hanoverians plunged themselves into all things Scottish. It was George IV who revived the service that his Stuart ancestor had instigated. William Howieson Crawford presented his ewer and basin to George IV, and the king broke the habit of a lifetime by washing his hands. ¶ Whenever called upon since to perform the service, three members of the family (now called Houison Craufurd) come from Craufurdland Castle with the silver basin and ewer made for George IV. The senior one holds the basin, while the other two pour the water and offer a linen towel from a salver.

The ewer, basin and salver holding fresh linen have been used to wash royal hands by the Houison Craufurd family since George IV revived the ritual in the early 19th century. This bridge across the River Cramond, near Edinburgh, may have been where the family's kind ancestor saved a king from murderous thugs in an act of courage that was well rewarded. Mr Craufurd washed George VI's hands when he was eight years old and Elizabeth II's soon after her coronation.

HEREDITARY ROYAL FALCONER

Just as John Howieson was presented with an honour from James V in gratitude for the service he had provided at a time of great danger, there were many others who received similar gifts from the Royal House of Stuart for services rendered. It was then customary for monarchs to give posts within the wider royal court, as these provided the recipient with a useful income and valuable access to the monarch. When power lay with the king, his court was the place to be, and no matter what task was required, it allowed the recipient to have the ear of those who counted. For this reason, the history of many royal courts is awash with utilitarian roles granted as hereditary offices to deserving nobles. However, it is doubtful whether many were actually fulfilled in anything more than a ceremonial way, the actual task probably being left to paid servants. ¶ Some of these appointments were given in such informal terms that no written evidence of them exists. In some cases, a change in family fortunes, particularly a lack of heirs, saw the appointments fade into obscurity. One such situation faced the Borthwick family, who claim to be Hereditary Falconers to the Scottish monarch. No Charter exists to prove the appointment, although there are references to their special role before the Union of the crowns. In 1672 the 9th Lord Borthwick died leaving no heir, so the title and its honours fell into abeyance. It was not until 1986 that the Lord Lyon King of Arms recognized a junior branch of the family and allowed both title and honours to be revived. ¶ The Borthwicks claim that, in return for services to the Stuart kings, they received the privilege of acting as Hereditary Royal Falconers. This was a service associated with leisure, and therefore a sign of the king's particular esteem and friendship. When James I of Scotland was imprisoned by the English, the head of the Borthwick family offered himself instead, and his self-imposed sentence dragged on for three years. When he was finally returned to Scotland in 1430, the grateful monarch allowed Borthwick to build his own castle and gave him a peerage 20 years later. Over the centuries, the Borthwicks continued to give valuable service to the Scottish kings; in fact, the 3rd Lord Borthwick lost his life fighting beside James IV at the Battle of Flodden. ¶ Falconry remained a very popular pastime until about the time that the Borthwick title fell into abeyance. In 1672, the 9th Lord Borthwick died leaving no heir, so the title and its honours fell into abeyance. It was not until 1986 that the Lord Lyon recognized a junior branch of the family and allowed both title and honours to be revived. According to the strict rules that governed what birds of prey could be owned by various ranks, eagles were restricted to emperors and kings; gerfalcons to other members of royalty; peregrines to earls; goshawks to yeomen; and sparrowhawks to priests. The 'hopeless' kestrel was for knaves and servants. ¶ In England, the appointment of Hereditary Master Falconer was given to the 1st Duke of St Albans, the 14-year-old son of Charles II by his mistress Nell Gwynn, in the 1680s. He was also given permission to ride in a coach along Rotten Row, the sandy track that runs through London's Hyde Park, a privilege usually restricted to the Sovereign. The eccentric Duke's descendant was invited to the Queen's coronation in 1953, but having said that he would arrive as Hereditary Master Falconer, with a live falcon, he was dissuaded and consequently did not attend.

The ancestors of the Hereditary Royal Falconer hunted with falcons across this land near Heriot, Midlothian, in the southern uplands of Scotland. Lord Borthwick, the 24th peer and current bearer of the title, is holding a female peregrine falcon into the wind. This species is still the most popular bird of prey to work these hills. A grouse would be flushed out by the pointer, a special breed of dog, before the falcon is released. The falcon would then swoop down onto the hapless grouse from above to effect the kill, in a skilled example of two species of animal working together with man to hunt another animal.

LORD MALLARD OF ALL SOULS

For over 300 years the Fellows of All Souls College, Oxford, have held revelries at which they sing their traditional Mallard Song. The festivities are presided over by one of their number bearing the title Lord Mallard. Chosen for his singing voice, he holds the office for several years. In the 17th century there were annual Mallard processions round the college, rather riotous and disorderly in character. Their traditional date was on 14 January. ¶ In the first year of each century since 1801, the Mallard procession has continued to take place, as a celebration of the college, while the song is sung each year at gaudies, or revelries. The Mallard Song, which was first written down in the 17th century, may have been sung from 100 years before, being passed orally from term to term. ¶ Centennial Mallard Dinners are controlled by the college's authorities. Gowned Fellows parade at night all round the college, not omitting the rooftops. They hold blazing torches, carry the Lord Mallard in a chair, and sing the song over and over again. At the head of the procession a mallard duck (nowadays a model, but in former times a real one) is carried on a pole. The procession is notionally a hunt for the mallard of legend, which allegedly flew up from an old sewer when the foundations for All Souls College were dug in 1438. No substantiated proof of this story has been discovered, although there is a false document, claiming to be a record of the foundation, which describes how the founder, Henry Chichele, Archbishop of Canterbury, had a dream in which he was advised where to build his college, and told that the 'schwopping Mallarde' appearing would confirm it. He dug in the place shown in his dream, only for the duck to fly from the drain as predicted. What is known as fact is that a seal was discovered in the foundations, on which was engraved an heraldic griffin and the name of a Clerk, called William Malard. Such a story, when exposed to time, creativity and nonsense, can easily develop into a good myth: this, in turn, provided the Mallard Song. Whatever the true source of the song, the fable has been dignified from observance by generations of Fellows, and the mallard now appears as a decoration on much of the college's tableware and other property. ¶ The College of All Souls of the Faithful Departed, to give its full name, was established by Henry VI, with Henry Chichele, who endowed it. In its patent of creation, the Warden and college are called to pray for 'the souls of all the faithful departed... who... in the service of [Henry V]... ended their lives in the wars of the kingdom of France'. Archbishop Chichele had been closely involved in the war and its diplomatic consequences, and had taken part in negotiating Henry V's marriage to Katherine de Valois, daughter of the French king; thereafter he crowned her at Westminster and baptized their son, the future Henry VI. Chichele died in 1443, just 10 days after sealing the completed statutes of his college, and was buried in a tomb he had taken trouble to prepare in Canterbury Cathedral. ¶ At the time of the 1901 procession, Cosmo Lang was the appointed Lord Mallard. Like the college's founder, he later became Archbishop of Canterbury. Perhaps it is not surprising then that he ended the habit of slaughtering a mallard and pouring its fresh blood into cups for all to drink: instead, he donated a silver mallard, from which Madeira was poured. A telegram was sent from the same 12-course dinner preceding the procession, to Lord Curzon, a former Fellow of All Souls who was by then Viceroy of India, in Calcutta. It contained one word: 'Swapping'. The reply from the potentate was just as simple and said, 'It was.'

Standing on the rooftop of All Souls College in Oxford, the Lord Mallard wears mortar board and gown and holds the duck — symbolic of the one reputed to have flown from a drain in 1438. He is singing the Mallard Song, which he did after the Centennial Dinner on 14 January 2001. On this occasion, women Fellows attended for the first time, as they were admitted to the college in the reforms of 1981. Commemorative medals, like the one he wears, were struck to mark the occasion. Behind him rises the dome of the Radcliffe Camera, which contains one of the university's libraries.

CHANCELLOR OF CAMBRIDGE UNIVERSITY

It has long been accepted that good learning thrives in a well-disciplined environment. Cambridge University has been regulated since 1231, when Henry III issued a writ to the Bishop of Ely granting powers for the governance of the assembled students. In the 13th century these rules were designed to protect the learned, many of whom had journeyed from overseas, from the townsfolk at a time when travel was rare and foreigners were more vulnerable than they are now. There were also strict rules from the outset on what constituted qualification for a licence to teach and universities gained their status by managing the standard of conferral. In most universities of northern Europe, this was controlled by a Chancellor Scholasticus who was generally part of a cathedral linked to the place of learning. He rigorously tested the examinations set by masters of study, in order to ensure that the standards of those seeking to teach in their own right were met. ¶ At the start of the 13th century Cambridge started to grow. It was on the main route from the east of England to the Midlands and there was increasing trade and wealth at either end. The impenetrability of the fens and the forested uplands forced roads into this crossing of the River Cam. Perhaps the story of the university can be traced to the establishment of an Augustinian house, dedicated to St Giles in 1092, founded by Hugoline Picot, the sheriff's wife. This attracted other religious houses, the Fransiscans, Dominicans, Carmelites and Gilbertines. But those who came to learn with these foundations were only taught what priests and monks needed for a prayerful life. ¶ In 1209 a group of scholars fed up with abuse in Oxford set themselves up among the religious houses of Cambridge. They took lodgings and by 1226 the various masters of learning had organized themselves, with a Chancellor at their head. However, the community disliked the young students and charged heavy rents. Thus Henry III's writ protected the fledgling university but highlighted a need for something better. ¶ This came when Hugh de Balsham, Bishop of Ely, founded the first college in 1281, called Peterhouse. It was the first of many that developed from Oxford's collegiate template. More colleges were founded by wealthy benefactors seeking the gratitude of a merciful God. The grateful teaching body, of Regent Masters, looked to their Chancellor to grant degrees of membership. The Chancellor then assumed the role of ecclesiastical judge over the university at the end of the 15th century, in a move that confirmed its independence from all but the Pope, and he was granted power over markets and fairs, in order to further protect the academic community. ¶ The privilege and licence to print books, confirmed by Royal Charter in 1534, gave the university considerable power and, just as the nation developed its mercantile empire under Tudor, Stuart and Hanoverian monarchs, so the discoveries of the new world challenged and opened up learning. The election of Prince Albert as Chancellor in 1847 brought one of the most challenging and methodical minds of the time into the fray and, following a Royal Commission, it was not surprising that the Cambridge University Act of 1857 was passed. In it the Senate was formalized as the authority of the university, along with the body of graduates and the titular presence of the Chancellor, with an executive Vice Chancellor. The power of royalty to convene and influence events had greatly reduced when Albert's great-great-grandson was elected to the chancellorship in 1976. But, like his forebear, Prince Philip brought an engaging mind to the role. Both princes sent their eldest sons to the university, namely the future Edward VII and Prince Charles. They matriculated, like every student, in a ceremony that links each graduate with the start of this and all universities.

The University Marshal, Chancellor's Train-Bearer, Chancellor and Esquire Bedells in Senate House Yard after the annual Congregation for the conferment of Honorary Doctorates by the Chancellor. One of the earliest recorded ceremonies was in 1493, when the university honoured the poet John Skelton. The office of Bedell is referred to in the original statutes of the university where the alternative title of 'apparitor' is also given. The Marshal is a university ceremonial officer.

BODLEY'S LIBRARIAN

Although now renowned as a centre of academic excellence with superb facilities, the University of Oxford has known hard times. During the mid-16th century, for example, it had no central library. Its book collections, built upon those bequeathed by Thomas Cobham, Bishop of Worcester, in 1327, and housed in a room over the old convocation house in St Mary's Church, had been dispersed, the final blow coming from the Protestant reformers in 1550, who were said to have given them away or sold them 'to Mechanicks for servile uses'. ¶ The first hints of organized learning at Oxford were the theological lectures given by Robert Pullen in 1133, though it is possible that Henry I's palace at Beaumont may have attracted scholars to Oxford's royal court before. The Bishop of Lincoln appointed a Chancellor there in 1214, and the colleges of Balliol, Merton and University appeared in the last decades of the 13th century. Cobham's library was therefore established fairly early in the university's life, though funds nearly fell short at the start. Help came from Henry IV, his son Henry V, and the Princes Thomas, John and Humfrey, Duke of Gloucester. The last of these donated a collection of rare manuscripts, many of which were new to England. When building of the new Divinity School was completed in 1488, the library moved into an upper storey. It was this collection that was dispersed during the religious upheavals of the 16th century and which left a 'great empty room' for 50 years where Oxford's growing heart had been. ¶ To this shell in 1598 came the Devonian Thomas Bodley, recently retired from court. He was a scholar of Hebrew, who had studied at Magdalen College and lectured in Greek at Merton. After a lifetime of service to Elizabeth I, he hoped now to serve his university. Twelve years earlier he had married a wealthy widow, and was now bent on benevolence: his ambition was to restore and restock the library. After just four years, the doors were opened to the scholars and they found shelves filled with books that Bodley had collected from all over Europe. The appointment of Thomas James as the first Librarian marked the fulfilment of Bodley's ambition. Although he had achieved all this within the last year of Elizabeth's reign, it was her successor, James I, who dubbed him a knight in recognition of his achievement. ¶ Sir Thomas went on to enter into an agreement with the Stationers' Company that would distinguish his library from all others at the time. He persuaded the Company to send a free copy of every book it licensed to his library. This privilege was forfeited with the collapse of the Star Chamber, Henry VII's civil and criminal court, during the Civil War. Re-established only fitfully in the half century after the Restoration, it was fully restored by the Copyright Act of 1710. The library continues to receive a free copy of every book published, so there is a never-ending demand for space. The Quadrangle built in front of the Divinity School between 1613 and 1619 was equipped by Bodley with a floor dedicated to book storage, but this was quickly filled, and it has been the responsibility of each succeeding Librarian to arrange further storage as required. ¶ It is impossible to quantify the benefits of the Bodleian collection on the increase of wisdom, but it has undoubtedly enabled some of the greatest minds in the world to pursue their academic endeavours. Sir Thomas Bodley's decision to spend the final years of his life turning the remains of a neglected library into a renowned place of study and research is one that has benefited generations of students. More than a memorial to a remarkable man, the library is a symbol of England's civilization.

The 22nd Librarian sits on Sir Thomas Bodley's Chair in Duke Humfrey's Library above the Divinity School. Through the window can be seen the Tower of the Five Orders of Architecture, which rises above the main gate to the library in the heart of Oxford University. Bodley's Librarian is supported in his role of maintaining this complete collection of all published books in Britain by four others, known as 'keepers'. They include the Keeper of the Printed Books, who supervises a constantly growing resource.

SENIOR CONSTABLE AND CONSTABLES OF OXFORD UNIVERSITY

Law and order are important parts of any civilized society and leaders have attempted to impose both since the earliest times. In England in 1285, Edward I passed a statute of Watch and Ward, which established formal surveillance of the streets of London. However, the Constables of Oxford University claim to be the oldest police force in the world, their Proctors who patrolled the city pre-dating Edward's initiative by 70 years. ¶ Until the 19th century saw the national introduction of officers and courts to keep the peace, civil order outside London was maintained by lords of the manor. Serious offences were referred to higher courts and ultimately to the king's mercy. Within the early manor courts the office of Constable was an influential one, inspired by the dignitaries that emperors employed to look after their horses. These 'counts of the stable' often commanded large and powerful armies for the emperor, but the title is now the lowest rank held by policemen in Britain. ¶ In the same year that Proctors first patrolled Oxford, the barons forced King John to sign Magna Carta, which curtailed royal power in favour of justice for the individual. Justice can only be exercised when the law is enforced, but despite this, British culture consistently rejected an organized force of law. People regarded such an institution with distrust and feared it would curtail their freedom. By the 19th century, however, as the Industrial Revolution brought urbanization and the power of religion declined, civil order deteriorated and people began to favour stricter law enforcement. ¶ Britain's earliest organized police force (based in London) was the Bow Street Runners, founded about 1745 by the writer Henry Fielding, who was a Justice of the Peace. In 1829, this force was reorganized by the Home Secretary, Robert Peel, but many people objected to the State assuming control of law and order. Over time, the blue-uniformed officers became familiar figures on the London streets and were nicknamed 'Peelers' or 'Bobbies' after their founder. In 1835 police forces were established in the London boroughs, and four years later they spread to the counties. ¶ In the same year that Peel's legislation was passed, the Vice Chancellor of Oxford signed the 'Plan for the Establishment of an Efficient University Police', in which the duties and powers of the Oxford Constables were formalized. University Constables, and the Proctors before them, were principally responsible for the supervision of scholars. They retained the power to issue avuncular reprimands, but the new plan also allowed them to act as quasi-policemen within the university precincts. ¶ Until the end of the Second World War, the Constables operated in loco parentis, which allowed them to remove students from pubs and get them back into college before the gates were locked. Misdemeanours, such as being out after curfew or being found with the opposite sex, were punished by either the college or the university on evidence presented by the Constables, nicknamed 'Bulldogs'. The punishments for minor transgressions have varied with the passage of time, but cheating has always been treated with the utmost severity. Formal hearings are now conducted into allegations of cheating, but Proctors were originally allowed to send down a student suspected of dishonesty without referring the matter any further. ¶ In 2003 the Oxford Constables were disbanded by the University Council and redesignated as Proctors' Officers, carrying out more or less the same duties but without the powers of police constables. A group of traders in Oxford had argued that the Constables were 'not accountable to any public authority' and described their role as an 'anachronism'. Previously they had full powers of arrest within the precincts of the university and within four miles of any university building.

Standing in front of Oxford's Clarendon Building, designed by Nicholas Hawksmoor in 1715, the Senior Constable is surrounded by the Constables of Oxford University, who are now known as the Principal Proctors' Officer and Proctors' Officers respectively. The bowler hats were introduced in 1946 when the uniform of top hat and cape was dropped.

A genealogical coincidence began the unification of the kingdom from two old enemies. Elizabeth, the Virgin Queen, died in 1603, and left the throne to her cousin James VI of Scots. James I of England, as he became, had written: 'God gives not kings the style of Gods in vain, For on his throne his sceptre do they sway,' hinting at the absolutism that would make the Stuart dynasty one of Britain's most controversial. This unification of crowns was the first step to political unity, joining the two countries both for economic advantage and for the defence of their interests against ideological opponents in Catholic Europe.

For Scotland, an absentee monarchy posed constitutional problems. With its single-chambered Parliament, the country was arguably easier to govern than its southern neighbour. But the growing power of the Kirk since 1560 proved a formidable opponent. To maintain his authority from London, James appointed Commissioners to represent him both at Scotland's Parliament and in the Kirk's General Assembly. The Union in 1707 removed any need for parliamentary Commissioners, but the Crown's relationship was maintained with an increasingly independent Kirk.

England offered negligible resistance to the new Scots dynasty of Stuarts. This was partly because James I was staunchly Protestant and sought to centralize power in the monarchy. However, in due course Charles I's disinclination to consult his Parliament, together with his wife's Catholicism, led to a fundamental breach between the king and the Commons. Charles was blind to the reality of the political situation, and civil war and the king's own execution followed. Succeeding Charles as ruler, Cromwell revived the title of Lord Protector, but stopped short of accepting the crown.

Scotland disagreed with England's regicide, crowned the late king's son Charles II, at Scone in 1651, and as a result suffered Cromwellian brutality and eventual unification with England under the Commonwealth, from 1652 to 1660. Autonomy returned with the Restoration of Charles II, who rewarded his supporters well. The army was thanked (or forgiven, depending on which side they had taken) with the establishment of the Royal Hospital at Chelsea, which provided shelter for elderly men-at-arms. When Titus Oates whipped up anti-Catholic fear against Charles in the fictitious Popish Plot, the king's natural son, the Duke of Monmouth, persuaded his father to protect himself better against personal attack: as a result Monmouth was made the first Gold Stick in Waiting in order to protect the Sovereign.

Following Charles II's death in 1685 and the unsuccessful Monmouth Rebellion, which ended in the Duke's execution, James II succeeded his brother, having been, as Duke of York, both High Commissioner in Scotland and Lord High Admiral. He fell quickly from favour, after failing to reassure Parliament that he was not seeking, in this Age of Reason, to establish a Catholic despotism. The Glorious Revolution of 1688 ended James's reign, and the reign of the Stuarts, and Parliament invited his daughter, Mary, and son-in-law, William of Orange, to take the throne, subject to terms that restricted royal powers.

Many in Scotland did not share the English wish to replace James II, and the imposition of the new regime was carried out brutally, culminating in the massacre of the Macdonalds at Glencoe in 1696. To prevent such a thing happening again, after Queen Anne succeeded William in 1702 Scotland's Parliament passed the Act of Security, to ensure that Scots could choose their own successor to Anne. This filled England with concern that James II's son, the Old Pretender, might inherit, and the Queen was advised to withhold Assent. However, she had to live with this legislation because she needed Scottish taxes for her army, fighting abroad under the leadership of the Duke of Marlborough. The English Parliament retaliated with the Aliens Act, by which Scots were treated as aliens unless they accepted Anne's Hanoverian heir. At around this time the queen granted a Charter to the Royal Company of Archers, which became in due course the monarch's official Body Guard in Scotland.

The political and economic tensions between the two kingdoms reached a point that could only be followed by separation or outright union. In 1707 the Act of Union came into effect. With the words, 'It is full time to put an end to it', power passed from Edinburgh to Westminster. Trading arrangements were shared, but Scots Law was retained, under the head of Scotland's legal structure, the Lord President of the Court of Session. It was not clear how the Union would function in reality, and so the new relationship of governance had to be forged in practice in the following years. The relationship was threatened early on by the spread of Jacobitism in the Highlands and Lowlands, and exacerbated by unpopular new taxes on basic goods, imposed to bring Scotland into line with England.

On Anne's death in 1714, while the crown of the United Kingdom of Great Britain was passed to George I, who was a distant Protestant cousin from Hanover, rebellion brewed in Scotland around the figure of James VIII, the Old Pretender. Many rallied to this cause in 1715, and again in 1745. The Jacobite rising was put down at the last battle on British soil, at Culloden in 1746. Thereafter, the Hanoverians undermined the ancient Scottish clan system. At around the same time, Freemasonry, a society of secrets, was becoming organized, and attracted members from the intelligentsia and aristocracy, first in Scotland, then in England; it thrived, too, in Ireland, among affluent Protestants. The Royal Family united the movement in the following century.

George I spoke few words of English; therefore business was conducted in his name by Privy Councillors, who formed a Cabinet of ministerial advisers. Despite coming from outside the English royal tradition, George was responsible for the revival of an ancient chivalric order, the Order of the Bath, prompted by the first de facto Prime Minister, Sir Robert Walpole, who saw it as an additional source of political rewards. George revelled in his new kingdom's wealth, just as James I had done. The kingdoms of Scotland and England were one (the union with Wales had taken place in 1536) and in 1801 Ireland would join the fold. Westminster was now the seat of Britain's government and the River Thames was the capital's thoroughfare: the Worshipful Company of Watermen and Lightermen saw business boom. But as the century progressed the chill wind of revolution began to blow through Europe and the British colonies.

QUEEN OF SCOTS, SOVEREIGN OF THE MOST ANCIENT AND MOST NOBLE ORDER OF THE THISTLE AND CHIEF OF THE CHIEFS

At the opening of the new Scottish Parliament by the Queen in 2004 the Presiding Officer referred to the monarch as 'Queen of Scots'. It was an emotional moment for a country that had pursued a long political path to recover an element of self-government, which was lost in 1707 under the Act of Union. The ancient title of Scottish monarchs generally differs from the English version, in that it derived its authority not from the land but from its people. Most Scottish monarchs used the title of King, or Queen, of Scots and the concept of familial chiefship was part of this concept too. ¶ The first ruler in the north was the King of the Picts, a title that defined his leadership over the Pictish people. In the 8th century Constantine was King of the Picts and Pictish supremacy survived until the 9th century, when Kenneth mac Alpin was the ruler of Dalriada, now Argyll, and leader of the Scots who had emigrated there from Ireland. When a Viking raid on the Picts killed their king and his principal chiefs, in around 839, Kenneth raided their lands too and claimed the title King of the Picts and Scots. Malcolm III Canmore, which means 'Great Chief', dropped the Pictish reference and was just plain King of Scots in 1058. David I, who became St David, used the Latin version of *Rex Scottorum*, and so it went on until the young Margaret Queen of Scots was killed in a shipwreck off Orkney in 1290. ¶ The English king, Edward I, arbitrated over the claimants and chose John Balliol but with the title King of Scotland, introducing the template of feudal ownership that shaped English kingship. After John's abdication, Edward took Scotland as his own possession. This was intolerable to the Scots and a campaign for independence was led first by Sir William Wallace and then by the claimant, Robert the Bruce, Earl of Carrick. He crowned in 1306, but with the title restored to King of Scots. However, he could not fully claim his kingdom until after the defeat of England's Edward II at Bannockburn in 1314. ¶ The title King of Scots passed from Robert I through to Mary Queen of Scots in 1542 and ended with her son James VI. When he inherited the English crown in 1603, his haste in leaving Scotland was almost shocking. He changed his title to King of England, Scotland, France and Ireland, and the ancient chiefly title of King, or Queen, of Scots was lost. But its visceral meaning has never ebbed and its use in the Scottish Parliament, in reference to Elizabeth, the descendant of Malcolm Canmore, Bruce and the Stuarts, ferments a warm reality. ¶ In 1687 King James's grandson, James VII of Scotland (and II), created the Scottish Order of the Thistle, similar to England's Order of the Garter and intended as a bargaining chip of patronage. It was to be a means of elevating his Scottish supporters and was given greater value by presentation as a revival of an ancient Scottish 'Order of St Andrew', which James III was supposed to have bestowed in the 15th century. The order's claimed age is referred to in its description as the 'Most Ancient and Most Noble Order of the Thistle' and was established for the Sovereign and 12 knights companion, reflecting Christ and his disciples. Within a year, James had been deposed by Parliament, and his son and daughter-in-law, William III and Mary II, were joint king and queen. In the instant of his deposition, the Edinburgh mob destroyed the abbey at Holyrood, where his Roman Catholic chapel of the order had been built. The present chapel for the order was not built until 1910. Queen Anne restored the order in 1703, even though her father and the Old Pretender had never stopped appointing Thistle knights of their own. The order is still the most senior accolade in Scotland, although, since George IV expanded the number to 16 knights, it has settled at that number, while the Queen opened its membership to women. ¶ The unification of Scotland was achieved to differing degrees by different monarchs. However, the diverse topography of the land made overall control arguably notional. The tribal structure of the past lived on through the families and clans, each of which, often further subdivided, was led by a patriarchal or matriarchal chief or head. These Chiefs and Chieftains often fought out quarrels amongst themselves, but the emergence of economic benefit, which came

from peace following the Jacobite rebellions, roads and the growing wealth of Britain's Empire, negated this thirst for violence and provided a greater cause. The logical focus for unity and cohesion formed around the King of Scots, who became the Chief of the Chiefs. When George IV visited Scotland in 1821, he symbolically planted the crown back in the national heartland. His niece, Victoria, went further by purchasing her beloved Balmoral estate and adopting the life of a Chief. Successive generations have built on this affection, and, despite great change in Scotland, the Crown has broadly held the loyalty of a nation during its reappraisal of its modern identity and constitution. Whenever Elizabeth II has returned to the Holyrood Parliament she has been welcomed not by her United Kingdom title but with provenance and fraternity as Queen of Scots.

Previous page: The wild landscape of the Scottish Highlands is where the culture and traditions of Scotland's Clan system developed. Here the Chief of the Chiefs stands by the Gelder Burn on the Balmoral estate, wearing her mantle as Sovereign of the Most Ancient and Most Noble Order of the Thistle. Although Queen of the United Kingdom, she is increasingly accorded the ancient title of her ancestors, as Queen of Scots. From her shoulders and held by white satin ties hangs the Collar of the Order, which is a chain made up of alternate golden thistles and rue sprigs, plants that abound in this terrain. From it is suspended the Jewel, showing Scotland's patron saint and his saltire cross. The star of the Order is also based on St Andrew's Cross, which legend says appeared in a vision to the Scots and Picts before they defeated the West Saxons. *Above*: A Knight Companion of the Thistle in the tiny Thistle Chapel at the High Kirk of St Giles, Edinburgh, where the order meets in conclave for the Sovereign to install new Companions.

CHIEF OF CLAN CAMERON

To those who lead a clan, no honours or titles can compete with the privilege of heading a great family. Scotland's history, geography and economy gave life to and sustained a large familial system in the wild and often inhospitable Highlands. ¶ In essence, the clan system operated like this: wherever life was sustainable, a group gathered to work the land and live on the food they grew. One among their number would emerge as leader. All would give him their allegiance in return for his protection. As the unit grew, increased resources were needed, and if they could not be sourced from within, a raiding party would be sent out to find what was required. As neighbours seldom had food to spare, these raids became skirmishes. Many died and the desire for revenge took root. This pattern of existence was common to all parts of the Highlands, but certain clans dominated. The greatest were those who wrested large tracts of land from their rivals and attracted the loyalty of sufficient clansmen to survive attacks from others. Tranquillity, like good weather, seldom dominated in the Highlands, and even today each clan jealously guards its identity. ¶ One of the great families is Clan Cameron, the name deriving from Cam shron, Gaelic for 'wry nose', the name of an early Chief. But the 15th-century leader from whom the family can trace a continuous line of descent was Donald Duibh (Donald the Swarthy). All his chiefly successors bear the name MacDhomnuill Duibh (Son of Donald the Swarthy). The clan's beginnings are obscure. It probably arrived in Lochaber from the islands after leaving the Lord of the Isles's protection to seek security and fortune elsewhere. Over the centuries, the clan and its Chiefs gained a reputation for tenacity and heroism, and this became enduringly established because of its support for the Jacobite cause. Lochiel, as today's Chief is affectionately known, still supervises the lands his family has held since the 14th century. ¶ In 1654 Sir Ewen, the 17th Chief, known as the Great Lochiel, fought the English at Lochaber, and in a fierce encounter had to use his teeth to tear out an Englishman's throat. Not surprisingly, he was said to have a 'look so fierce might fright the boldest foe'. Later, in the steep pass of Killiecrankie, Cameron's men fell on the English army and inflicted a heavy defeat, albeit at great cost to the clan's numbers. ¶ Infirmity prevented the Great Lochiel from fighting in the 1715 Jacobite Rebellion, but he told his son John to lead the clan into battle anyway. The result was disastrous: John was exiled, leaving his son Donald to take the helm as 19th Chief. The young man, less aggressive than his grandfather, became known as the 'Gentle Lochiel'. When news of the arrival of Bonnie Prince Charlie in Scotland reached him, he was horrified to hear that the Prince had landed with only seven men and no French support. The Gentle Lochiel failed to dissuade the Young Pretender from marching south to claim the English throne, and was persuaded to call out the clan in support of him. Of the 800 men he led from Lochaber in 1746, more than 300 were killed in the Battle of Culloden, the last battle fought on British soil. This defeat sounded the death knell for the ancient clan system. ¶ Following that decisive battle, Clan Chiefs became owners of land rather than stewards of it, and had to apply hard-headed economic criteria to their land management. A collapse in the rural economy in the late 1700s led to the Highland Clearances, in which tens of thousands were evicted to make way for large-scale sheep farming. ¶ This policy was enforced with great brutality, even by some of the Chiefs themselves – a betrayal of their original role as protectors that has left an enduring sense of bitterness in some of the worst affected areas. People already on subsistence level were forced into a life of hunger and destitution, and many had no option but to migrate to America and elsewhere. ¶ The clan system, once again benign, is overseen by a Standing Council of Chiefs, which aims to maintain the fundamental principle of the clans – kinship.

The 26th Chief stands near Loch Arkaig in Inverness-shire, looking across land on which Camerons have lived for centuries. His cap's eagle feathers mark him out as Chief, as do his shoulder-borne 'plaid' of the chiefly tartan and cromach (shepherd's crook). His kilt is Clan Cameron tartan.

CAPTAIN GENERAL OF THE QUEEN'S BODY GUARD FOR SCOTLAND, ROYAL COMPANY OF ARCHERS AND GOLD STICK WITH OFFICERS AND MEMBERS OF THE ROYAL COMPANY OF ARCHERS

The Battle of Flodden, in 1513, tied Scots monarchs close to their archers. It is said that James IV, who died along with most of the 'flowers of Scottish Chivalry' on that day, fell among a close escort of French archers. His great-grandson, James VI, respected the skills of archery so much that he passed an edict banning football in favour of bowmanship. When James rode south to claim his English throne in 1603, he found two English Body Guards waiting to protect him in the palaces he inherited. His grandson, Charles II, could have done with a Scottish Body Guard when he sailed to Scotland in 1650. He could not be sure what reception would be given him, after less than a year since his father, Charles I, had been executed. ¶ The Royal Company of Archers started out as a private club in 1676. The Constitution it drew up still governs the Company today. The Scottish Privy Council not only granted a request for recognition, but also established the Queen's Prize for shooting. In addition it granted the title the King's Company of Archers, which Queen Anne confirmed with a Royal Charter in 1704. In return, the Archers are expected, if asked, to provide the Sovereign with a Reddendo, comprising three arrows. Since then, a vast roll has been kept that every Archer signs on appointment. ¶ George IV's visit to Edinburgh in 1822 provided the Royal Company with a chance to bid for the vacant position of Scotland's King's Body Guard. Walter Scott dressed it in a fanciful uniform based on his own whimsical imagination; the Duke of Montrose swore the Company in and the Earl of Elgin marched it to the quay at Leith to await the arrival of the Royal Barge. Throughout the visit the Archers escorted the king in State, and a grateful monarch made the Duke the first Gold Stick for Scotland. ¶ William IV was so glad to inherit his brother's throne, in 1830, that he busied himself signing documents 'William R' to the point of having to ease his painful hand in a bowl of warm water. Among these papers was one granting a new Gold Stick, with a Silver Stick and ivory ones for the Royal Company's council members. There were more replacement sticks in 1837, when William's 18-year-old niece, Victoria, inherited the throne. ¶ Royal visits to Scotland had been rare; hence Victoria's first State visit went badly. No rehearsals and a change of plan meant that, when the young queen climbed into her carriage, the Royal Company was still shaking itself into formation. The Archers were left in a cloud of dust as the queen's cavalcade sped off, and despite a valiant attempt they failed to catch up. This was soon put right by the queen, who ensured that she was properly escorted the next day when she claimed the keys of Edinburgh Castle. ¶ Traditionally only a Scot may join the Company, and many famous people have served in its ranks. Its senior officers and a good number of its 400-odd members are noblemen, many of whom have also served as distinguished military officers. Each member is still encouraged to be proficient with bow and arrow. ¶ Each year, the Queen's Body Guard parades at events during the Queen's stay at Edinburgh. Most ceremonies take place around Holyrood Palace. Here, across the wall and dominating the city's remarkable skyline, is the craggy feature of Arthur's Seat. Its name reputedly evolves from Archer's Seat: the predecessors of the Royal Company were said to have rested there after practising in the valley beneath.

The Archers, commanded by the Captain General as Gold Stick for Scotland, carry longbows with a 'graith' of three arrows tucked into their belts. The Captain General carries a symbolic gold-topped stick and, like Clan Chiefs, wears three eagle feathers in his cap. Archer's Hall is where the Royal Company meets and practises the skills of toxopholy before matches, where each Archer tests his bowmanship on targets called 'clouts'. Every summer, the Royal Company of Archers shoots for the Musselburgh Arrow. Started in 1603, this is the oldest continually held sporting event in the world.

SISTERS OF THE HOSPITAL OF THE MOST HOLY AND UNDIVIDED TRINITY

While the Dissolution of the Monasteries made Henry VIII a wealthy man, its adverse effects were many and various. The 16th century closed with ruins where great abbeys had once stood, and while there may have been little sympathy for the religious orders they dispossessed, the work they had done in caring for the elderly was sorely missed. As the old and destitute wandered around in search of food and shelter, they fell victim to a law that branded them idle beggars and imposed a fine on those who failed to apprehend them. Into this welfare vacuum stepped patrons of varying wealth, responding to the moral imperative that successful men should fulfil their Christian obligations by helping those in need. ¶ One such beneficiary was Henry Howard, the Earl of Northampton, whose family had garnered wealth through ownership and development of land in Norfolk, particularly at Kings Lynn, where a thriving port attracted good revenue. Born at the beginning of the Dissolution, the Earl lived through the worst of the Reformation and saw his brother Thomas, 4th Duke of Norfolk, lose his head after plotting against Elizabeth I. Like most Howards, the Duke held proudly to Roman Catholicism and died in the faith. ¶ The Earl himself was a powerful man, being Lord Privy Seal for James I, as well as Constable of Dover Castle and Warden of the Cinque Ports. Having established charitable institutions at Clun and Greenwich, in 1616 he went on to found the Hospital of the Most Holy and Undivided Trinity at Castle Rising in Norfolk. He stipulated that 12 local ladies were to be cared for in the new Hospital, but they had to meet strict criteria for admittance as the Earl was determined that his money should support only the most reputable of the less fortunate: 'They must be of honest life and conversation, religious, grave and discreet, able to read, if such a one be had, a single woman, her place to be void on marriage, to be 56 years of age at least, no common beggar, harlot, scold, drunkard, haunter of taverns, inns and alehouses.' ¶ Having satisfied this range of requirements and gained admittance, the ladies, who were known as Sisters, were to pray for the lives and souls of Howard's noble family. (Their benefactor might have been influenced by a pre-Reformation practice whereby wealthy people built chantry chapels and funded priests to say Masses eternally for their soul – a sort of spiritual life insurance.) In return, the Hospital provided a welcome refuge for those admitted to its secure environment at a time of religious upheaval. ¶ Qualifications for membership and the rules to be observed by the Hospital inmates have changed considerably since the 17th century, in line with evolving compassion and growing respect. In 1959 the building was completely renovated and reorganized to the Charity Commission's approval, but its primary function – to look after 12 needy women – remains its raison d'être. ¶ The Sisters wear a uniform based upon that approved by their historic benefactor. The high-crowned hats, originally worn over white, coif-like headpieces, were considered highly fashionable when first adopted. Their cloaks, originally made from dark blue and brown fustian, were changed to red during the 20th century at the request of the Sisters themselves. Full uniform is now worn only on special occasions, such as the swearing in of a new Sister. Such events are supervised by the Warden and attended by a member of the Howard family because the Hospital remains a Howard family concern.

For the annual ceremony of Founders Day and the swearing in of a new Sister, which takes place in the Hall of the Hospital of the Most Holy and Undivided Trinity, the Sisters wear conical hats and distinctive scarlet capes, which are embroidered with the Howard of Northampton family arms.

GOLD STICK IN WAITING

One of the oldest and closest of royal Body Guards, Gold Stick once served a vital role as the Sovereign's protection officer. The post emerged at a time of crisis, during the fictitious Popish Plot – a 'hellish' conspiracy to kill Charles II and to put his Catholic brother James on the throne and massacre all Protestants. The Popish Plot was a tissue of lies, fabricated by a mischief-maker, Titus Oates, who hoped to win fame by discovering, if not inventing, Catholic plots. In a country where Catholics were passionately hated and pathologically feared, Oates's elaborate plot threw London into panic, precipitating the judicial slaughter of 35 innocent Catholics. Religious tension escalated to fever pitch. Parliament passed an Act excluding all Roman Catholics from sitting in either House. ¶ When the Popish Plot gathered momentum, the Duke of Monmouth, Charles's illegitimate son, implored his doubting father to take precautions. Combining his responsibilities as Colonel of the First Troop of Life Guards with his filial concern for Charles II, Monmouth recommended a new appointment that would be directly responsible for the Sovereign's safety. The king concurred and created the post of Gold Stick in Waiting, the holder of which would be in constant attendance on the king 'from his rising to his going to bed... carrying in his hand an ebony staff or truncheon with a gold head engraved with his majesty's cipher and crown'. The post was thereby attached to colonels in the Household Cavalry and, if they were unable to be in attendance, an officer immediately junior could step in and be called Silver Stick in Waiting. ¶ The growing anti-Catholic sentiment led Parliament to persuade Charles to exile his brother James and make the Protestant Monmouth his heir. Later he changed his mind, and Monmouth lost his appointment as Gold Stick and was exiled in turn. ¶ When James II succeeded in 1685, Monmouth returned to challenge him for the throne. Monmouth's vainglorious hopes were dashed at the Battle of Sedgemore, where he fled the field, leaving his wretched peasant followers to certain butchery. By a quirk of just deserts, he was captured by his old regiment, the Life Guards, led by the Earl of Faversham. For his part in saving the Sovereign, Faversham was chosen as the next Gold Stick. Colonels of the Life Guards have since served as Gold Stick, with their lieutenants ever ready to stand in as Silver Stick. ¶ After the tumultuous times of the Stuarts, royal security relaxed for some centuries. Apart from occasional risings in Scotland, any domestic threat seemed minimal. The greatest potential threat came from abroad, during the Napoleonic wars with France, until the Duke of Wellington swept the French from the field at the decisive Battle of Waterloo in 1815. For his part in the action, Wellington was made colonel of a regiment called the Blues by George IV, and the regiment was raised to the status of Household Cavalry in 1820. Ever since, colonels of the Blues (now merged with the Royals) have shared the duties of Gold Stick with those of the Life Guards. ¶ The duties now are mainly ceremonial, accompanying the Sovereign on all State occasions and passing the Sovereign's orders to the Household Cavalry. Today the job of round-the-clock, front-line royal protection is carried out by a hand-picked squad of policemen, who field ever-present threats to the monarchy. Gold Stick still accompanies the Sovereign when riding, travelling by carriage or walking through London. As cavalry officers, all Gold Sticks have been excellent horsemen.

Holding the gold-tipped stick of office that gives this title its name, as guardian of the Sovereign's personal security, Gold Stick in Waiting stands in the Officers' Mess at Knightsbridge, home of the Household Cavalry Mounted Regiment, which performs ceremonial duties and provides mounted escorts for the Sovereign. The appointment is shared between the colonels of Britain's two most senior regiments that make up the Household Cavalry, the Life Guards, the colonel of which is shown on duty, and the Blues and Royals.

GOVERNOR OF THE ROYAL HOSPITAL

Following his defeat by Oliver Cromwell at the Battle of Worcester in 1651, Charles II became a fugitive and spent several years trying to evade capture by Cromwell's men. During his years in the wilderness, he found many protectors, but none so sturdy and silent as the Boscobel Oak in Shropshire. The future king hid in this tree to avoid capture, and thereafter celebrated the part it had played in his return by wearing a sprig of oak on 29 May, the date of his Restoration in 1660. ¶ In days that followed his resumption of the throne, Charles II searched for ways to show his gratitude to the people who had fought for and supported him. Some say that it was his mistress – the infamous Nell Gwynn – who gave him the idea to build 'an hospitall for maimed soldiers at Chelsey'. However, it seems more likely that he took the idea from the Hôtel des Invalides in Paris, which had been established some years earlier and was widely admired. ¶ Sir Christopher Wren was commissioned to design the Royal Hospital, as it was to be known, and the king laid the foundation stone in 1682. Ten years later it was ready to admit 476 retired military men. The In-Pensioners, as the residents are known (to differentiate them from Out-Pensioners, who include most retired soldiers), are looked after by five retired officers, known as Captains of Invalids, who are answerable to the Governor of the Hospital. ¶ It is the Governor's duty to ensure that the In-Pensioners are looked after according to the highest military traditions while also imposing a gentle discipline. This, of course, must be done with sensitivity, as the old soldiers represent thousands of years' service between them. Above all, the Governor must ensure that the Pensioners' lives are dignified, as they follow in the footsteps of the Roundhead and Cavalier veterans who first occupied Wren's large and elegant building. ¶ The Hospital is one of the great landmarks in London and was designed to command an uninterrupted view of the Thames and the boggy ground of Battersea beyond. Unfortunately, that vista has altered over the years. Now traffic thunders alongside the river, while trees struggle to blot out the un-Wren-like structure of Battersea Power Station. Internally, however, the Hospital has lost none of its appeal. In a dining room hung with regimental colours and paintings the red-coated Chelsea Pensioners take their meals, surveyed by a vast allegorical portrait of Charles II. In return for being housed, fed and clothed, the veterans surrender their army pensions. Across the hall, the chapel is almost always open, and the Governor's stall beside the door is set at a slight angle so that he can survey his congregation. ¶ The open quadrangle of the Hospital, known as Figure Court, is colonnaded and lined with memorials to previous Pensioners and Governors. Along its length, benches provide rest for the residents and, as the Hospital is open to the public, visitors converse with the old comrades. In the centre of the grassy quadrangle stands a statue of Charles II by Grinling Gibbons. Rather oddly, the king is depicted as a conquering Roman emperor, with laurels at his temples. ¶ To commemorate the founder's birthday, which was also the date of his restoration as king in May 1660, the Chelsea Pensioners parade around the statue on 29 May (Oak Apple Day) every year and each participant wears a spray of oak leaves to recall the king's lucky escape from Cromwell in 1651. In similar time-honoured fashion, the Governor ensures that the statue keeps the lion's share of the leaves for camouflage. Each year a member of the Royal Family is invited by the Governor to inspect the In-Pensioners, which maintains the link between the monarch and the loyal In-Pensioners. In 2009 the male soldiers welcomed the first female soldiers, which was a further step in the gradual progress the United Kingdom's institutions are making towards gender parity. After all, both men and women have fought side by side for many years now and their aftercare is of equal importance to Charles II's descendant.

Beside the gilded statue of the founder, King Charles II, the Governor of the Royal Hospital is joined by In-Pensioners, one woman and three men. They all wear oak leaf sprigs, which represent the tree in which the king hid from Cromwell's army, to celebrate Oak Apple Day.

GRAND MASTER FOR THE
UNITED GRAND LODGE OF ENGLAND

Ten centuries before Jesus Christ walked the banks of the River Galilee, King Solomon ruled the kingdom of Israel. One of the symbols best associated with the wise king was the temple he built in Jerusalem. Legend has it that the building was perfect in every way – an achievement that resulted from the quality and character of the masons and their leader. The historical links with the reign of King Solomon may be doubtful, but the existence in the British Isles of free and accepted Freemasons can be argued from documents that survive from around 1390, which record rituals that are still in use now. The Royalist antiquarian Elias Ashmole was made a mason in Warrington in 1646 and records in his diary visiting other Lodges (places where Freemasons meet). ¶ The first Grand Master was chosen in 1717, when four London Lodges came together at the Goose & Gridiron tavern near St Paul's Cathedral. (Most Lodge meetings were held in pubs, as the ceremony was also a sociable event with food and drink.) On this historic occasion, the four Lodges established a central authority, known as a Grand Lodge, and elected their first Grand Master, Anthony Sayer. A few years later, Dr John Desaguliers followed into the Grand Master's Chair and brought direction to the Grand Lodge. Among other innovations, he introduced the aristocracy to the Craft, as Freemasonry was called, thus providing a major fillip to the movement. ¶ The advantages of incorporating the aristocracy were to be seen almost a century later. The movement by then had developed into a number of separate, independent factions, with a central and ongoing conflict existing between the two main groups, the Premier Grand Lodge and the Antients Grand Lodge (started by Irish Masons in 1752). In 1813 this all changed when Prince Augustus, then the Duke of Sussex, became Grand Master of the Premier Grand Lodge, and his brother Prince Edward, then the Duke of Kent, became Grand Master of the Antients Grand Lodge. The bickering that had existed between both Grand Lodges was almost instantly resolved by a fraternal pact. By the end of the year, the princes had solved the remaining problems and the United Grand Lodge of England was formed with the elder of the two princes in the Chair. ¶ The creation of the role of Grand Master provided the leadership and direction that the movement needed, while the union of the principal Masonic groups consolidated the strength of the Craft. By the 19th century the fraternity's appeal stretched across the Empire, as far away as Australia, New Zealand, Canada and India. In 1901 the Duke of Connaught became Grand Master, a post he held for longer than any other, until 1939 – a period of office that enabled him to oversee the construction of Freemasons' Hall in London's Covent Garden, built as a memorial to the thousands of Freemasons from all over the Empire who died in the First World War. ¶ The United Grand Lodge of England is made up of 8,500 Lodges with some 350,000 members. Much ritual in Masonry, based on customs and masons' tools, is misunderstood by outsiders. The main challenge of the leadership today is to explain the Craft's purpose and recruit new Freemasons, while also reassuring a public sceptical and suspicious of any institution that appears to operate through hidden signs. Meanwhile, the royal links continue, and hospitals, schools and other support organizations are funded by the generosity of Freemasons throughout the world.

Chequered flooring symbolizes the light and shade Freemasons experience in life, and represents the floor of Solomon's Temple – the building of which is the allegory around which Craft rituals are constructed. The Grand Master for the United Grand Lodge of England stands by his throne in the Grand Temple at Freemasons' Hall, in London's Covent Garden, where he holds the gavel first used by his great-grandfather, Edward VII. The stylized Mason's apron and a gilt collar carry emblems of his rank. As First Grand Principal of the Grand Chapter of Royal Arch Masons he wears a neck badge. The flags are the Grand Master's personal standard (left) and the standard of the Grand Lodge (right). The Bible sits on the pedestal, with the Square and Compasses, representing virtue and morality, placed on top. Beside them is the State Sword of the United Grand Lodge.

QUEEN'S BARGEMASTER AND
THE ROYAL WATERMEN

George I, the first Hanoverian to rule England, decided to hold a great water pageant on the River Thames on 15 July 1717. George Frideric Handel, the composer and sometime Master of the King's Musick, wrote the Water Music especially for the occasion. The king liked it so much that he commanded that it be played three times. George I had been on the throne for just three years, spoke little English, and, frankly, was not much interested in Britain. But he loved music, and his vivacious, if ageing, mistress, Madam Kilmanseck (popularly nicknamed 'Elephant and Castle'), loved a party. Another guest – the cuckolded husband – was left holding the £150 bill for the musicians alone. ¶ At his concert on the river, George I was attended by Royal Watermen, led by the King's Bargemaster. Watermen had ferried British monarchs up and down the Thames since medieval times, when the river was London's most used highway. When King John signed Magna Carta in 1215, for instance, his barge was in attendance at Runnymede. In the Tudor period especially, with Hampton Court, Greenwich and Westminster spaced out along the Thames's winding banks, the Royal Barges frequently bore the monarch, his family and courtiers from one palace to another. ¶ The formal royal appointment of Watermen dates from the 14th century. When roads improved in the 19th century, carriages took over, and today, Watermen are used as royal coachmen on duties originally carried out by the Royal Barge, especially when the Sovereign opens Parliament. On this occasion, the Watermen act as Footmen on the carriages bearing the Symbols of Sovereignty – the crown, Sword of State, maces and Cap of Maintenance – which in earlier times had come by river to Westminster. Even today, when the carriage arrives at Westminster, the Queen's Bargemaster formally hands the crown over before it is borne into Parliament. Royal Watermen still take part in the State Ride during State visits, originally a river duty for the Royal Barge. ¶ The Queen's Bargemaster and the Royal Watermen accompany the Royal Family when they travel ceremonially along the Thames. When the Queen is embarked, the Queen's Bargemaster takes eight Watermen. This is because the fastest of the old Shallop barges used eight oarsmen. ¶ All Royal Watermen belong to the City of London's Company of Watermen and Lightermen, which was established by an Act of Parliament in 1514 and provided a reliable taxi service for City merchants and regulated the waterway and the fares charged by Watermen. The Watermen's comrades, the Lightermen, essentially moved cargo around, thus lightening the ships, but they also shared some skills with the Watermen, whose licence is for carrying passengers. Together, they worked the merchants' grand city barges, each of which was run by a Bargemaster. ¶ Another thread connecting Watermen, Lightermen and George I's water concert is Doggett's Coat and Badge Race, an annual event initiated by Thomas Doggett to mark George I's accession on 1 August 1715. Doggett, an enterprising Irish actor, Whig and comedian, decided to mark the occasion by setting the Watermen a wager. The prize, which included money, a red livery and silver badge, was hotly contested each year by six Watermen. Doggett faithfully set the wager every year until his death in 1721, at which he left funds for the race to continue. The responsibility for the race was taken up by the Fishmongers' Company, which still stages the annual event, now one of the oldest annual sporting events in Britain. Every August opens with this unique competition to mark the anniversary of the music-loving Hanoverian's arrival. Most Watermen compete, and the liveried coats and badges are highly prized.

The Queen's Bargemaster (wearing white socks) and the Royal Watermen are all experienced boatmen chosen from the ranks of the Thames Watermen. Nowadays, conveying the monarch from Hampton Court to the Tower of London by barge is no longer necessary. In Tudor times, however, it was the safest route, and the multiple oarsmen made sure it was also the quickest.

LORD GREAT CHAMBERLAIN

The post of Lord Great Chamberlain dates from the time of the Norman Conquest, when William the Conqueror appointed his compatriot Robert Malet to the office. In this role, Malet supervised the improvements at the Palace of Westminster while the Tower of London and other fortifications were being built under the watchful eye of the new king. ¶ The Chamberlaincy is one of the Great Offices of State and was made hereditary by Henry I in 1133, when Aubery de Vere was granted the appointment. De Veres continued in the post until 1526, when the last male of that line died. Mary and Elizabeth Tudor then appointed a distant male heir, and his descendants inherited the post until the same problem occurred again in 1626. The final beneficiary was Lord Willoughby d'Eresby, and yet again his line ended without male issue. As a result, several families disputed the right to the post, so the House of Lords reached a decision in 1902 to let them share the privilege, according to a complicated arrangement whereby one claimant shares the duty with two others, who take it in turns to fulfil the privilege. The appointment survives, but nowadays it is largely ceremonial and without much power. ¶ The Palace of Westminster, which was once entirely the Lord Great Chamberlain's domain, is now his responsibility only as far as ceremonial matters are concerned: he plans the domestic arrangements whenever the Queen visits her Parliament, such as for the State Opening. When her carriage draws to a halt under Victoria Tower, the Lord Great Chamberlain greets her and leads her inside. He carries a white stave, which is a little over six feet long, and on the back of his uniform he wears a golden key, an entirely symbolic emblem of his office. ¶ In former times monarchs always stayed the night at Westminster prior to their coronation, and a custom arose whereby the Lord Great Chamberlain had the privilege of handing the monarch his shirt, stockings and drawers on the morning of the coronation and helping him to dress. In return for this service, the Lord Great Chamberlain was entitled to claim the bed, bedding and night-gown used by the king on the eve of his coronation, plus all the furniture, valances and curtains used in the royal chamber. ¶ In addition, the Lord Great Chamberlain was entitled to demand the clothes worn by the king at the coronation, which included his underclothes, socks and other personal belongings. Quite what was done with these items is not known, and some monarchs objected to the claim anyway, even though there was little room for negotiation as the terms were framed in law. James I, who had just arrived from chilly Edinburgh to claim his English crown, would not part with any of his clothes or belongings, and paid a fee of £200 in lieu. Queen Anne was similarly disconcerted by the demand and sent £300 to keep her 'bottom drawer intact'. Things are different now, as monarchs prefer to spend a quiet night at Buckingham Palace before their coronation. Since 1821 the complex processions from the Hall at Westminster to the Abbey are no longer necessary, so the duties of the Lord Great Chamberlain have been reduced still further. ¶ As the Palace of Westminster is now a royal residence in name only, the Lord Great Chamberlain's remit no longer extends very far, and others now carry out his ancient responsibilities. The Lord Chamberlain, for example, is the full-time Managing Director of the Royal Household, while Black Rod keeps order in and around the House of Lords.

By 'antient… just and lawful right' the Lord Great Chamberlain keeps the Consort's Throne and the Prince of Wales's Chair in the Stone Hall at Houghton, his home in Norfolk: when needed, he takes them to Parliament. He wears a symbolic ceremonial key on his back to show that he once had responsibility for domestic arrangements at the Palace of Westminster. The white stave of office is held throughout a reign and broken at the monarch's graveside. When leading the Sovereign to the Lords the Great Lord Chamberlain walks backwards.

MEMBER OF THE MOST HONOURABLE
THE PRIVY COUNCIL

When looking for the real power in Britain, a good place to start is the Privy Council, the source of the present-day Cabinet's legal powers. Its structure derives from the Normans' Commune Concilium, which in turn was based on the Anglo-Saxons' Witenagemot, a council of nobles and clergy who advised the king. This advisory body has had several titles during its evolution, but the current name, Privy Council, emerged in the 13th century because its members met in private. ¶ Apart from acting in an advisory capacity, the Council saw that justice was done, that the royal will was exercised and that the monarch's executive power was kept in check, thereby guiding the Royal Prerogative. The relationship between monarch and Council changed with each incumbent. The Council would exert greater influence over a weak king, just as a capable monarch could swing the pendulum in the other direction. Early Norman Councils consisted of the Chancellor, Chief Justiciary, Treasurer, Steward, Constable, Marshal, the Archbishops of Canterbury and York, and others the king selected. Many of these titles still exist, though most play their part only at the Accession Councils and coronations of new monarchs. ¶ In Plantagenet times the Curia Regis (King's Court), as the Council was then known, grew fairly large and often misused its power to draft legislation from petitions submitted by the relatively impotent House of Commons. The Tudors believed that a small Council was vital to good government, and it suited Henry VIII to limit it to any but the most essential Councillors. The Civil War led to the Council's temporary disbandment, and the Restoration saw its return, but not immediately. Charles II's experiment of appointing 30 new Privy Councillors was not a success: he felt there were too many to keep business confidential, so he returned to having a small inner clique, which helped set the pattern for how the Council is organized today. While the Glorious Revolution of 1688 saw constitutional supremacy move from the Crown to Parliament, the Privy Council continued to help monarchs exercise their remaining powers, carry out any judicial obligations and fulfil any other responsibilities. ¶ It was the arrival of George I, who spoke no English, that necessitated the passing of greater executive power to the Privy Council. A gathering similar to Charles II's cabal, known as the Cabinet, incorporated the king's Ministers. ¶ The progression from the Hanoverian Cabinet to the parliamentary executive of today has come about largely through the emergence of an increasingly representative democracy and the decline of royal influence. As a result, the Privy Council has waned in importance and membership of it has evolved into little more than part of the honours system. Nonetheless, every member must take an oath of confidentiality to facilitate cross-party briefing by the executive, which means that party-political differences are set aside. They also swear 'to give good advice, to protect the king's interests, to do justice honestly, [and] to take no gifts'. ¶ Nowadays, every member of the Cabinet is a Privy Councillor, but the Council's total membership of nearly 400 also includes other parliamentary figures, judges, bishops and members of the Royal Household. All the appointments are for life. ¶ Once a month, or whenever necessary, the Queen meets in Council with just four Councillors from the Government to give formal approval to legislation drawn up in advance by government departments. In return, Privy Councillors are available to provide advice on constitutional matters at any time to the Queen and her Ministers.

A Privy Councillor stands in the National Liberal Club, close to Parliament and London's Whitehall. Once a select band of trusted advisers close to the king, the Privy Council now has around 500 members, some of whom are drawn from the Commonwealth. Court dress is seldom worn these days, but it was once the ceremonial wear of imperial potentates who drew on the status conferred by their Privy Council membership to exercise power in various parts of the world.

KNIGHT GRAND CROSS OF THE MOST
HONOURABLE ORDER OF THE BATH

By comparison with other orders of chivalry, the Most Honourable Order of the Bath, founded in 1725 by George I, is relatively modern. Its inspiration, however, is more ancient, as it derives its name and many of its symbols from the rituals associated with the creation of knights in the Middle Ages. For instance, to repeat the sacramental immersion in water of Christian baptism, a symbolic bath was taken, and allegorical robes symbolizing purity put on. When the order was revived, mulberry-coloured satin, lined with white taffeta, was selected for the robes, these colours symbolizing the blood of Christ and the purity of the Virgin Mary. ¶ It was deemed necessary for a warrior preparing for the accolade of knighthood to undergo certain rituals that would purify his body and soul so that his commitment could be worthy of God, in whose name the honour was conferred. First the candidate fasted, spending time in religious contemplation and confession to prepare his soul for the obligation ahead of him. Then he had to have a bath – a rare act of cleanliness in those days – to ensure that his bodily purity was on a par with his spiritual state. When the washing was complete, the dripping candidate was led by his squires to a bed, where the covers absorbed the wetness and symbolically drew any remaining impurities from his body. After this, the knight was believed to be 'of a pure mind and of honest intentions, willing to conflict with any dangers or difficulties in the cause of virtue; to take care both in his words and actions to follow the maxims of prudence; and religiously to observe the rules of fidelity and honour'. ¶ Before the Norman invasion of England, it was the tradition for Anglo-Saxon knights to visit a cleric in some place of worship and spend a night in contemplation before being dubbed with a special sword by the priest at dawn. The medieval Knights of the Bath also symbolically offered their own shield and sword at the altar as instruments of God's will. The only part of this ritual to be retained in modern times is the use of a sword for the dubbing ceremony. ¶ Another link to the history of knighthood and to the spiritual lives of Norman and Plantagenet kings can be found in the upper floors of the Tower of London's White Tower. Here, at the Chapel Royal of St John the Evangelist, knights of old observed many of their rituals. Kings also did vigil here before their coronations, and it was here, before his crowning in 1399, that Henry IV founded the original order. Forty-six Knights of the Bath were initiated, having 'watched all that night, each with his own chamber and bath, and the next day the Duke of Lancaster made them knights at the celebration of Mass... and the said knights had on their left shoulder a double cordon of white silk, with tassels hanging down'. This last detail was incorporated into the robes currently worn. ¶ The old Order of the Bath fell into disuse under James II, but, according to the writer Horace Walpole, was revived in 1725 on the suggestion of his father, Sir Robert Walpole. Although intended to be a military order of knighthood, it also included many civil members. The new order's statutes still required knights to bathe before doing vigil in Henry VII's chapel at the east end of Westminster Abbey, where the stalls are decorated with the plates of knights and festooned with the heraldic banners of the most senior living Knights Grand Cross. The order burgeoned in classes and membership after the defeat of Napoleon at Waterloo in 1815. While bathing is no longer mandatory, it is hoped that all those honoured do so anyway.

To achieve spiritual purification, medieval candidates to become Knights of the Bath kept vigil with their swords overnight in a holy place – sometimes here in William the Conqueror's private chapel in the White Tower at the Tower of London. They also achieved bodily ritual of preparation by taking a bath. The 1725 Order of the Bath has no formal links with the original order, but the robe of a Knight Grand Cross of the Most Honourable Order of the Bath retains the double cordon of white silk first worn on the left shoulder in 1399.

GROWING AN EMPIRE
1750–1901

After the kingdoms of England, Scotland and Wales were united there followed a gradual rationalization of national Offices of State, particularly in Scotland. Those with specific historical provenance survived, especially if they belonged with a single family or if they embodied moments in history, as did the Royal Banner Bearer of Scotland, whose rights carried the hallmark of the Scottish wars of independence. Many English appointments, however, were elevated to encompass the whole of the newly named United Kingdom of Great Britain and Ireland: the Earl Marshal, for example, took responsibility for Britain's State ceremonial because it took place mostly in London.

Britain had united to protect itself politically and from the continuing threat of Roman Catholicism. It also sought to increase its wealth through trade by establishing favourable trading links with distant corners of the world, in an ongoing quest for raw materials and markets. Conflicts of interest in these new places often led to the use of arms, either in defence or aggression, and so markets and plantations usually became colonies. More by accident than design, a colonial structure developed that encircled the globe. It was expensive to maintain these colonies and, although they offered economic opportunity, they were resented. The British Museum helped to change this, by alerting the public to discoveries from the far corners of this new world. Also the Colonial Reform Movement in the 1830s persuaded people that there was a moral imperative to invest in the colonies as well as exploit them. Colonial service became popular.

To head these colonial structures, Britain sent governors provided with blueprints for administration. Communication between Westminster and the governors of the colonies was maintained through the Corps of King's Messengers. Britain had established colonies first in America; but in 1776, rejecting the burden of taxation without representation, these declared themselves independent. It was India that became the focus of imperial effort. Traders became executive Governors, Clive of India advanced British interests and, after the Indian Mutiny of 1857 and the nationalization of the British East India Company, which had ruled much of India, Governor Generals became Viceroys. Disraeli formalized the Empire's existence by the Royal Titles Act of 1876, under which Queen Victoria proclaimed herself Empress of India. Orders of chivalry were created, including the Order of the Crown of India for women. The Empire became the largest the world has ever seen.

Hanoverian rule was secure, following the defeat of the Jacobites in 1746, and for the first time the United Kingdom could confidently celebrate itself. As a result, the pageantry today recognized as British heritage was largely invented in the 18th century. This new ceremonial echoed historical patterns, revived history and quickly became tradition: it met the requirements of a growing Empire, hungry for symbolic expressions of splendour.

The French Revolution in 1789 changed Europe. Its secular and republican ideology and its territorial ambitions set France against most of the Continent and, when Napoleon Bonaparte's military successes had earned him enough power, his army and navy challenged Britain. Nelson's victory at Trafalgar in 1805, as Commander-in-Chief of the Mediterranean Fleet, thwarted invasion and earned the Royal Navy unchallenged supremacy. Wellington's victory in 1815 against Napoleon at Waterloo gained him a reputation to match the Field Marshal's baton recently presented to him by the Prince Regent, the future George IV.

George IV succeeded to the throne in 1820 and in the euphoria still felt in Britain after Napoleon's defeat, Parliament indulged the profligate king's desire for a splendid coronation – not just to please him, but to celebrate the nation. This was perhaps the most magnificent coronation ever, including the appointment of the king's old friend as Herb Strewer. Later, to heal the wounds from Culloden, the king visited Scotland to celebrate its Highland revival. Quashed practices, such as playing the bagpipes and wearing tartan, were resurrected, and eventually George's niece, Victoria, was to make a home in Scotland and appoint her own Piper. It was to Balmoral, in the Highlands, that the queen fled when her husband died in 1861. Stricken by grief, Victoria completely withdrew from public view, even refusing requests from Government to return to London to open Parliament. Politicians began to question whether Victoria was earning the money she received from the Civil List. Public discontent at their sovereign's absence bolstered calls by some Radical MPs to abolish the monarchy and replace it with a republic but the Crown was saved by her reluctant return to public duty. Her popularity grew with old age.

As the 19th century progressed, people became increasingly interested in local and indigenous customs. In Wales and Cornwall druidism was re-established, no longer as a cult religion but as a means to celebrate cultural inheritance.

Feudal responsibilities that had lingered as a way of administering the land died away. Cities mushroomed as industry grew to meet the demands of the burgeoning Empire, and with these new urban centres came challenges to law and order. Sir Robert Peel's police force was established from the roots of existing constabularies, such as the force responsible for order among the undergraduates at Oxford University. The Great Reform Act in 1832, which enlarged the franchise and altered Parliament's make-up, was a further step towards democracy. The Lords, however, maintained the significant connection between land and power.

Britain's Empire gave the Church of England's missionaries access across the world. Funding for the splendour of Anglican cathedrals was scrutinized by Parliament but administered by Commissioners, while the tidal wave of Victorian morality carried bishops and their doctrines to greater authority. Since Wesley's conversion, Methodism had grown to challenge orthodoxy, and its adherents reflected the shift towards personal empowerment that reform engendered.

Victoria's Diamond Jubilee in 1897 was the ceremonial apogee of the western Empires. Describing in her diary her progress in an open carriage to St Paul's Cathedral for a service of thanksgiving, she wrote: 'No one ever, I believe, has met with such an ovation as was given to me… The cheering was quite deafening & every face seemed to be filled with real joy.' As her carriage approached the steps of St Paul's she was surrounded by an establishment preening itself in splendour: from Indian princes, ministers, ambassadors and governors to flag-waving children, this was a great display of confidence. Beneath the display, however, this establishment was also to prove vulnerable to the unprecedented pace of change that the new century would bring.

GOVERNOR AND COMMANDER-IN-CHIEF
OF GIBRALTAR

Britain's Empire was the largest the world has ever seen: it once included much of the United States, Africa, India, Australia, New Zealand and the Caribbean. It was built through trade and the exploitation of opportunity, and was distinguished by a sense of duty and purpose. Started by accident in the 17th century, it was seen as a mixed blessing during the 18th, became a valued asset in the 19th but finally proved to be untenable in the 20th. ¶ The spread of territories it encompassed presented a major administrative challenge, and it became necessary to improve communication and strategic support from the mother country. In 1704 one such opportunity arose during the War of Spanish Succession. English troops, under the command of Prince George of Hesse Darmstadt, attacked the Rock of Gibraltar as part of their plan to put Archduke Charles of Austria on the Spanish throne. The job was finished by Admiral Sir George Rooke, who took possession in the name of Queen Anne – a step ratified by Westminster and confirmed in the 1713 Treaty of Utrecht, but which Spain has never accepted. Possession of the Rock did three things: it gave the growing Empire a strategic hold on the Mediterranean's entrance, started a long-running feud with Spain over sovereignty and produced another outpost to be governed. ¶ Britain thought it governed colonies well, but it took time to get the attitude and balance right. Mirroring Britain's constitution, representatives of royal authority were needed. They were called Governors and graded according to the size of the territory they governed – Lieutenant-Governors for the smallest, through Governors up to Governor Generals for the largest. In both Ireland and India they were given the title Viceroy for additional status. ¶ Power went to the head of some early Governors, who became as despotic and absolutist as medieval monarchs. Over time, however, checks and balances were introduced and each colony followed its individual path to democracy and independence, while Governors became constitutionally aloof. In the case of the few remaining dependent territories, of which Gibraltar is one, this aloofness retains diplomatic clout. ¶ The British troops who secured the Rock had to defend it from a succession of Franco-Spanish counterattacks, notably during the Great Siege of 1779-83, when a Captain Fisher and 17 men defended the Round Tower from 500 French grenadiers. Following the small band's remarkable success, it became the custom to demonstrate that the Rock was secure by the Port Sergeant delivering the Keys of Gibraltar to the Governor at his official residence. In memory of both events, the colony's coat of arms depicts a fortress and keys. ¶ Gibraltar's strategic importance meant that, until the late 1990s, the Governor was always a senior officer from the Armed Forces. This continued a line of military governance dating back to 711, when Al Walid Ibn Abdulmalic became Caliph on the Rock. That military significance is now marked only on special ceremonial occasions. ¶ The Governor's diplomatic role has increased to reflect a broader European outlook and to address Spain's continued claim to the Rock: recently non-military diplomats have filled the post. Gibraltar's House of Assembly, which opted for membership of the European Union, must leave responsibility for external affairs, defence and internal security to the Governor, and therefore indirectly to the Government of the United Kingdom. Gibraltar may choose to end its governance by Britain at any time, but sovereignty would then revert to Spain. Recent surveys indicate that Gibraltarians wish to continue with things as they stand, but the British Government is discussing the province's future with Spain for the first time.

The State dining room in the Governor's official residence, which is called the Convent, in the centre of Gibraltar, awaits his guests. The walls are hung with portraits of previous Governors, dating back to the Moors of the 8th century. The Port Sergeant hands the Governor and Commander-in-Chief the Keys to the Fortress of Gibraltar, proof that the Rock – so strategic in building an empire and fighting two world wars – is a secure dependent territory of Britain for another night.

HEREDITARY BANNER BEARER AND BEARER OF THE NATIONAL FLAG

In centuries past, two Scottish families – the Scrymgeours and the Maitlands – claimed the right to carry the Royal Banner of Scotland, and both had a strong legal argument for doing so. Their dispute was eventually resolved in the 20th century when it was decided to use the two flags that have represented the nation's identity since before the 14th-century wars of independence. ¶ The Scrymgeours (a Gaelic word meaning 'skirmishers') gained their name and their position of Bannermen when a 12th-century ancestor called Carron led a Scottish army to victory. In gratitude, the king asked Carron to carry his standard. ¶ Little more evidence of the honour exists until William Wallace's charter of 1298, which confirms that Alexander 'called Skirmischur' carried the Royal Banner. He supported Robert the Bruce's bid for the crown in 1306 and paid for it with his life. A further charter after Bannockburn in 1317 confirmed the privilege on his son, along with the Constabulary of the Castle at Dundee. ¶ Having served as Royal Bannermen of Scotland through the 13th- and 14th-century wars of independence, the family turned out for subsequent battles against the English, including the tragic Battle of Flodden in 1513, when John Scrymgeour fell beside his king with the Royal Banner in his hand. The banner was again aloft for Charles II at the Battle of Worcester in 1650, and after the Restoration in 1660, Scrymgeour was rewarded with the earldom of Dundee. Following his death eight years later, the terms of the inheritance to these privileges were not adequately clear. This prompted the powerful Duke of Lauderdale, who was head of the Maitland family and Secretary of State for Scotland, to take possession of the Scrymgeour estates. The story goes that he sent a troop of dragoons to the Scrymgeours' home, Dudhope Castle, in order to carry off all the family's deeds of ownership. Naturally, this is not how the Maitland family records the event and there is no way of knowing which version to believe. Without written evidence, it was impossible for the Scrymgeour claimants to regain their lands. In 1790 the Royal Banner and Saltire were added to the Lauderdale arms, confirming their role as Royal Bannermen. ¶ In 1910, however, the Scrymgeours went to the Court of Claims and once again asserted their right to carry the Royal Banner – this time for George V's coronation. This court convenes only for a coronation and hears claims that stem from feudal rights, principally where there is what is called 'Grand Sergeanty' at stake. This is when land carries feudal duties that are to be carried out at a coronation and many rights were jealously protected to carry these out. After hearing the evidence, the House of Lords gently strictured the Lauderdales for treachery in 1668. The stolen lands were no longer available for return, but the Lauderdale successors were required to pay all the costs of the hearing. Consequently, in 1911 George V was the first monarch since Charles II to have a Scrymgeour as his Royal Bannerman. ¶ Following Elizabeth II's coronation in 1953, the year when the earldom of Dundee was restored to the Scrymgeour family, a meeting was held between the Earls of Dundee and Lauderdale, the heads of the feuding families. At their request, Sir Thomas Innes of Learney officiated in his capacity as the Lord Lyon King of Arms, and the meeting produced an agreement, subsequently confirmed by the Queen. The agreement drawn up recognized that both families held legitimate and long-standing claims to be Royal Bannermen and laid down that the two Scottish flags should thereafter be included in national ceremonies so that both families would have a role. However, it reaffirmed the 1603 ruling that the Royal Banner took precedence over all other flags. Thus, from 1954 onwards, the Scrymgeours of

---

Victory on the field of Bannockburn in 1314 earned Scotland its independence, and the standard that Robert the Bruce flew as King of Scots has been carried by Banner Bearers ever since. A 20th-century ruling returned the right to be Hereditary Banner Bearer for Scotland to the Scrymgeour family, whose ancestors stood beside the king in that decisive battle. The lion rampant design can be seen in the caparison covering Bruce's charger in the statue on the left, sited on the battlefield near Stirling.

Dundee have been Hereditary Banner Bearers for Scotland and carry the Royal Banner, showing the lion rampant within a double treasure (two frames), surrounded with red fleurs-de-lis on a gold ground. This flag represents the chiefly status of the monarch's leadership over all Scots. It has inspired generations of Scots to fight, including those who followed William Wallace and Robert the Bruce against the English. Meanwhile, the Maitlands of Lauderdale, who are now recognized as Hereditary Bearers of the National Flag of Scotland, carry the Saltire. This flag, which is also the Scottish ingredient in the Union flag of Great Britain, shows a white diagonal cross on a blue background and symbolises the crucifixion of St Andrew, Scotland's patron saint. ¶ St Andrew was crucified by order of the Roman Governor of Patrae in Achaira, during the time of Emperor Nero, possibly in AD 60. He was bound, not nailed, to a decussate cross – one shaped like an X – in order to increase his suffering. Although the saint is reputedly buried at Amalfi on the Italian coast, the belief is that a missionary, called St Rule, brought some of his relics to Scotland, landing on the east coast at a place that has been called St Andrews ever since. ¶ In 832, not long before Scotland became a united nation with a single king, an extraordinary portent was supposed to have galvanized an army. Angus MacFergus, the High King of Alba, faced the Northumbrian army at Athelstanford in Lothian. As he prayed for victory, so the legend goes, St Andrew appeared to him in a vision. The next morning, above the battlefield, clouds formed in the shape of a great white decussate cross against the blue sky. This gave the troops courage and rallied them to victory. This is the reason that the flag that came to represent the Scottish nation has a white cross on a sky-blue background. It is the oldest national flag in the Union but, in order to combine the red cross of England, which represents the English patron saint, St George, in 1707 with the flag of Scotland, the blue adopted was much darker. The union with Ireland in 1801 presented heralds with a further problem because St Patrick was not identified by a symbolic cross. One was invented and allocated to St Patrick. Inspiration came from the coat of arms of the FitzGerald family, one of Ireland's oldest Norman families. The red saltire on white would fit perfectly into the existing design. However, in order not to extinguish Scotland's position in the union, a compromise was reached. In the 'hoist' or senior side of the flag, the white cross would appear uppermost, whereas in the 'fly' the red of Ireland would take precedence. The conclusion has been an amicable one for both families, but the history of their dispute is rather like that between Scotland and England, and this is borne out by the design of the English Royal Banner. Two years after Wallace was defeated by Edward I, the 'Hammer of the Scots', at Falkirk in 1298, a chronicler described how the English Royal Banner, which shows three lions, reflected Edward's political agenda for the subjugation of Scotland. The king, however, reckoned without his son's failures and without the success of the Scottish army under Robert the Bruce. Whenever Scotland holds a major national occasion, either for the Scots monarch or for her Lord High Commissioner of the General Assembly of the Church of Scotland, both Hereditary Banner Bearers play out the amicable settlement, side by side.

The Hereditary Bearer of the National Flag of Scotland, a member of the Maitland family, is standing on the lower part of Salisbury Crags, close to Arthur's Seat, which dominates Edinburgh's skyline. This spot overlooks the Palace of Holyroodhouse and the site of Scotland's new Parliament building.

PERPETUAL WARDEN OF THE WOODMEN OF THE ANCIENT FOREST OF ARDEN

At the centre of what was once a wooded wilderness in the Midlands, which encompassed the forests of Sherwood, Hatfield, Cannock Chase, Charnwood and Wye, is the ancient Forest of Arden. It was one of the wild areas that provided a buffer between the Saxon settlements that formed the kingdom of Mercia. At its heart is the town of Meriden, where, on 15 November 1785, Heneage Finch, the 4th Earl of Aylesford, and five enthusiastic friends gathered at the Bulls Head. In one of England's most traditional settings, they laid the foundations for the Woodmen of Arden. It would become the country's most exclusive society of archers – one that maintained and celebrated the longbow's story. ¶ From the Saxons to the Tudors, the longbow's military effectiveness earned it a significant place in England's history. It was developed from a rough and cumbersome implement into a mass-produced and inexpensive military weapon. In particular, Edward I recognized the longbow's possibilities and ensured that, by his grandson's reign, the improved properties of tensile strength and performance combined to provide English kings with an armament that was almost to win the crown of France in the Hundred Years War. ¶ Among the victories it gave to Edward III, Edward the Black Prince and Henry V were the battlefields of Crécy, Poitiers and Agincourt. A position overlooking the battlefield added both height and the force of gravity to the longbow's effectiveness, and the records of the Woodmen of Arden describe how longbowmen were deployed to strategic effect: 'On word of command they shot rhythmic volleys of arrows into the ranks of their charging opponents, shifting their targets successively until every living one of them was killed, or maimed or routed.' Edward III, like his successors until Edward VI, made practising this military skill mandatory after Sunday Mass. ¶ When saltpetre and guns propelled the efficiency of war a further macabre step along the path of barbarity, archery became more of a noble pastime than a vital military skill. The Tudors developed the sport, with Henry VIII proving a formidable shot. London became a venue for matches, led by the Society of St George. By the middle of the next century small archery societies proliferated as far north as Warwickshire. ¶ The 4th Earl of Aylesford had been loosing off arrows at his Meriden estate for years before founding the Woodmen. Since then, succeeding Earls have presided, first by the traditional toxophilite title of Captain of the Grand Target, which was changed in 1786 to Warden of the Forest. And, before the year was out, the prefix 'Perpetual' had been added. The Lieutenant of the Grand Target was also renamed by the Woodmen as Senior Verderer. Membership of the Woodmen has always been limited to 80, though in 1835 it was increased by one to include the police reformer Sir Robert Peel. The society remains a fairly closed shop, with preference given to applicants related to or descended from former members. Each new member is given a number and must record his cresting, a unique mark, on the shaftment of all his arrows and on the aschams, or bow lockers. There is both a Captain and a Lieutenant of Numbers, and the first to score a Gold, or bull's eye, in Grand Week becomes Master Forester for the year. The uniform was established in 1786, with the hat following 100 years later. Forest ground was bought and, according to the records for 1788, 'after a long interval, a Wardmote [meeting] was first held by the Woodmen'.

The Perpetual Warden of the Woodmen of the Ancient Forest of Arden, the 12th Earl of Aylesford, surveys the Forest Ground. The Earl is the eighth Warden in 228 years. The only Earl not to have been Warden was the 9th, Michael, who was too young when he succeeded to the earldom to have been elected as a Woodman. His uncle was elected to the post instead, and when Michael was killed at Dunkirk without an heir, his uncle became the 10th Earl. The 11th Earl of Aylesford was one of only a handful of Woodmen to have been shot by an arrow, when his upper arm was pierced while he was marking during a practice day.

QUEEN'S TRUSTEE OF THE
BRITISH MUSEUM

The British Museum is generally acknowledged to house one of the finest collections of antiquities in the world. Here, treasures of ancient civilizations are admired by a general public who regard accessibility to such works as a national right. Yet the notion of public ownership – and guardianship – of works of art is only relatively recent, as the story of the British Museum, and its Trusteeship, shows. ¶ Up until the end of the 17th century, collections of art and science had been gathered by the wealthy in order to decorate their homes or, occasionally, to display cultural interests. But with the coming of the 18th century, disillusionment at the restrictive attitude of religion to the world and its creation, coupled with a reaction against the Church's power, led to the Age of Enlightenment. This reappraisal of man's secular, rather than spiritual, role on Earth gave birth to a new hunger for knowledge. At the same time, the world was opening up to discovery, and the Imperial Age was dawning. As a result, explorers and scientists were returning from journeys of discovery with ships filled with artistic and scientific treasures. ¶ One such collector was the noted physician and scientist Sir Hans Sloane (1660-1753). Perhaps most widely remembered for the London square that bears his name and the Chelsea Physic Garden he created, Sloane had a long life during which he amassed one of the finest collections of plants, animals, coins and general antiquities of his time. Anxious that his work should survive, he bequeathed his collection to the British nation on his death – an act that forced Parliament to accelerate plans for a national museum. After protracted discussion, the Government purchased the Sloane Collection and combined it with the library of Sir Robert Cotton to create the nucleus of the British Museum. On 7 June 1753 the British Museum was formally established by Act of Parliament and a site was selected at Montague Square in Bloomsbury. In honour of the fact that the collection belonged to the nation, the museum was held in trust by a Board of Trustees, whose main task was to ensure that the collection was preserved for the benefit of internal scholarship and the enjoyment of the general public. ¶ In the years that followed, the museum's status was enhanced by several royal contributions, such as the addition of the Royal Library by George II in 1757, and Egypt's Rosetta Stone, offered by George III – himself a keen collector and patron – in 1802. The increasing size of the museum led, in 1832, to changes in the make-up of the Board of Trustees. For the first time the Sovereign was given the right to make an appointment, and other families whose forebears had made significant donations to the museum could also nominate a Trustee each. King William IV nominated his first cousin, Prince William Frederick, the Duke of Gloucester and Edinburgh, and a succession of royal princes, dukes, and two Deans of Windsor have been appointed as Royal Trustees ever since. ¶ The present holder of the title of Queen's Trustee of the British Museum is the Duke of Gloucester, appointed by Queen Elizabeth II soon after the introduction of the 1963 British Museum Act, which established a Board of 25 Trustees: one appointed by the Sovereign, 15 by the Prime Minister, four by learned societies, and five by the Trustees themselves. One of the Trustees' most important tasks was the supervision of the radical Millennium Project, caused by the relocation of the world-famous British Library and the construction of the museum's latest addition, the glass-roofed Great Court, said to be the largest covered public square in Europe.

The Norman Foster roof over the British Museum's Great Court, in London, joins the façades of the museum's four main wings, built by Robert Smirke, with the old circular Reading Room that sits in the centre. The result is an exciting mix of architecture, lines and light. Each Trustee of the museum has a supervisory curatorial responsibility; the Queen's Trustee of the British Museum took responsibility for the Coins and Medals Department. Here he holds a gold medal, struck for George II, which shows the king's family. The medal belonged to George III and was given to the collection by George IV. All three monarchs were involved with the early development of the museum.

KEEPER OF THE ROYAL ACADEMY SCHOOLS

When Louis XIV built the Palace of Versailles it became the catalyst for incredible patronage, attracting painters, sculptors, architects and masons anxious to play their part in elevating the Sun King and his Roman Catholic glory. Great artists from both France and wider Europe gathered to construct the final and most spectacular temple of the *Ancien Régime*. In 1648 the Royal Academy of Painting and Sculpture had been established in Paris to provide the highest level of artistic training and this drew further skills to help with the visual and political manifestation of France's greatness. ¶ The reputation that this school of artistic discipline achieved was not overlooked in Great Britain, which sought to nourish its own messages of reformed religion, mercantile trade and evolving political freedom through art. In one of his many wise investments of royal patronage, King George III responded to the suggestion by Sir William Chambers, his former architectural tutor and architect of Somerset House, that London needed an academic home of excellence for the arts. In 1768 this became a reality with the king's establishment of the Royal Academy of Arts. Its first president was Sir Joshua Reynolds, the English portrait painter, who led a list of 34 founder members, who were to be called Royal Academicians, with the initials 'RA' after their names. Chambers was appointed the Academy's first treasurer, and other founder members included Thomas Gainsborough, Mary Moser and Angelica Kauffman. In his group portrait entitled *The Academicians of the Royal Academy*, Johann Zoffany (himself a founder member) showed the members gathered around a nude male model. Since women were excluded from life classes in order to protect their modesty, Zoffany included these two female Academicians as portraits hanging on the wall. The painting is now part of the Royal Collection. ¶ Among the lasting achievements of Sir Joshua Reynolds when he was president was the establishment of the Royal Academy Schools, which were based on the French template. He shaped the studies that had been set in Paris in accordance with his adherence to the 'Grand Style' and gave them a uniquely British philosophy, albeit based upon the need to learn about the great masters along with the styles and methods of their discipline. Responsibility for these schools was placed with the Keeper of the Royal Academy Schools. Then as now, the longest possible term for learning was offered, free of charge, to the most deserving of graduates. During this virtual apprenticeship, Royal Academicians, who were and still are deemed to be the best in their skills, would guide the pencils, texture the paints and angle the chisels of their students' developing expressions. ¶ Over two and a half centuries since the Royal Academy Schools first opened their doors in 1769, artists of great renown such as Sir John Soane, Sir Edwin Landseer, Thomas Rowlandson, William Blake and Sir Thomas Lawrence have sat where students still work today. There are now about 60 postgraduate students, selected from an enormous number of applicants, who benefit from a three-year course in the oldest school of fine art in the country. Every three years a new Keeper of the Royal Academy Schools is selected to supervise the school's work. The Keeper is selected from the existing Royal Academicians, who never exceed 80 in number, made up of 50 full RAs and 30 associates. The Keeper was originally responsible for setting the tuition programme by drawing from the other Royal Academicians and visiting professors but, since between the two world wars, full-time teachers have been on the staff. ¶ While the Royal Academy of Arts continues to celebrate the highest achievements and aspirations in the fine arts for the United Kingdom, the Keeper of the Royal Academy Schools continues to nurture and challenge future talent.

In the studio where artists have been tutored since the Royal Academy of Arts was established in Piccadilly, stands the Keeper of the Royal Academy Schools, who is elected from among the Royal Academicians for a period of three years. During this period, the Keeper attends in the Schools for at least two days a week during term time.

SCULPTOR IN ORDINARY IN SCOTLAND

A walk along Princes Street in Edinburgh provides the most remarkable aspect of, arguably, Britain's most beautiful city. The chill foreboding of the craggy castle stands above the bustle of life, commerce and a vibrant appetite for art. The view is interrupted by a vast 200-foot-high grimy Gothic spire that celebrates the Romantic historian and novelist Sir Walter Scott, who did so much to engineer Scotland's international reputation for literature, history and tradition. Juxtaposed beneath and hallowed by it is a striking white sculpture of the pensive Scott and his hound. It was fashioned in Carrara marble by Sir John Steell, with whom Queen Victoria was so impressed that she appointed him to be her own sculptor, as Sculptor in Ordinary in Scotland, and a member of the Scottish Royal Household. ¶ Queen Victoria had a romantic appetite for Scottish culture, particularly the version she read in Sir Walter Scott's books. Soon after her marriage, the mountains, glens and rivers of her imagination became manifest in the journeys she and Prince Albert enjoyed together. Both queen and consort were avid collectors of art and employed, among other skills, sculptors to capture the likeness of their nine children. Their houses resembled something of the macabre with white marble limbs, hands and feet of each son and daughter resting on red velvet cushions to provide the tactile Victorian equivalent of a photograph album. ¶ The rise of John Steell from being the son of a Dundee carver to become both a knight and the queen's personal sculptor was remarkable. He had demonstrated talent for art in his father's eyes and, after training in Edinburgh, went to Rome where his skill was honed. Returning to Scotland, he was quickly commissioned to sculpt and cast in bronze some of the prominent statuary in the city. He must have met the new queen in the first year of her reign for it is believed that she appointed him as her personal Sculptor in Ordinary in 1838. No formal document is recorded that marks this appointment but later in the reign his post appears in the official lists of the Scottish Royal Household. For the queen, no event was more traumatic than the death of Prince Albert in 1861 and no figure was more worthy of sculpture than him, as if to keep him alive. Steell performed this task and his representation of Albert, astride his horse in Field Marshal's uniform, stands in Edinburgh's Charlotte Square. Victoria was so delighted that, after the unveiling in 1876, she dubbed him a knight. ¶ Another Victorian favourite, Sir Joseph Boehm, was also appointed Sculptor in Ordinary in a similar, rather personal manner. His preferment came in 1881, when the monarch was much older and wiser. He had earned the queen's respect for his representation of her father, the Duke of Kent, that stands in St George's Chapel at Windsor Castle and also for his many sculptures of the monarch. In addition, he was a tutor in sculpture to the queen's daughter, Princess Louise, whose carving of her mother still stands outside Kensington Palace in Kensington Gardens. The princess was so fond of her tutor that she was with him when he died in 1890. ¶ With his death and that of Steell the next year, no further appointment was made until the title was revived by George V in 1921. With brief gaps there has been a Sculptor in Ordinary ever since, though now it is less a matter of the monarch's personal choice. The Queen takes advice on the appointment from the First Minister of Scotland.

Studies surround the Sculptor in Ordinary in Scotland in his studios on the Paisley campus of the University of the West of Scotland. From left to right, they are a working model for the Adam Smith statue for Edinburgh's Royal Mile, a study of the head of Robert Adam, the back of the statue of James Clerk Maxwell on George Street in Edinburgh, a bust of the sculptor's father, a colossal head and a small study of Ossian, the original plaster for the Pimlico Priapus, a study of Robert Burns, a Station of the Cross, a study of St Nicholas of Tolentino and a study for the rectification of Chambers Street in Edinburgh, part of the Playfair Statue project.

HERB STREWER

Poor drains and noxious gases were a fact of life in Britain until the 19th century as nobody had found a clean and efficient way of dealing with human waste. James I remarked on the problem when he arrived in London from Holyrood in 1603, but little could be done to rid the court, or anywhere else, of unpleasant smells. The most common solution was to try to disguise them with other, more fragrant, aromas, such as strewn herbs. ¶ Following the Restoration, Herb Strewers were employed to wander through the royal apartments, distributing rue, mint, sage and camomile along with roses and lavender. Theirs was a vital role as it brought relief to everyone. The herbs scattered about were probably gathered from the King's Herb House in the grounds of the old Palace of Whitehall. Herb Strewers spread their fragrant items wherever the monarch went, but were especially valued when the route led out among the 'great unwashed' for ceremonies such as the Royal Maundy or for meeting scrofula victims, believed to be cured by royal touch. ¶ The first recorded Herb Strewer was Bridget Rumny, who served from 1660 until 1671. She received £24 per annum, as did all her successors, until the appointment fell into abeyance the year before Victoria came to the throne. To this generous income was added an annual grant of two yards of superfine scarlet cloth for livery. ¶ Many Herb Strewers served for considerable periods, while successors waited in the wings. One such hopeful, Anne Edwards, died waiting for Elizabeth Jux to expire. The longest-serving, full-time Herb Strewer was the last, Mary Rayner, who spent 43 years in the post and served George III and two of his sons. ¶ When George IV finally inherited the throne from his father in 1820, he celebrated by planning the most flamboyant coronation Britain had ever witnessed. Improved hygiene meant that a Herb Strewer was no longer needed to keep the air sweet, but the new king decided to use the role to inject another note of fashion and display into the proceedings. He had already promised the post to an old friend, 56-year-old Anne Fellowes, who had supported his brother, the Duke of Sussex, by witnessing his secret (and illegal) marriage to Lady Augusta Murray in Rome. Some thought Miss Fellowes too old to add lustre to the show, but the king kept his word and provided her with a gleaming badge of office. ¶ Perhaps to offset Anne's fading charms, it was decided that six maidens of gentle birth would attend her. This excited much competition, but Anne had the final say and, unsurprisingly, two of her nieces were chosen. They carried silver-gilt baskets and scattered flowers along the rich blue carpet from Westminster Hall to the Abbey, and it was reported that 'a more interesting or lovely group never was exhibited on any occasion'. Anne was reported to have 'scattered exotic flowers and aromatic herbs, from time to time filling a small hand basket from the large baskets of her attendants, who always made a profound obeisance as they presented their fragrant burthen to the mistress'. ¶ Anne Fellowes applied again for the post of Herb Strewer at William IV's coronation and was granted the job; however, cutbacks in the ceremony left no role for her to perform. Queen Victoria eschewed any extravagance, so did not have a Herb Strewer at her coronation, and Edward VII followed suit. However, this did not deter the Fellowes from petitioning for the position as of right. They still defend the claim in the name of the senior unmarried daughter of the family, who waits for the chance to sweeten the air at Westminster Abbey once again.

The Herb Strewer sits at the West Door of Westminster Abbey in London – the coronation church of England's monarchs since 1066, when William the Conqueror was crowned. Her predecessor led the procession of the most flamboyant coronation Britain has ever seen when George IV was crowned in 1821. Then, as depicted here, she and her ladies strewed herbs and petals across the royal path.

SUPERINTENDENT OF THE CORPS OF
QUEEN'S MESSENGERS

Discretion and loyalty are valuable qualities at any time, but they become particularly important during periods of intrigue and war. Monarchs have always known this and have taken great pains to find people who can be trusted with delicate, often confidential information. ¶ The first record of royal Messengers occurs in clothing accounts of 1199. Those chosen for the task were noblemen or trusted courtiers, and they performed a range of services from collecting taxes to escorting felons accused of High Treason. ¶ Medieval heralds later acted as royal Messengers and were sometimes entrusted with basic tasks of diplomacy. The first record of a person with the title of King's Messenger dates from 1454, when Henry VI appointed Robert Asshewell. It was not until the reign of Henry VII that an emblem was chosen for the Messengers. The king selected the silver greyhound of Richmond as one of the heraldic beasts to support his royal arms, and, perhaps to speed them on, it was embroidered across the tunics of the Tudor Messengers. When the future Charles II was in exile during the Civil War, he is supposed to have broken off silver greyhounds decorating the edge of his dish and given one to each of his English and Dutch couriers to enable them to be recognized. Then, it is said, he decreed that his Messengers should wear silver greyhounds on Garter-blue ribbon around their necks. Many of these were stolen and not a few were lost when Messengers fell from their horses. Today these emblems are worn only on special occasions. Henry VIII formed the first Corps of Messengers in 1547, when they were known as the Gentlemen of the Great Chamber in Ordinary or Extraordinary and were members of the Royal Household. During the mid-17th century the Corps gave invaluable service to Charles I when he and his troops were fighting against the New Model Army of Oliver Cromwell. But, as executive power was transferred from kings to their ministers, so the Messengers began to serve the Government rather than the monarch. On 6 May 1722, a group of 16 was transferred into the King's Foreign Service Messengers, and the Corps left the palace for the Foreign Office. ¶ During both world wars, King's Messengers played a vital role in carrying secret communiqués to and from Germany, thus helping Britain to defeat first Kaiser Wilhelm and then Adolf Hitler. The Messengers also worked as encoders and decoders, which helped safeguard the contents of the messages they carried. ¶ As international correspondence increased, so did the need for permanent ambassadors abroad, and they in turn needed a secure and reliable means of passing information back and forth with their Government. Under the terms of the Vienna Convention for Diplomatic Relations, bags containing official government communications can be carried by appointed people without fear of interference. In Britain the Queen's Messengers still undertake this task, and each Messenger travels about 250,000 miles a year, the diplomatic bags they carry never leaving their sight. ¶ The Corps, which was led by the Superintendent but is now under the jurisdiction of the Head of Classified Bag Services, undergoes continuous financial review, and ways of improving the service are under constant scrutiny. Even though the security of electronic communication is improving, hand carriers remain the safest way of exchanging confidential messages. As a result, the Queen's Messengers will probably continue to be needed to carry sensitive and sometimes bulky items of Her Britannic Majesty's diplomatic business around the world safely and discreetly.

In modern parlance they are referred to as 'secure logistics experts' and are part of the Foreign and Commonwealth Office Services, but the Queen's Messengers still operate as diplomatic couriers with over 800 years of experience. The Superintendent of the Corps of Queen's Messengers, as the title was until recently, stands on the Grand Staircase of India House, in the Foreign Office, surrounded by specially sealed diplomatic bags. The silver greyhound badge around the Superintendent's neck is suspended from an oval containing the Queen's cypher. HBM stands for Her Britannic Majesty's.

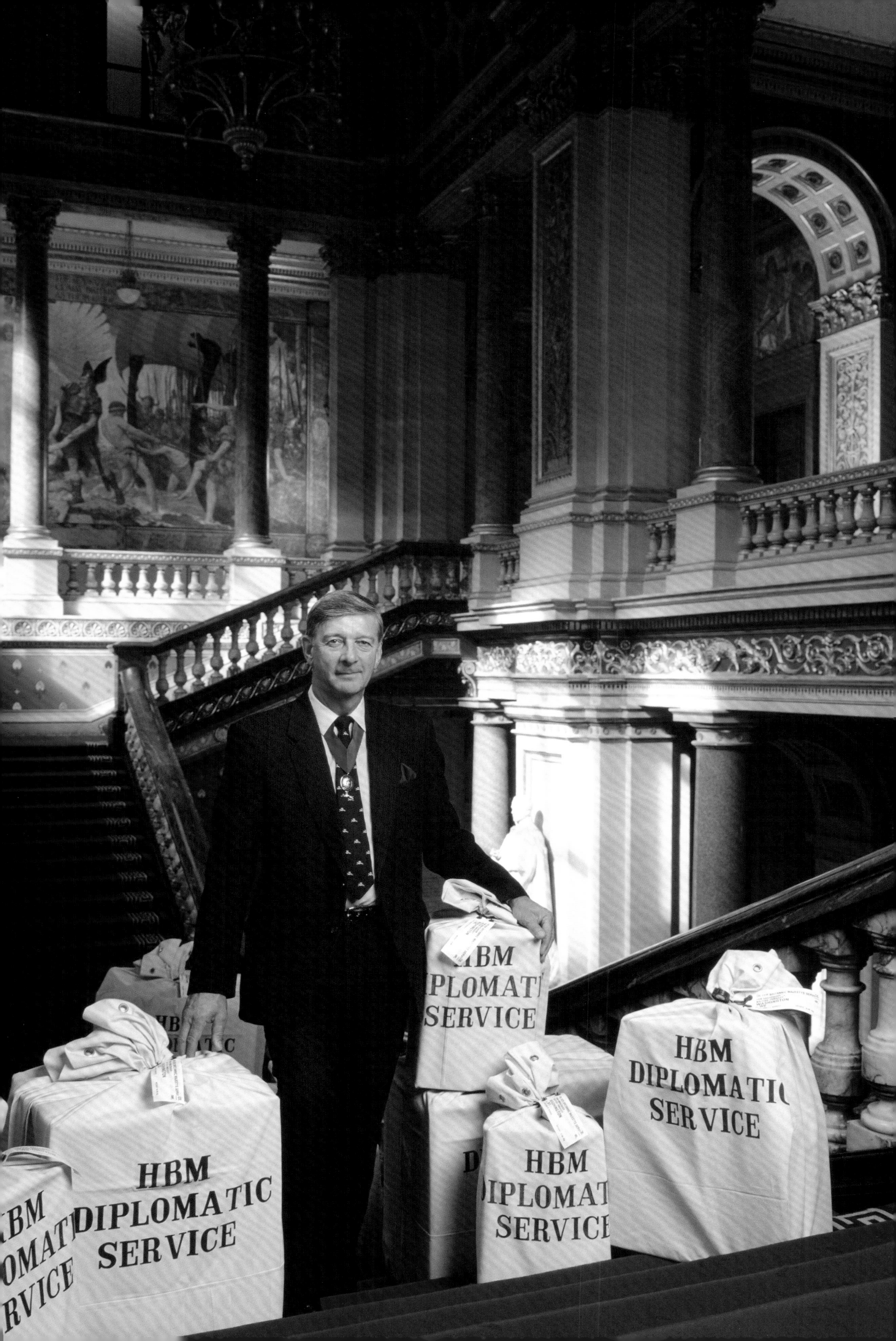
HBM
DIPLOMATIC
SERVICE
HBM
DIPLOMATIC
SERVICE

PRELATE, BAILIFF OF EGLE, CHANCELLOR AND LORD PRIOR OF THE MOST VENERABLE ORDER OF THE HOSPITAL OF ST JOHN OF JERUSALEM

After Napoleon's defeat in 1815 Britain was able to concentrate once again on its overseas interests and, as the Empire continued to grow, so did the need for medical support for all in its colonies. What better than to dust down the traditions of the Knights Hospitaller of St John, who had held sway in many places? Britain's largest voluntary first-aid service was created, first unofficially and then formally by a Royal Charter granted by Queen Victoria in 1888. The Most Venerable Order of the Hospital of St John of Jerusalem was established in the remnants of the knights' priory at Clerkenwell in London, and had branches in New Zealand, Australia, South Africa and Canada. ¶ The history of the order stretches back to the First Crusade, called by Pope Urban II in 1095. He urged the faithful to recapture the Holy Land from the Muslims and, in return, offered blanket forgiveness for their sins. Knights and their servants were mobilized under the authority of the Church and, on 15 July 1099, an international army led by Geoffrey de Bouillon retook Jerusalem with pious hearts but bloodstained hands. ¶ A hospital run by Blessed Gerard, the Custodian of the Poor in Christ of the Hospital of St John, had been established in the city for half a century at least, caring for all who were wounded, and many Crusaders were inspired to offer themselves to 'serve Our Lords the Sick'. They formed an order of military monks, the Knights Hospitaller, which was recognized by the King of Jerusalem in 1104 and by Pope Pascal II in 1113. The English Hospitallers formed one of the order's eight langues, or tongues, and a domestic headquarters was established just north of the City of London where, between 1130 and 1145, Prior Walter of England built the Church of St John. Its crypt still survives. ¶ The Second and Third Crusades saw the Hospitallers fighting beside their brother orders, the Knights Templar and the Knights of the Holy Sepulchre. But the Crusaders lost their hold on Jerusalem and withdrew first to Acre, which fell in 1291, then to Cyprus and, finally, to Rhodes in the early 14th century. The Knights Hospitaller became one of the most powerful naval forces in the Mediterranean. They were finally driven from Rhodes in 1522 by Suleiman the Magnificent, and eight years later an English knight, William Weston, sailed into Malta's Grand Harbour to take possession of the island for St John. ¶ Philip IV of France had charged the Knights Templar with heresy in 1307 and when Pope Clement V confirmed this in 1312 the order was stripped of its European possessions in favour of the Hospitallers. Egle, an estate near Lincoln, was included in the booty that fell into their hands – its Bailiff was one of the order's principal officers until 1999, an appointment that has since been revived by the new Priory of England and the Isles. Henry VIII dissolved the Knights Hospitaller along with the monasteries, and although Mary I revived the order it was soon suppressed again. However, it lived on in Malta until the French Revolution cut off vital resources. Napoleon subsequently took the island and ousted the knights. ¶ The order, which was reorganized in 1999, is responsible for many voluntary associations that provide first-aid support and training in the United Kingdom and abroad. It also retains a link with its origins: it runs the St John Eye Hospital in Jerusalem, which provides help close to the religious strife that is still a feature of the city.

The Prelate of the Venerable Order of St John of Jerusalem kneels in prayer at the crypt altar of the order's 12th-century church in Clerkenwell, which is close to one of the City of London's gates. In the foreground are (from left to right) the Bailiff of Egle, the Chancellor and the senior non-royal appointment, the Lord Prior. All three wear the sopravest (cassock) and mantle of Bailiffs Grand Cross. They coordinate the work of an army of volunteers throughout the United Kingdom, the Commonwealth and in the United States, who all wear, like them, the eight-pointed cross of St John. This symbolizes the four Christian virtues – prudence, justice, temperance and fortitude – and the eight beatitudes that spring from their practice.

PRESIDENT OF THE
METHODIST CONFERENCE

Methodism can be said to have begun when a 15th child was born to the Reverend Samuel Wesley in 1703. The infant John, steeped in clerical tradition, was to found a religious movement that would have far-reaching consequences. ¶ When Wesley senior's Rectory was burnt to the ground, the Duke of Buckingham provided money for John's education at Charterhouse, which eventually led to his studying at Oxford. At the age of 26, John was appointed Father of the Holy Club, a small society that met every Sunday to study the Greek Testament, and that fasted each Wednesday and Friday. The club followed a simple 'rule', the Greek word for which is 'method', and in time this became the foundation of the Methodist Church. ¶ The evangelical pursuit of Jesus Christ among the precepts and rituals of the Established Church of England has often caused tension within the Anglican Communion. This was particularly true when John Wesley became an ordained member of England's dominant church. He did not find fault with the 39 Articles, which form the foundations of Anglican faith, or with Archbishop Cranmer's Book of Common Prayer. However, this was the Age of Reason, and his egalitarian belief that the word of God should reach beyond the church door, out into the kingdom's roughest communities, was one that contradicted established practice. He led a revival that 'spread Scriptural holiness over the land'. Methodism was to become another strand of factionalism, which was identified more by the zeal of its adherents than by the nature of their faith. They believed that the Gospel was for everyone. ¶ The doors of Anglican churches were closed to Wesley and his adherents, so they made street corners their pulpits and travelled widely in search of souls. They found people hungry for ministry, many of then having been cast out of churches when they could no longer pay the rent demanded for pew space. Travelling preachers visited communities and established Methodist Societies with their own local preachers. Each was dedicated to worship, fellowship, service, prayer, Bible study and responsible giving. Shunned by Anglicanism, Wesley had to ordain his own preachers: thus Methodism took independent root. ¶ All human institutions developed for the worship of God seldom match the demands placed upon them by individual members: this was true of Methodism, which could not contain the aspirations of its fast-growing Societies. Many of these splintered into different groupings, among them America's Episcopal Methodists, the Calvinistic Methodists and even the Salvation Army. ¶ Wesley understood mavericks, having been one himself. Perhaps he also anticipated the fallout that followed his call in 1784 for a 'Yearly conference of people called Methodists'. While many initially rebelled against the idea, it subsequently provided a means for uniting them all. ¶ Wesley died leaving no nomination for his Church's leadership, so by default responsibility fell to the Methodist Conference. During the period of disunity, the appointment of President was held by Wesleyan Methodists, often for long periods. However, by the time all the Methodist factions were reunited into the present-day structure, this system had been changed and it is now the practice to select a new President every year. Unchanged, however, is the tradition of pulpit evangelism. Few Methodists are unaware that during Wesley's first sermon at his purpose-built Chapel in the City of London on All Saints' Day, 1778, he launched into a tirade against the sea of expensive hats that filled the building. To him they symbolized wealth and privilege, which were at odds with Gospel simplicity.

John Wesley's pulpit stands at the centre of his Chapel in London's Old Street. Methodist symbolism surrounds the President of the Methodist Conference, who holds aloft a copy of the Gospel, which Wesley believed was for everyone.

QUEEN'S PIPER AND PAGE OF THE PRESENCE

In 1842, when Queen Victoria and Albert visited Scotland and saw the wild scenery of the Highlands for the first time, the Marquess of Breadalbane and his Highlanders, dressed in Campbell kilts, greeted them at Taymouth Castle, at the head of Loch Tay. 'It seemed as if a great chieftain in olden times was receiving his sovereign,' Victoria wrote in her diary on Wednesday 7 September, and later, to her mother, she wrote, 'We have heard nothing but bagpipes since we have been in the beautiful Highlands & I have become so fond of it that I mean to have a piper.' The playing of Breadalbane's piper, John Ban Mackay, had so impressed her that soon afterwards she wrote and asked the Marquess for his help in recruiting her own bagpipe-player. A year later, on 25 July 1843, Angus Mackay was sworn in as Piper to Her Majesty. ¶ In 1847 Prince Albert took the lease of the estate of Balmoral, in Aberdeenshire; negotiations were finally settled in 1852. To celebrate, a cairn, or pile of stones, was built on a nearby peak called Craigowan while Mackay played his pipes. Beside the old castle a new one was built, where Victoria and the Prince Consort sought to live the life of Highland lairds. Each morning the Queen's Piper played under their windows, and on expeditions into the hills they were attended by staff including a growing number of pipers. Most of these wore the Balmoral tartan, designed by Victoria and Albert in grey and red and quite different from the majority of red and green setts proliferating in the romantic revival of clan symbols that had begun with George IV's visit to Scotland in 1822. ¶ When Mackay retired in 1854 the army provided his replacement, a custom that has been followed ever since. Pipe Major William Ross, of the Black Watch, was the Queen's Piper during the period of Victoria's domestic happiness at Balmoral with Albert. It was also Ross who played laments when Albert died. With the death of the Prince Consort the atmosphere at Balmoral immediately changed, as did the uniform, to black. Another Highlander on the staff, John Brown, encouraged the queen to resume excursions into the hills. On one of these she decided to build a new house in a remote place called the Glassalt, or 'grey burn'. It was located on the shore of Loch Muick, surrounded by steep craggy hills and below the mountain Lochnagar. Here she felt safe, at peace and close to Albert. As at Balmoral Castle, the Queen's Piper played each morning outside her window. It was the Scottish idyll she first imagined possible at Taymouth in 1842. ¶ William Ross's successor, James Campbell, led Victoria's coffin from Osborne House in 1901. Edward VII retained his services, and each of the king's successors has loved Balmoral and appointed Pipers. The Balmoral season lasts approximately 12 weeks, and it is also the Piper's responsibility to teach members of the Royal Household the Scottish dances for the Ghillies' Ball, which he organizes on behalf of the Queen. When the Queen is at Buckingham Palace, Holyroodhouse or Balmoral her Piper plays under her window every morning. He wears the Balmoral tartan when on the estate; elsewhere he wears the green Hunting Stewart in the morning and the red Royal Stewart for his evening duties. ¶ Today the Queen's Piper is also one of the three Pages of the Presence whose responsibilities include attending royal visitors and supervising the arrival and departure of Ambassadors and other guests at Buckingham Palace's Grand Entrance. This dual role requires tact and discretion as much as it does musical ability.

The Queen's Piper wears Royal Stewart tartan when he plays outside Windsor Castle. His rank is embroidered on his sleeve and his drone carries the Sovereign's Piping Banner.

MARSHAL OF THE DIPLOMATIC CORPS

The Marshal of the Diplomatic Corps acts as a link between the Sovereign and foreign diplomats. He is a member of the Royal Household and has an office in Ambassadors' Court at St James's Palace, which is still the official residence of the Sovereign. The Marshal supervises the attendance of diplomats at ceremonies. ¶ The present-day position of Marshal of the Diplomatic Corps originated in the first years of James I's reign (1603–25), in order to ensure that all meetings between the Sovereign and Ambassadors were conducted properly. The new Master of Ceremonies – as the Marshal was then called – and his Assistant were responsible for conducting court ritual, including the visits of diplomats. An abundance of different ranks then formed diplomatic missions, depending on the size of a territory. An empire would field an Ambassador, either 'ordinary', meaning permanent, or 'extraordinary', being appointed for a specific purpose; smaller states would send either Residents or Agents. All sought access to the king's court, though some had achieved their status by paying for the privilege in their own country and were therefore effectively fraudulent. The Master of Ceremonies had to establish a form of precedence that would satisfy all. In the end, this was done by giving seniority according to time served at the Court of St James's, with the senior diplomat becoming head of the corps, or Doyen. ¶ The Master also became responsible for the Levee, a ceremonial reception within the court. The name comes from the French word *lever*, to rise, and from the bizarre court practice in the *Ancien Régime* at Versailles, whereby Louis XIV's rising from bed was witnessed at its various intimate stages by different grades of the nobility and Ambassadors. The British equivalent was less eccentric, being more of a stylized gathering to which diplomats were given special access: Buckingham Palace was constructed with a Levee Entrance, through which Ambassadors still technically have special access to the monarch, which is regulated by the Master's successor. ¶ In 1714 the appointment became the sinecure of the Cotterell family but this practice proved unsatisfactory. Later it was vested in a retiring senior military officer. Constitutional changes in the 19th century led to the end of the monarch's direct influence over foreign policy. In 1930 George V changed the title of Master to Marshal of the Diplomatic Corps, which better described the function as the king's link with visiting diplomatic missions. By this date, the monarch's role in directly influencing foreign policy had ceased, though the Royal Prerogative remained intact and was vested in the hands of the Foreign Secretary. With the establishment of the Dominions within the Empire it was not appropriate for territories over which the monarch was Head of State to send Ambassadors to their own king's court, and a new appointment of High Commissioner was established. Later, when some of these nations not only gained independence but also became republics within the new Commonwealth of Nations, the need for them to present Credentials was re-established. To mark their special status, the Marshal was instructed to escort High Commissioners of republics in landaus drawn by four, rather than two, horses. ¶ The number of diplomats in London soared in the second half of the 20th century. As recently as 1938 there were just 16 Ambassadors and seven High Commissioners accredited to the Court of St James's. Now, as a result of both the break-up of empires and the growth of new nations, these numbers have risen to around 120 and 50 respectively. The Marshal still escorts those with Credentials to the Queen and organizes the annual Diplomatic Reception.

The Marshal of the Diplomatic Corps escorts all newly appointed foreign Ambassadors and most High Commissioners to present their Credentials to the Queen. Here, he escorts the Zambian High Commissioner, in a Semi-State landau drawn by four horses. The High Commissioner carries Letters of Credence for the Queen from the President of Zambia. There is a special purpose to the Marshal's badge of office, which is suspended from a chain around his neck. The side visible here shows the dove of peace but on the reverse is a sword of war; according to the situation between Britain and the relevant country, the badge can be turned around.

The Reform Acts of the 19th century precipitated fundamental changes in British society. Government became increasingly democratic, and the queen empress evolved into more of a figurehead than an influential participant in government. Her passing heralded a new century, and new voices made the case for change.

In 1909 the Chancellor of the Exchequer delivered a finance bill that included a 'super tax' on wealth and land to pay for the modest social measures expected by voters. The House of Lords threw it out, and the Liberal Government reacted to this with outrage, firmly returning the bill to the Lords to be accepted. It was the Lords' rebellion that eventually precipitated the Parliament Bill, which began a steady erosion of the old powers so long vested in the landed peerage.

Both 'people' (Commons) and 'land' (Lords) have always been represented in the English Parliament, a situation that enabled balance between urban and rural interests to survive, even after universal suffrage gave increasing power to densely populated places. The primacy of the Commons was firmly established by the Parliament Act, and successive evolution in practice has confirmed this. Increasingly the nation's elected representatives, or Members of Parliament, are expected to stand before the Court of Public Opinion through the prism of media. When the hereditary peerage finally disappears from the Legislature its titles will survive as clues both to the reasons for their creation and the roles each has played in history. When some no longer have heirs, as happened in 2011 with the death of Earl Kitchener of Khartoum, a part of that history is lost.

The two world wars and the conflicts since have established the Armed Forces in a strong position with the nation. Their traditions, and the values and standards they project, are still maintained in the delivery of excellence and ceremonial that is recognized around the world. The Royal Navy is known as the 'senior service' because, as an island, it is the nation's first line of defence. Its most senior serving commander, the First Sea Lord, carries a title that resonates from the timbers of an oak navy but which is every bit as potent today.

After each conflagration the monarch has looked back to the foundation of chivalry in the 14th century and honoured great commanders and political leaders with the Orders of the Garter, Thistle and St Patrick. The latter went into disuetude with the independence of Ireland but the oldest, the English Order of the Garter, continues to embrace the great English men and women of the age. The 1,000th place in this list of Knights and Ladies was given to a future king, his investiture a reminder of the first knight's when Edward III placed the Garter around the left leg of the Black Prince. The Queen appointed her son, Prince Charles, to be Prince of Wales and Earl of Chester when he was nine, and invested him formally later, in 1969, at Caernarfon Castle. She also marked the 100th anniversary of Edward VII's foundation of a British Order of Merit by granting one to her heir for his charitable work. This extraordinary honour, which carries no rank, is arguably the most highly prized royal affirmation.

Following the signing, in October 2012, of a deal between Westminster and Edinburgh over terms for a referendum, Scots will vote in autumn 2014 on whether or not to become an independent nation. The date is significant because it marks the 700th anniversary of Robert the Bruce's victory over England's Edward II at Bannockburn. It is another change to Britain in its evolution from great imperial motherland. The development of former colonies into a Commonwealth of Nations included some countries that chose to keep the monarch as their Head of State. As a consequence, the role of Counsellors of State had to change. Counsellors before had been selected from the political establishment, but within the new Commonwealth this could have led to a British politician influencing the affairs of a former colony. To avoid this, Counsellors are now only drawn from the ranks of the Royal Family.

Millions watched the coronation of Elizabeth II in 1953 on television. During the ceremony, according to an ancient practice, the Lord of the Manor of Worksop's glove was presented to the Queen in a link to the feudal appointments that once existed to order the nation. In the last few decades, these old feudal honours have been bought and sold, like quaint oddities, and often by foreigners keen to own something of the British way. It was around this time that the Church approved the removal of the prefix 'Lord' before the title of High Almoner, and began to invite office bearers of other religions to take part in national ceremonies. Interestingly, the Royal Household still retains the full title of Lord High Almoner.

One of the country's oldest appointments is that of Sheriff. In order to maintain the relevance of this Saxon post, the Shrievalty Association is striving to alter its selection to ensure that holders represent society more fully. It is interesting that the largest creation of new appointments ever made in Britain has come about within the last few years. The Labour Party's landslide victory in 1997 brought forward legislation that considerably altered the constitutional form of the United Kingdom. The creation of a Parliament in Scotland, and Assemblies in Wales and Northern Ireland, will have long-term effects – just as the Reform Acts of the 19th century did long after they were enacted. This desire for reform carried through into the Judiciary, where the old links between the High Court of Parliament and the Queen's courts, which was bridged by the Lord High Chancellor, was deemed no longer acceptable under European law. The Supreme Court provided a new ultimate court of appeal, with various limitations for different parts of the United Kingdom.

Sentinel amid all the change that the nation's modern democracy, diminishing wealth and fervent need for reform demand, stands the office of Sovereign. A reign of more than 60 years has brought a steady wisdom and reassurance in this effervescence for change. But there is reform afoot here too. The Heir to the Throne has suggested that his wife may not be called 'Queen' in due course, but rather 'Princess Consort'. And, as his heir awaits the arrival of a child, the needs of equality have united the Governments of the 16 nations that still hold the British Sovereign as Head of State, in order to pass primary legislation through their respective Parliaments. Once passed, the issue of male gender preference in the Order of Succession, forged by the need for masculine strength in the Middle Ages, will disappear. This is further evidence that Britain's institutions survive through constant reinvention designed to meet the evolving expectations of the people. New offices, posts and appointments continually emerge to meet new needs but, while Britain remains confident in its present, it will continue to be comfortable with the survival, among us, of these clues from the past.

SUPERIOR GENERAL OF THE
TYBURN NUNS

The Tyburn Nuns, a cloistered community situated close to the bustling commercialism of London's Oxford Street, have their roots in Paris where Mother Marie Adele Garnier, their first Superior General, founded the Adorers of the Sacred Heart of Jesus of Montmartre, Order of St Benedict, in 1898. Within three years, however, the anticlerical French government passed the Laws of Association. These ordered the dissolution of all religious communities that were not authorized by the State and in 1901 the congregation was forced to leave France. In a reversal of the journey that had been made centuries earlier by English Roman Catholics, who fled to the Continent in order to keep both their faith and their lives, the French nuns crossed the Channel and came to England. After two years their foundress settled the community close to Tyburn, famous as a site of martyrdom during the English Reformation. By popular acclaim its members were instantly known as the 'Tyburn Nuns'. ¶ Tyburn was London's public place of execution for six centuries, from 1196 to 1793, and during this period more than 50,000 criminals were hanged on its 'King's gallows'. The first martyr of the English Reformation to die there was John Houghton, a Carthusian prior, who was hung, drawn and quartered on 4 May 1535. It was less than a year after Henry VIII had created the Church of England with himself, and not the Pope, at its head and Houghton's crime was that he had refused to acknowledge Henry's supremacy. Such a refusal was considered to be treason, as was, later, being a Catholic priest or associating with Catholic priests. In the 150 years that followed, more than 350 people died for their faith. At Tyburn alone, where a triangular gallows – the Tyburn Tree – was in use from the reign of Elizabeth I, 105 men and women were martyred. The last of these was Oliver Plunket, Archbishop of Armagh, whom Titus Oates, an anti-Catholic agitator, implicated in a fictitious plot to murder Charles II and re-establish the Catholic Church in England. Plunket was executed on 1 July 1681 and canonized nearly 300 years later, in 1976. ¶ Close to the monastery a stone marks the site of the gallows, and within Tyburn Convent itself there is a shrine to the martyrs of the English Reformation. Visited by people from all over the world, its altar is surmounted by the three crossbeams of the Tyburn Tree, transformed into a religious symbol. The monastery is now the senior of eight convents, in the British Isles, Australia, New Zealand and South America, and in all of them the nuns – Mothers who have dedicated their lives to the order and Sisters who have yet to make this final commitment – live according to the Rule of St Benedict. This was established in the 6th century, at Monte Cassino in Italy, and although Benedict described it as 'a little rule for beginners' it became the basis of Western monasticism. Benedictine orders are disciplined communities within which the emphasis is on contemplation and prayer, and the Tyburn Nuns meet seven times a day to chant the offices stipulated by the Rule, led by the Superior General. Sisters also take it in turns, two at a time, to pray in an unending vigil at the martyrs' shrine for the many thousands who died on the Tyburn Tree, for mankind as a whole – and for the Pope, the head of the Roman Catholic Church, and the Queen.

Flanked by nuns at prayer, the Superior General of the Tyburn Nuns, also known as the Mother General, kneels before two candles inscribed 'For the Pope and the Church' and 'For the Queen and England'. The Tyburn convent was established by Mother Marie Adele Gamier, foundress of an order called the Adorers of the Sacred Heart of Jesus of Montmartre, on Bayswater Road in London. This was the site where 105 Catholics were martyred during the English Reformation, at a permanent gallows called the Tyburn Tree.

HIGH ALMONER

Every year on Maundy Thursday, in the week before Easter, the Queen continues a royal tradition by making a journey to a cathedral city and giving specially minted coins to a group of women and men equal in number to her age. The ceremony is the responsibility of the High Almoner and the Royal Almonry, which is administered by the Queen's Privy Purse. ¶ The Royal Maundy is one of the duties and observances that Christian monarchs have carried out to show that they remember and follow Christ's example at the Last Supper, when he showed humility to his followers. The Christian calendar of high days illuminated important events in red, and these 'red letter days' required the monarch's attendance at Mass, sometimes a crown-wearing ceremony (coronamenta) and sometimes preparatory fasting. The most important period in the Christian calendar is Holy Week, the seven days leading up to Easter Sunday when Christ rose from the dead. On the eve of Good Friday it was usual to observe the mandatum (commandment) of Jesus, who said, 'I give you a new commandment: love one another as I have loved you.' (The word 'Maundy' is actually a corruption of mandatum.) ¶ To observe this command, monarchs were expected to follow Christ's example of humility, which he displayed by washing his disciples' feet at the Last Supper. On the night before his crucifixion, Christ 'laid aside his garments and took a towel and girded himself. After that he poureth water into a basin, and began to wash the disciples' feet, and to wipe them with the towel wherewith he was girded.' Many early monarchs followed his example literally and washed the feet of the poor, but this practice had ended by 1730 because most could not stand the dreadful smell and were also worried about other health dangers associated with close contact with the poor. ¶ Specially minted silver coins were always part of the monarch's charity, as Maundy Money is today. Other traditions of giving out food and cast-offs from the royal wardrobe were later replaced with more money, which was popular with paupers, who could do more with a full purse than clean feet or fine clothes. ¶ Only since the late 19th century have monarchs started to take an active part again in the annual Maundy Service. For years preceding that time the Lord High Almoner (as he was then called) would distribute the purses on the monarch's behalf to a gathering of men and women who equalled the number of the monarch's age. When attending the service, the High Almoner now wears towels made in 1883, which symbolize those worn by Jesus. However, he was once charged with controlling much more. ¶ In the Middle Ages the Lord High Almoner would strew the route with money from the king's Treasury in order to attract an enthusiastic crowd when his master passed through towns. He could give the fish dish from the king's table to 'whatever poor person he pleased'. Also, he received all 'deodand' – any moving thing that had caused the death of a person – which, by dint of its action, became forfeit to God, in the person of his representative, the Sovereign. So the Lord High Almoner received horses, carts and ladders, which he distributed to the needy after taking a small percentage. This practice was abolished in 1846. ¶ The first Lord High Almoner was appointed in 1103 to assist in the religious service on Maundy Thursday and to administer the Sovereign's obligation to give alms to the poor. His status was emphasized by inclusion among the Great Officers of State. It has always been an ecclesiastical appointment filled mostly by bishops, but occasionally by archbishops. Now the High Almoner concentrates solely on planning the Queen's annual act of humility.

The High Almoner, in the Sanctuary of his cathedral at St Albans in Hertfordshire, wears his badge of office, which shows the three-masted ship instituted as the symbol of the Royal Almonry by Cardinal Wolsey in 1512. He is girded with towels in remembrance of the days when monarchs, who were anxious to follow Christ's mandate of humility, washed the feet of the destitute. Bishops have filled this post since 1103.

COUNSELLORS OF STATE

In order for the Crown to fulfil its constitutional obligations, the Sovereign has to enact or approve certain elements of government business. However, in the event that the monarch is unable to perform this role, Counsellors of State are appointed from within the Royal Family to act on the Sovereign's behalf. It is perhaps the least known of the family's responsibilities, but this is the only occasion when members of the family, apart from the monarch, take on an entirely necessary function within the constitution. ¶ The abdication crisis of 1936, when Edward VIII renounced the throne, brought the family of his younger brother, the Duke of York, into the limelight. Albert, Duke of York, had married Lady Elizabeth Bowes-Lyon, who later came to be known as the Queen Mother, in 1923, and together they had had two daughters, Elizabeth and Margaret Rose. The abdication of Edward meant a change of destiny for them all, and one of their worries was the thought that King Edward's desertion could have made the monarchy unpopular. Therefore one of the main tasks for the first years of the reign of King George VI, as he became known, was to restore public confidence after the abdication. This was largely achieved by the time of the Second World War. ¶ The constitutional implications for the new king were considerable, both for himself and for his eldest daughter, who was 10 years old and now only a heart's beat from the throne. The last 'minor' to succeed to the throne had been Edward VI, in 1547. With this in mind, George VI asked Parliament to make statutory provision to deal with four scenarios: the monarch being a minor; the monarch being permanently incapacitated; the monarch being temporarily incapacitated; and the monarch being temporarily out of the country. ¶ The changing form of the Empire made the drawing up of these provisions quite complicated. The existing arrangements for Counsellors of State, drawn up at the start of the 20th century, allowed for Great Officers of State, such as the Prime Minister, as well as members of the Royal Family, to act on the Sovereign's behalf. This was acceptable within the United Kingdom, but George VI was also Head of State in many other countries. Some of these had once been colonies of Britain but were now self-governing dominions and they rejected the idea that members of the British Government might, as Counsellors of State, exercise constitutional power over them. ¶ King George's request was eventually dealt with by the Regency Act of 1937. This established that minority or the permanent incapacity of the monarch would be met by establishing a Regency, with the next adult heir in order of succession acting as Regent. Meanwhile the absence of the monarch abroad, or temporary incapacity, would necessitate a Council of State being established. Membership of this, however, was restricted to the Royal Family. The Council would include the Sovereign's consort and the next four adult members in order of succession. Complete incapacity of the monarch had to be confirmed by three of the following: the Sovereign's next of kin, the Lord High Chancellor, the Speaker of the House of Commons, the Lord Chief Justice and the Master of the Rolls. In 1953 the Regency Act was altered to allow the Queen Mother to continue serving and to provide for Prince Philip to act as Regent, if Prince Charles came to the throne prior to his 18th birthday. ¶ Counsellors of State are restricted in what they can do: in particular they may not dissolve Parliament or sign acts that alter the order of succession. However, without them the process of constitutional government is unable to operate.

The 1844 Room in Buckingham Palace is where the Queen receives her Privy Council. In the monarch's absence abroad or through ill health, two Counsellors of State must take her place, when government business dictates. They stand where the monarch does – before the fireplace and beside a table laid, according to long-established custom, with paper, pens and letter openers – to receive a quorum of Councillors. This generally consists of the President of the Council and three other Ministers, with the Clerk of the Council. All stand for the brief meeting. Candle and sealing wax are to hand, but seldom used.

LIEUTENANT-GOVERNOR AND
COMMANDER-IN-CHIEF OF JERSEY

'Our dear Channel Islands are also to be freed today.' So did Churchill broadcast on 8 May 1945, bringing to an end the German occupation, which had lasted nearly five years. Within a short time, the Duke of Normandy's gubernatorial representatives on the various islands were re-established in their respective residences, providing a figurehead for the many differing constitutional arrangements enjoyed by these self-governing ducal dependencies. Government House in Jersey had always been a symbol of the Duke's rule and it was Britain's instinct to name the house where its colonial governors lived by that name. There are Government Houses spread across the globe, though many have been renamed since independence. In the Falkland Islands, it was at Government House that the significant moments of the 1982 war with Argentina took place. The Government House of India was in Calcutta and built as a copy of Kedleston Hall in Derbyshire, but, when the great imperial city was built in Delhi, this was replaced by a massive Viceroy's House, now the President of India's residence. So it was that, after the swastika was removed from Jersey's Government House and the flag of the Governor returned to the flagpole, that symbolic importance was enhanced. ¶ Lieutenant-General Sir Arthur Grasett arrived at Government House in August 1945. His ducal appointment was signed by the Duke, King George VI, and he was to be Jersey's first Lieutenant-Governor and Commander-in-Chief; before the suffix had just been 'Commanding the Troops'. This change met both the new appointments throughout the Empire and also gave a robust response to the recent occupation. He was succeeding to an appointment that evolved from 1204 when King John lost the duchy of Normandy to King Philip II Augustus of France. The king appointed a warden to look after what was but a few island possessions off the coast of France. ¶ Normandy first grasped the Channel Islands in 933, when its duke, William Longsword, acquired them from Brittany. When his descendant, William the Conqueror, took England in 1066, the Channel Islands were but part of his growing suzerainty. Henry II built further upon the size of these possessions, particularly through marriage when he gained Aquitaine, creating what was known as the Angevin Empire but, all the time, the dukedom of Normandy remained its cornerstone. So, it was a great loss when Henry's younger son, John, who was called 'Lackland', lost all these French possessions in the period of about 16 years. ¶ His son, Henry III, formally renounced possession of the dukedom's historic lands in the Treaty of Paris but retained the title and the Channel Islands. The monarchy has maintained Jersey and the other Channel Islands as a separate dukedom and, hence, it is still separate from the United Kingdom and the European Union but it is a Crown Dependency, which brings with it certain responsibilities. ¶ John did provide something very constructive out of his loss, which was the Constitutions of King John. By these, the islands developed their own form of government, under the Crown, which became the template for modern self-government. The Wardens represented a succession of dukes. They were replaced by two appointments, those of Governor of Jersey, which was a titular sinecure and generally absentee, which began in 1503 but was abolished in 1854, and the Lieutenant-Governor, who was both resident and active. The first Lieutenant-Governor took office in 1703, the first year of a new Duke's reign, Queen Anne having come to the throne the previous year (all monarchs, whether male or female, are always dukes). ¶ Duke Anne's uncle, Charles II, stood in Jersey's capital, St Helier, to be proclaimed monarch after his father's execution in 1649. After his Restoration in 1660, the king rewarded the island for its loyalty with a large gift of land in America, which was called New Jersey. Unfortunately, this possession did not survive American independence in 1776. The French language was retained in formal business until 1901 when the States of Jersey, which is its Parliament, started to use English for debates. ¶ Indeed, there is often some disagreement between the States of Jersey and the British Government. In these situations, the Lieutenant-Governor

is the go-between. Perhaps, for this reason, in 2010 it was announced that the next Lieutenant-Governor would be recommended to the Crown by a panel in Jersey rather than by British Ministers. This is a subtle but important evolution and may well end the long association of the island with British military commanders, such as admirals, generals and air marshals. Perhaps, today, the synergy between a figurehead who also possesses the capability to defend the islands seems less relevant. But in 1945, military assurance at the apex of the democratic process was unction to the islanders recovering from occupation.

Government House on the island is the symbolic residence of the Lieutenant and Commander-in-Chief of Jersey. Appointed by the Sovereign, as Duke of Normandy, the office represents independence and security for the islanders.

KNIGHT COMPANION OF THE MOST NOBLE
ORDER OF THE GARTER

Quite how such a strange item as a garter became the symbol of the oldest and most senior order of chivalry remains a mystery, but the order is now over 650 years old and its badge crops up everywhere, even on cereal packets and marmalade jars. In fact, wherever the royal arms are shown, the order's dark blue buckled belt with its golden motto neatly encircles the shield. ¶ The actual date of the order's foundation is unclear, as are the events leading up to it. What we do know is that Edward III encouraged chivalry among his nobles, leading them into great wars and celebrating victories with banquets, wine and women. The motivation for the order's creation was political but its inspiration came from the legend of King Arthur and his Knights of the Round Table. As early as 1344, Edward told his court that a new Round Table of knights would be mustered for jousting tournaments. There would be two teams of 12: he would lead one, and his son, the Black Prince, the other. The meetings would take place at Windsor, where halls suitable for the festivities were to be built. ¶ No sooner had the building work begun than Edward was off to war, this time to claim the French throne for himself: after all, his mother was the late king's sister. Aware of how quickly domestic problems could develop in his absence, he knew that conquests must be delivered to keep the barons in check. First his son achieved success at Crécy in 1346, then Calais fell into Edward's hands. Needing to secure his supremacy on his return to Windsor, he evolved his embryo Round Table into an order of chivalry, specifically one that imposed a grave oath of loyalty upon the membership. Few dared to break such oaths in those superstitious times. ¶ The knights' symbol was then, as it is now, a blue garter marked in gold with the motto, 'Honi soit qui mal y pense' (Shame to those who think evil of it). Blue was the French royal colour and its use was a deliberate slight to the French and underlined England's claim to their throne. The motto's provenance is less easy to define. Possibly the fanciful story of Joan, Countess of Salisbury, losing her garter while dancing and causing laughter among the courtly onlookers could be true. Edward supposedly picked it up, tied it round the heroic Black Prince's leg and uttered the words that became the motto of the order. Other sources say it was Edward's queen who dropped her garter and the motto was how she replied when Edward said it would one day be a symbol of reverence. However, the most tantalizing theory is more recent: it points out that witchcraft was still practised in the 14th century and that the garter would have been recognized as a symbol of coven membership. Edward therefore defused a potentially hazardous situation by stepping in to save a lady's embarrassment. ¶ The Order of the Garter has evolved to suit the needs of successive monarchs. The Tudors, anxious to legitimize their dynasty by currying favour with foreign monarchs, used it as a powerful political tool. Henry VIII's excesses led to the most frequent use of Degradation, a ritual that humiliated any treasonable knight: his banner, sword and helm were thrown from their position above his stall in St George's Chapel in Windsor Castle, to be kicked by heralds out of the gates and into a ditch. ¶ Today, the order includes among its members former Prime Ministers, retired generals and admirals, and a number of familiar ducal names. Recently, the statutes were altered to include women.

The order was founded by Edward III when he invested the first knight, the Black Prince. The 1,000th Knight Companion of the Most Noble Order of the Garter holds the Garter he was invested with at the site of his investiture: the Throne Room in Windsor Castle. He also wears the mantle and collar, which is a chain of gold knots alternating with enamelled medallions showing a rose encircled by the Garter. From the collar hangs the George, an enamelled image of St George slaying the dragon. The red velvet hood is connected to the right shoulder by a sash to hold it in place. He holds the plumed hat with his right hand through the opening in the mantle designed so he can use a sword in combat.

KEEPER OF THE GREAT CLOCK

The Diamond Jubilee gave Parliament the opportunity to rename the clock tower of the Palace of Westminster in honour of the Queen. It is now the Elizabeth Tower and stands in partnership with the Victoria Tower, at the other end of the building, celebrating both Diamond Jubilee monarchs. The Elizabeth Tower contains the Great Clock and its phenomenal hour bell, 'Big Ben', by which the national timepiece is both heard and known. The workings of this mechanical chronometer, which remain vital even in a world now run by split-second digital precision, rest in the care of the Keeper of the Great Clock. This title has evolved, along with its status, from that of an unsung Victorian functionary into a skilled and high-profile character responsible for the care of a national treasure. ¶ The fire that devastated the medieval Palace of Westminster in October 1834 consumed something of England's political heart. Gone were many of the halls once lived in by Edward the Confessor, the chamber nearly blown to smithereens by Guy Fawkes and then violated by Charles II and his soldiers. ¶ The great conflagration provided Great Britain and Ireland, as the nation had become in 1801, with an opportunity to build from the rubble a great new Parliament as an icon of fairness to both the nation and its emerging Empire. Perhaps in homage to the power that Time holds over Man, Charles Barry, the architect of the new Palace of Westminster, planned for a vast four-faced clock to remind Parliamentarians of their limitations. ¶ The clock tower was built in the 1840s and '50s and Barry took advice from Queen Victoria's clockmaker, Benjamin Lewis Vulliamy, about the clock itself. Other clockmakers demanded the opportunity to compete for this prestigious commission and the Commissioner for Works decided to hold a competition, judged by the Astronomer Royal, Sir George Airey. Among the conditions were that the hour bell had to strike within one second of the correct moment, and the clock's performance had to be checked twice daily, by telegraph, against the Greenwich Royal Observatory. These challenging requirements set the standards by which the winning mechanism still performs today. ¶ The strict competition delayed the selection of a clockmaker for seven years but, in the end E.J. Dent won the commission to build it in line with the design virtually imposed by Lord Grimthorpe, who had interceded as a co-judge. In 1859, after further delays in the construction of the tower and the casting of bells, the clock began its life of timekeeping for London. ¶ Daily it was wound and cared for by keepers; their role made easier over the decades by the arrival of an electronic winding mechanism. It has almost never failed, though when it does the news is sensational because of the clock's status and reputation. ¶ Literature has woven the icon of the clock and Big Ben into the consciousness of Britain. The imaginations of children have flown with Peter Pan past the clock faces on their imaginary journey to Neverland and countless spies have stubbed out their cigarettes in black and white films under the streetlights of a fog-filled street close by. The Elizabeth Tower and its clock survived its own real drama, as the bombs of the Blitz landed around its avuncular symbol of Britishness, sending out its own message of tenacity. Today, the voracity for news and information finds political commentators anchored to any vantage point that can hold the image of the clock to bring visual provenance to their content. ¶ All the time the relentless supervision of the Keeper of the Great Clock must ensure this timepiece never misses its moments. Armed with old pennies he weights the mechanism to gain, or lose, seconds in the hour and, under his supervision every year, an army signaller is posted beside the mechanism to ensure that the gun fires exactly as the clock strikes 11 on Remembrance Sunday.

This utilitarian role has gained notoriety because the four clock faces that look out from the Elizabeth Tower high above the United Kingdom's Parliament is known throughout the world. Standing beside its original Victorian mechanism the recently named Keeper of the Great Clock holds one of the winders and the coins used to tweak its speed, in order that the great bell, Big Ben, which has come to stand for the clock tower too, always strikes the hour exactly and to the second.

MASTER GUNNER OF ST JAMES'S PARK

The Bible describes King Uzziah of Judah, around 750 BC, as making machines 'to shoot arrows and hurl large stones', proof that the use of artillery in warfare is ancient. English kings first used cannon against the Scots in 1327 and first fired them abroad in the Battle of Crécy in 1346. ¶ Maurice of Nassau achieved a means of field gun mobility with his Kartouwen, a gun that could be moved around in a cart and perhaps the first piece of field artillery. The concept was developed and deployed to good effect by Sweden's King Gustavus Adolphus in the Battle of Breitenfeld in 1631. Moving his 12 heavy and 42 light guns around the field helped ensure his victory. ¶ The English Civil War left a hangover of fear throughout the land. The Restoration of 1660 was the healing catalyst that brought Charles II to the throne, but with him came the need for a proper standing army. The king's protection was evidently part of this army's mission and around London's palaces piquets were posted to warn of potential threat. Among these were artillery pieces, sited where appropriate. In 1678 the king appointed Captain Thomas Silver to be Master Gunner of Whitehall, a responsibility soon extended to include St James's Park. ¶ The Master Gunner of St James's Park, as the appointment

became known after guns were removed from Whitehall in the 1720s, quickly attracted officers of fairly senior rank. These officers seem to have held sway over just six guns, which were probably now kept for salutes. Inevitably, these officers were part of court life, so providing a link between the army's artillery and the monarch. George I raised two regular companies of artillery at Woolwich in 1716 and named them the Royal Regiment of Artillery. The number of artillery regiments increased and in 1793 the Royal Horse Artillery was added to support the cavalry. ¶ The relationship between the Royal Regiment of Artillery and the Crown was touchingly reaffirmed in 1947, when George VI visited the Riding Troop, which was retained in the traditional ceremonial uniforms of the Horse Artillery, and renamed them the King's Troop. They still fire salutes, perhaps as the direct successors of those six guns in St James's Park. The appointment of the Master Gunner of St James's Park is given by the monarch to a senior officer with distinguished artillery service, acting as the link with the Sovereign in her capacity as Captain General of the Royal Artillery.

The Master Gunner of St James's Park stands proud of the gun in Green Park, with the Queen Victoria Memorial in the distance, through Buckingham Palace's Canada Gate, and St James's Park beyond.

[219]

GARRISON SERGEANT MAJOR, LONDON DISTRICT

Carved into the memory of almost every soldier is a clear image of the Sergeant Major. He is placed by custom, a history of social engineering and the need for professionalism in combat, at the emotional heart of the military will to serve and fight. Whilst never the commander, the Sergeant Major holds the commanding authority in his office to supervise, enforce and deliver the highest standards of military capability among both officers and private soldiers in order that the commander can achieve his intent. ¶ The birth of film and television came during and after the two world wars and was pioneered by men, predominantly, who had been called up to serve and fight in the Armed Forces. Their collective memory of the Sergeant Major, which shaped and hardened their military lives for war and National Service, led to a gradual establishment, through drama, of the Sergeant Major as a fear-inducing, high-principled and screaming figure who was unquestioningly loyal to the core as he bellowed relentlessly into the ears of generation after generation of army recruits. ¶ England was feudally managed by Norman kings, with the key purposes of maintaining order, gathering taxes and recruiting soldiery as required. The feudal system simply demanded, in time of need, that tenants of the land must provide the king with rough trained soldiers from the peasantry who were ready to fight. Many of the specific feudal demands placed on tenants in this and other ways were referred to as acts of Sergeanty. This word derived from the ancient French word for 'service' from one who owes allegiance, and that central principle has grown with the word ever since. ¶ An English standing army was formed after the Restoration of Charles II in 1660. The lessons of the Civil War and the success of Cromwell's standing army, both good and bad, were merged into a structure that Parliament was content to acknowledge and, where necessary, fund. The army's establishment would herald the status of England, and later Great Britain, as a formidable power in the world. Like all organizations, it needed its own internal management system in order to deliver command effectively to the soldiers in the field. Inevitably, the template for this system was taken from that prevailing in society at the time and the very real differences that existed between the families of power and influence, who generally provided the officers, and those who either had none or less. The latter were the majority and filled the ranks of soldiers who delivered the army's punch, and the best of them served by training the others, with the rank of sergeant. Selected by merit, they marshalled, drilled, equipped and organized men to fight. In 1680 the first use of Sergeant Major was applied to the man overseeing a number of sergeants. ¶ When many regiments or battalions were located close together, they became a garrison, possibly evolving from the French word *garnir*, which means 'to equip'. These concentrations were often commanded by brigadiers or senior generals and, in London, there was the additional garrison responsibility of protecting the monarch. The first Garrison Sergeant Major, London District was appointed in the early 1950s to shape State ceremonial drill in the Household Division's pursuit of excellence. Since then there have only been five Garrison Sergeant Majors, each holding office for many years, making them the residual authority on drill. With an eye for detail shaped from the first step marched by an enlisted Guardsman, this office bearer sets a template that is rigorously applied.

The ultimate arbiter of ceremonial excellence in a land that does pageantry better than any other is the Garrison Sergeant Major, London District. Always from one of the five Foot Guards Regiments of the Household Division, this appointment wears the revived badge of rank, consisting of the Royal Coat of Arms over four gold chevrons. He stands in the Tilt Yard of Horse Guards. The arch is part of the ceremonial entrance to the Sovereign's London residence and, in the distance beyond the Trooper who guards the office of the Major General Commanding the Household Division can be seen the Guards Memorial, which is still marked by bombs that fell during the Blitz. Designed by Gilbert Ledward between 1923 and 1926, it commemorates soldiers of the Foot Guards regiments who died in the First World War. The bronze figures were cast from German guns captured in the war.

FIRST SEA LORD AND CHIEF OF THE NAVAL STAFF

The Queen appointed her husband, the Duke of Edinburgh, to be Lord High Admiral of the United Kingdom on his 90th birthday in 2011. She had held the office since 1 April 1964. On that day the Board of Admiralty, which consisted of Their Lordships the Commissioners, ceased to exist, their duties subsumed into the Joint Chiefs of Staff in the Ministry of Defence, where the three service chiefs report to the Chief of the Defence Staff, the senior serving officer in uniform. ¶ The boardroom of the Admiralty is only used for special ceremonies now but from here the Royal Navy, which won supremacy at sea for Great Britain and explored much of the globe, was sent forth 'By the Commissioners for Executing the Office of Lord High Admiral of the United Kingdom of Great Britain and Ireland, etc'. Two roles that survived the establishment of the Ministry of Defence were those of the First and Second Sea Lords. The First Sea Lord had also become Chief of the Naval Staff during the First World War, while the Second Sea Lord also became Commander-in-Chief, firstly of Portsmouth and more recently of Naval Home Command. Recent changes in the structure of the Royal Navy have changed this further. ¶ In medieval times, the English navy was supplied by the Cinque Ports under the same feudal system by which the monarch administered the land: the barons of these wealthy Channel ports served the king by supplying ships. In Henry III's reign, they were expected to supply 57 fighting vessels with 1,197 men and boys for 15 days at sea every year, after which the king would pay the expenses. Unfortunately, this feudal fleet tended to engage in piracy. For instance, while travelling to Flanders in 1297 they attacked and destroyed 20 ships from Yarmouth as Edward I looked on in horror. ¶ By the reign of Edward III, the Lord Admiral's duties and jurisdiction were fixed: he selected the ships offered under the feudal system, and chose the officers who would take them to sea. In fact, choosing captains to take command remains a responsibility of the First Sea Lord to this day. ¶ Manning the navy remained a problem for many years. Indeed, Henry IV was forced to apply to private enterprise in the 15th century in order to protect his shores. Eventually, Henry VIII reorganized the navy completely, placing it upon the foundations that govern it still. He built ships with the money he plundered from the Dissolution of the Monasteries and established the Navy Board in 1546. This was chaired by the Lord Admiral and his deputy, the Lieutenant of the Admiralty. (It was not until 1623 that the title Lord High Admiral came into being.) ¶ When James II was Duke of York and Lord High Admiral, he was served by the energetic reformer Samuel Pepys, who acted as his Secretary. After 1688 power passed from the Navy Board to the Admiralty Board, created in 1690 by William III, who appointed nine Commissioners to act as if they 'were the Lord High Admiral'. Chief among these was the political post of First Lord of the Admiralty, which was sometimes occupied by senior admirals until 1806. From this time on, the senior serving officer on the Board of Admiralty was called First Naval Lord, a title that evolved into First Sea Lord. The appointee thereby became the senior serving officer in the Royal Navy. ¶ The post of First Sea Lord survives as a link with the past and also, because geography does not change, Britain remains an island and needs a strong navy to protect its interests at home and abroad.

The First Sea Lord and Chief of the Naval Staff sits in the Admiralty Boardroom of Old Admiralty Building, off London's Whitehall. It is dominated by the weathervane that still spins with the wind to indicate whether it is 'Fair for France'. The ornate wood carvings by Grinling Gibbons are rich in naval symbolism, including ropes and anchors, astrolabes and bearing rings. It was in this room that plans were drafted for Captain James Cook's exploration of the globe. *Overleaf*: The First Sea Lord stands on the flying bridge of HMS *Dauntless* with HMS *St Albans* alongside and a Merlin helicopter from RNAS Culdrose flies overhead, during weekly 'Thursday War' war-fighting and damage control exercises off Plymouth. Training constantly keeps the Royal Navy ready for war.

ORDER OF MERIT

The christening of Queen Victoria's eldest son, the future Edward VII, in 1842, came at a time when Britain's more liberal constitutional monarchy was rare in autocratic Europe. It was also a time when the ascendancy of a united Germany was foreseen, with militaristic Prussia well placed to take the lead. Perhaps for this reason, King Frederick William IV of Prussia was invited to stand as his Sponsor, or Godfather. Ironically, soon after the Prussian king returned home, he expanded his nation's well-respected order of merit, called the Order Pour le Mérite, to include a Civil division. This was limited to 20 recipients: the same size as the Military one that Frederick the Great had established in 1740. ¶ In a bid to mark the incredible expansion of Great Britain's imperial power, along with its recent industrial and mercantile developments, there was a move to evolve the honours system, so as to reward the wide range of service in this great venture. This was especially necessary at the start of the 20th century, when society was changing and the traditional aristocracy was diminishing in its monopoly of venture and praise. ¶ Many attempts at creating an honour for the arts and sciences emerged, only to splutter and fail. Queen Victoria was engaged at different points in her reign but, stripped of her husband's visionary zeal for these disciplines, she never quite managed the leadership to push it through. In his time, the Prince had summoned the statutes of Prussia's order and considered it as a template; perhaps his interest was displaced by the business of preparing the more practical means of celebrating British capability that resulted in the Great Exhibition of 1851, where the industrial inventions, scientific discoveries and design advances of the Empire were flaunted before the world. ¶ Thus, in 1901 Victoria died and her fun-loving son became the seventh King Edward. Not renowned as a man of either the arts or sciences, he had both a completely natural comprehension of his role as figurehead for the Empire and also an almost naive excitement at being the Fount of all Honour. Preparing for his coronation, he also sent for the statutes of the Prussian order, now managed by his nephew, the German emperor Wilhelm II. The plan was for the new Order of Merit to be restricted to 24 members, divided into two divisions, Military and Civil. Its unique power was that it carried no rank: this in a time when rank was all. But, what it did carry was rarity, something that could be more highly prized and respected. ¶ On Coronation Day 1902 the list of new Members of the Order of Merit was published, but, due to the onset of acute appendicitis, Edward's coronation did not take place for several months. Among the list of military luminaries were Field Marshals the Lords Roberts and Kitchener, famed for having just saved the Empire from ignominy during the Boer War. Lord Lister was also named, the pioneer of preventative medicine and antiseptic surgery. ¶ The Order of Merit was left in the monarch's own gift. Here it thrived as the recipients from the arts, sciences, literature and Armed Forces knew that no politician or ministry had been involved in their selection. The ribbon for the simple neck decoration was equal widths of the Order of the Garter's blue and crimson. The badge in red and blue enamel is surmounted by the imperial crown but dominated by its central wreathed roundel, on which are the words 'For Merit', which echoes again the Prussian order's cross. The last military appointment, which has crossed swords between the arms of the cross, was Lord Mountbatten: he was the first Chief of the Defence Staff, an Admiral of the fleet but also a Lieutenant-General and Air Marshal. ¶ He was but one of the many appointments made to the order by Elizabeth II, who has reigned for 60 of the order's 110 years. All her appointments have been captured in portraits kept at Windsor Castle, the only such record kept by any Sovereign.

Each holder of this order has been selected because of a meritorious service that the Sovereign deems to be immense. In this case, the simple insignia of a Member of the Order of Merit is worn around the neck of a recipient who has made his contribution to the arts and public life of the nation, quietly. This office contains clues to his interest and motivation, not least the painting of Jerusalem on the wall behind and the reference to architecture waiting for scrutiny on the desk.

CHIEF BUTLER OF ENGLAND

Norman kings handed out land to nobles with strings attached, each manor held of the king in consideration for certain duties. Mostly these consisted of Knight Service, the promise to provide troops or pay in lieu. Others were given under Sergeanty, which required the regular offering of some specific service. This latter group was divided into two: those who offered service at regular intervals or when asked, which was Petit Sergeanty, and those who did service at the coronation only, called Grand Sergeanty. ¶ The manor of Kenninghall was given as a reward by Henry I to William de Albini, in recognition of the support he gave in the king's battle against his elder brother, Robert Curthose, for the throne. Because it was a royal manor it came under Grand Sergeanty and the service expected was Pincera Regis, or King's Chief Butler at the coronation banquet. There were perquisites of 'the best gold cup with a cover, which is on the table, and all the wine under the bar of the [Westminster] Hall'. The Butler could rely on none other than the Lord Mayor and Corporation of the City of London as his assistants. ¶ Manors were not vested in families but were feudal in character; hence they could be inherited, bought or sold like anything else. The Dukes of Norfolk inherited Kenninghall and the duties with it but in 1872 they sold it to John Oddin Taylor of Norwich. In the 1990s it changed hands again and was bought by a European, who lives in Sweden. His family came from Aquitaine and served Richard the Lionheart in the Crusades, while one member attempted to save the French royal family and faced the guillotine. ¶ The last time a coronation banquet was considered was in 1902 for Edward VII, though his sudden illness put a stop to the plans. At the Court of Claims that preceded the event three people claimed the right to act as Chief Butler: the Duke of Norfolk, Mr Taylor of Kenninghall and a descendant of William de Albini. The court did not consider their cases and so no decision was taken. ¶ Nor did it decide on the Earl of Denbigh and Desmond's claim to act as Grand Carver. His claim was up against Scotland's Hereditary Carver, a post fully recognized today. The last person to perform the task at a coronation was the Earl of Lincoln, by right of his earldom, in 1399, at the coronation of Henry IV; as it happened, it was the king himself. However, the Denbighs maintain their right but it would need the Court of Claims to adjudicate. Other banquet appointments of Grand Sergeanty include the manor of Ashele to act as Naperer, the manor of Addington to serve a Mess of Dillegrout, the manor of Nether Bilsington to present three Maple cups and the manor of Sculton to be Larderer. ¶ It is the right of the Lord of the Manor of Worksop to attend the coronation itself in order to present 'A Glove for the King's Right Hand' just before the sceptre is given to the monarch, and then to remain available to support the arm if necessary. This silent but deeply symbolic task has been performed at every coronation since medieval times. Whoever owns the manor of Worksop is entitled to perform the unique services of Grand Sergeanty, but at the time of the Queen's coronation it was owned by a limited company, and allowing a commercial organization to take part was deemed unacceptable. As a compromise the Chancellor of the Duchy of Lancaster presented the glove in proxy. ¶ When feudalism ended little remained but the title 'Lord of the Manor', which is intrinsically valueless unless it retains some rights, such as minerals or markets. Nevertheless there is some pride in ownership of a description of such antiquity associated with real territory, even when all the freehold, leases and copyholds have been taken up by others.

Outside the royal manor of Kenninghall in Norfolk stands a display of the heraldry of its historic owners. The arms of King Edward the Confessor take precedence, along with the families of Howard, Mowbray and Dacre, who provided the Butlers of England.

HIGH SHERIFF OF THE BAILIWICK
OF NORFOLK

It is significant that the legendary English folk hero Robin Hood challenged authority in the form of the Sheriff of Nottingham. For the medieval English yeoman, the Sheriff had power over life and death. As the king's representative in the shires, he could preside over the shire court in the Earl's absence, arrest and imprison criminals to preserve the king's peace, collect taxes and fines, raise and lead the local fighting force (Posse Comitates) and enforce regulations covering trade, currency weights and measures, fairs and markets. ¶ The foundations of local administration in England were laid towards the end of the 10th century. Reeves, or bailiffs, scattered around the kingdom gathered taxes and enforced the king's writs. During the reign of Aethelred II (978–1016), the senior shrieval position in each shire was the Shire Reeve. The holders of this post became the 'Sheriffs' inherited by the Norman victors in 1066. The Anglo-Saxon Sheriff of Norfolk, Toli, retained his bailiwick for several years, but by 1076 Normans had been installed in every shrieval post. Roger Bigod, who held the Norfolk office in 1086, acquired extensive lands in East Anglia after the Conquest. ¶ The function of the Sheriff's office that most concerned the reigning Sovereign was gathering taxes. In the 12th century Henry I made his new Exchequer Court responsible for supervising the shrievalty of England. To avoid disagreements over what was due, many sheriffs paid Sheriff-Geld, a set sum. Any excess produced by tax in the shires, they would keep as profit. Families became wealthy on shrieval income and took over more shires. Monarchs found other ways to improve their finances: Richard I auctioned off sheriffdoms to the highest bidder to raise money for the Crusades, and gave a clutch, including Nottingham, to his brother John, in order to secure his loyalty. ¶ Magna Carta, the great Charter that John was forced to sign at Runnymede in 1215, curbed the power of the king, thereby controlling the Sheriffs. Their position was eroded further in the 14th century by the introduction of Justices of the Peace, and in the 16th century by the appointment of Lord-Lieutenants to deal with military and administrative matters. As the Sheriff's workload gradually increased and the income declined, the position became less attractive: people would even nominate their enemies, in the hope that the job would bring financial ruin. ¶ The Sheriffs Act of 1887 redefined the duties of the post, stating that 'if a sheriff finds any resistance in the execution of a writ he may arrest the resisters and commit them to prison'. This long arm of the law was effectively removed by the Courts Act of 2003 and today the High Sheriff's judicial reach is restricted to attendance at royal visits in the county and support for High Court Judges when on circuit. The High Sheriff's support of voluntary sector organizations involved in crime reduction and social cohesion, as well as the police and prison services, is today the core role of the office. ¶ Every year, lists of three new names are still prepared for each shire. The Sheriffs Roll is subsequently taken to the Queen, in Council, and she 'Pricks the List' with a bodkin, a tradition that may have started with Elizabeth I in the 16th century. And since 1254 it is to the High Sheriff that the monarch's writ to hold a General Election in the shire is still sent. ¶ In 1997 the incoming Labour Government sought to update the appointment, which had been an almost exclusively male preserve and had a narrow social base. Through the Shrievalty Association, the nation's bailiwicks were encouraged to recruit more widely, achieving a greater degree of representation from women and ethnic minorities.

Saxon rulers had reeves to govern in the shires. The office of High Sheriff in rural post-Conquest England had extensive powers within its remit, including being able to enforce law and gather taxes in every corner of the shire. Today they act as official returning officers for parliamentary elections, proclaim the accession of a new sovereign and support the work of the crime prevention agencies both in the public and voluntary sectors. The High Sheriff of the Bailiwick of Norfolk wears the traditional black velvet court dress with gilt buttons, sword, jabot and breeches.

MEMBER OF PARLIAMENT

When the Sovereign arrives at the Palace of Westminster to open the High Court of Parliament, the building is awash with the panoply of State in scarlet and gold. Carpeting adorns every marble paving and step that the monarch might use, while everyone taking part in processions are in court dress, some versions of which have hardly been updated since the 18th century. It is another ironic moment in British life, the reality being the opposite of what appears. The real power in this pageantry that brings together the Crown, Lords and Commons is in direct contrast with what the witness observes. ¶ The story of British history is about the capture of power from the monarch and vesting it with the people. The people's representatives are the elected men and women who travel from their constituencies to hold the Executive to account, as Members of Parliament. Watching how this is done and constantly probing into the decisions, views and morals of those representatives is a media no longer able to keep up with its own technological capabilities. ¶ Parliament was originally unicameral, with the knights and burgesses meeting with peers from 1265. From 1341 Parliament divided, with peers forming an upper chamber and the knights of the shires a lower chamber. The latter became known as Members of Parliament from 1477 and the initials 'MP' have been used ever since abbreviated honours became common practice. 'House of Commons' may have evolved from the French word *commune*, which means 'community of the realm'. MPs are chosen in a 'first past the post' election when the Returning Officer inscribes the name of the winner, but not the party, on the Writ of Summons, which constitutes the individual's right to attend Parliament and call him- or herself a Member of Parliament. ¶ When William defeated Anglo-Saxon England and took possession of the State, root and branch, there was no limit to his autocracy. The barons he raised to greatness loyally supported him and his successors, but time gave perspective and they soon challenged royal authority. These barons represented the land and secured power and justice from the monarch through Magna Carta and later the Provisions of Oxford. Henry III's determination that Westminster Abbey be built higher than any other church placed demands on a nation it refused to endure and Simon de Montfort again checked the king and wrested further power from royal hands. The struggle between Monarch, Parliament and Church is the chart along which the ship of British history has navigated, because similar struggles occurred in Scotland, Ireland and Wales. Charles I walked into the Commons fixed on arresting his detractors, igniting a conflict that ended with his execution by a Parliament that never again let a monarch through its doors. The Reform Acts, particularly that in 1832, set the scene for an increase in both suffrage and expectation. The further the monarch's powers withdrew, the greater were the expectations of MPs and short was the moral authority with which the Lords held their stake. As the Church's influence declined and universal suffrage from the age of 18 arrived, the Commons' power increased. Reform continues to stab unsuccessfully at a solution for the Lords. The Crown retains huge authority but its remaining Royal Prerogative is only to be used as advised by an executive rooted in the Commons. ¶ Thus, when the MPs are summoned to the Bar of the House of Lords by the Gentleman Usher to the Black Rod, but only after slamming the door of their chamber in his face as a reminder of privilege, they shuffle towards the glare of scarlet and ermine with power in their wrinkled boots. They are the power now, theirs is the firmament of Executive authority and we, the people, have made it so.

On Lambeth's Albert Embankment, with the Palace of Westminster in the background, stands a Member of Parliament. Henry VIII handed this Palace over for the use of Parliament. To the left of the Victoria Tower is Westminster Abbey where Simon de Montfort supposedly convened members of England's first Parliament. She wears a brooch that shows the Crowned Portcullis, which was a Badge used by the family of Henry VII's mother, Margaret Beaufort. It has recently been formally adopted as the symbol of Parliament. Today's media is ubiquitous in its pursuit of political detail, and advancing technology only increases this power.

PRESIDENT OF THE SUPREME COURT OF THE UNITED KINGDOM

In the firmament of constitutional change that began this century, a new appellate court was established in the United Kingdom, called the Supreme Court. It was a completely new beginning for a justice system that has evolved since the Anglo-Saxon Court Moots and, when it opened in 2009, the tradition of the House of Lords, or judges sitting within it, operating as the highest and final court of appeal in the land was brought to a halt after centuries of judgement. Whereas the House of Lords, in its judicial capacity, had been led by the Senior Lord of Appeal in Ordinary, the new court has a President at its head, which reflects a more egalitarian time. ¶ The Constitutional Reform Act of 2005 was a flagship for the second Labour Government, led by the reforming zeal of Prime Minister Tony Blair. It came in the wake of his first five-year term, which began with almost the largest landslide victory in history and it followed the national expectation of change implicit in a new millennium. When the second term began, the Constitutional Reform Bill was crafted and debated, while in the very chamber of Parliament where some of the keenest debate took place, time was set aside for judgements of the Lords of Appeal in Ordinary to be heard. ¶ The name, Supreme Court, echoes the one that is central to the constitution of the United States of America. But, whereas the US court, founded in 1789, has the Federal power to overturn primary legislation from Congress and any of the States, the United Kingdom one can not. This respects the sovereignty implicit in Parliament. However, its interpretations of law, which are expressed in the appeals it addresses, can shape the interpretation of that legislation, which then becomes Common Law, one of the great resources of law in the respective parts of the United Kingdom. ¶ Another comparison comes with the make-up of each court. In the States there is a limit on nine members, each nominated by the President but subject to the affirmation of Congress. In England the President and his Deputy have 10 further puisne judges, while the constitutional link with the Crown and the separation of powers is maintained. Justices of the Supreme Court are selected by a commission that includes its President and Deputy President along with representatives of the three judicial traditions over which the Supreme Court has jurisdiction: Northern Ireland, England and Wales, and Scotland (though the High Court of Justiciary keeps its primacy over its criminal cases). Nominations they deduce are given to the Prime Minister, who advises the monarch whom to appoint. ¶ In 2009 the Queen put the President of the Supreme Court in the Order of Precedence for the United Kingdom, taking his place immediately after another new appointment created by the same rash of constitutional reform, the Lord Speaker of the House of Lords, and before the Lord Privy Seal. This Order of Precedence is rich with appointments and titles, many reflected in this book. Some no longer hold the power they once did, like the Lord High Chancellor. Nearly abolished by press release one minute, this ancient office was reinstated the next and remains one of the Great Offices of State, something that the raw fibre of the nation needs at any coronation. The Order of Precedence jogs memories for the nation like a scrapbook can for any life. The President is undeniably the top of the judicial tree but he remains five below the Lord Chancellor, and so the subtle inconsistencies of the United Kingdom's stricture and identity go on. The President's addition is a reminder that things will always change. Precedence of some sort exists in every part of the world but the United Kingdom has chosen to keep history as an influence in this choice. It may be eccentric, it may seem wrong to many, but in Britain these things often make no sense. The core thread through every appointment is the aspiration to make a better life for all.

Presided over by the President, the new location of the Supreme Court is highly symbolic of the United Kingdom's separation of powers, balancing judiciary and legislature across the open space of Parliament Square, with the other two sides occupied by the executive – the Treasury building – and the Church – Westminster Abbey.

THE SOVEREIGN

Britain's monarchy sparked from the smouldering ruins of Rome's empire, which had reached into the British Isles but never conquered them all. During the Roman Empire's decline, opportunities to attack the islands were seized by barbarian tribes from the German plains. Roman legions were unable to hold back these warrior hordes and were forced to retreat, leaving Britain in 409 to be picked over by an unending stream of invaders, including Picts, Scots, Attacotti, Franks, Jutes and Saxons. One such invasion force, a group of Saxons led by Cerdic, landed on Hampshire's coast in 495. Cerdic founded the kingdom of the West Saxons, or Wessex, in 519 and his direct descendant, Elizabeth II, continues the unbroken line of succession that he established: a line that follows the evolution of kingship from warrior chief to constitutional figurehead. The changes in fortune that affected this line of succession over more than 1,000 years can be read in the titles that each ruler held. ¶ Cerdic, like many rulers from the Continent, claimed his own legitimacy as King of Wessex by descent from his eight-times great-grandfather, the God-king Woden. Without this genealogy, pagan society might have had little reason to respect one man in preference over another outside the fact that the order of precedence in this anarchy was hammered out by brawn and military prowess. Britain's invading tribes fought for their destiny against the ancient Britons, whose reputed 5th-century king, Coel the Old, is also numbered among the Queen's ancestors. A nursery rhyme recalls that he was 'a merry old soul and a merry old soul was he'. Bardic genealogy declared Coel the descendant of another god-king, called Beli Mawr, associated with the Druids' Beltane, or May Day festival, which is still a public holiday. At about the same time, the Pictish king Fergus the Great ruled Albany, now known as Scotland. He is a predecessor of Elizabeth II through the Picts' favoured system of matriarchal descent, a tradition that the Scots have always recognized and respected. ¶ For most of the second half of the first millennium A D, Angle Land, or England, was divided into a number of small kingdoms known as the Heptarchy: similar divisions existed in other parts of these islands. Christian missionaries converted their monarchs by offering to replace legitimacy, based on descent from Woden, with that offered by the sacrament of unction. With Holy Oil, the Sovereign, or supreme ruler, was anointed as God's vice regent on Earth, just as Zadok the priest and Nathan the prophet had anointed Solomon as king in the Bible. Missionaries also confirmed a genealogy, recorded in the Anglo-Saxon Chronicle around 840, that extends the line of royal descent a further 15 generations back beyond Woden to Sceaf, the son of Noah and thence to Adam. It was brilliant spin because it offered a more venerable status and made regicide, killing the anointed king, a sin. One consequence was that the Church in Rome gained influence over the titles claimed by English kings. ¶ Offa, King of the Mercians in the 8th century, was the first monarch to claim all England under his rule, as *Rex Totius Anglorum Patriae*. But Wessex was flourishing at this time and in 973 St Dunstan crowned its king, Edgar the Peaceable, as Emperor of Britain, in a coronation ritual that has remained broadly unchanged since and which was the basis of that used for Elizabeth II. The Normans grasped Saxon rituals to give their conquest of England legitimacy in 1066. William I was crowned on Christmas Day in Edward the Confessor's new abbey at Westminster, setting a precedent followed ever since. He styled himself *Willelmus Rex Anglorum* and his son prefixed this title with *Dei Gratia*, 'by Grace of

---

The Sovereign sits beside the Symbols of Sovereignty in the Throne Room at Buckingham Palace. The Imperial State Crown has a sapphire in the top cross, which came from Edward the Confessor's ring; below it hang Elizabeth I's pearl earrings. The massive ballas ruby, owned by the Black Prince and worn by Henry V at Agincourt, sits above the bright second Star of Africa diamond. The Sword of State was traditionally the monarch's personal weapon and is the symbol of both her authority and power. The Throne, with the Royal Cypher, was used when the Queen made her Oath during the coronation in 1953.

God', perhaps to add legitimacy to the conquest. Other medieval kings added to this with the dukedoms of Normandy and Aquitaine, as the vastness of possessions accumulated by Henry II and his wife, Eleanor of Aquitaine, made England the mere backyard of the Angevin Empire. Most of these territories were lost in a single generation by their son, John 'Lackland' who, perhaps to make up for his losses, was the first to add lordship over Ireland to his title. ¶ Edward I may have been nicknamed *Scottorum Malleus*, or 'Hammer of the Scots', but he never completely conquered the country. It was in Wales that his knights and a necklace of massive castles brought him success, with an end to the ancient line of Welsh princes. Edward's wife, Eleanor of Castile, produced a son at Caernarfon Castle in 1284 who was subsequently created Prince of Wales, beginning a new tradition. But since then the blood of the displaced princes, including Llewellyn the Great, has found its way back into the genealogies of British sovereigns. ¶ Edward III claimed France by inheritance through his mother, Isabella, who was the daughter of King Philip the Fair of France. The French fleurs-de-lis were added to the three lions of England on his coat of arms and he was proclaimed as *Rex Angliae et Franciae*. He also laid claim to the blue livery of France by dressing his new Knights of the Garter in dark blue robes. His claim to France led to the Hundred Years War and shaped England's diplomacy in Europe for generations. Even when the claim was technically made good by victory, at Agincourt in 1415, it was lost again within a generation. Despite this, the titular claim endured. ¶ Pope Leo X awarded Henry VIII the suffix *Fidei Defensor*, or 'Defender of the Faith', for writing a polemic against Luther. The title, intended for Henry alone, was retained in a deliberate display of irony against the superiority of Rome by his successors. Following his marriage to Anne Boleyn, Henry made it treason not to recognize him as 'of the Church of England and also of Ireland, on Earth the Supreme Head' and he elevated Ireland to a kingdom in his title. This list of kingdoms was made complete in 1603, when Elizabeth I died and James, the King of Scots, came south to claim his cousin's titles in what was described as the Union of the Crowns. For the sake of uniformity, the ancient Scottish title was changed from 'of Scots' to 'of Scotland', so ending a tradition that reflected that these were monarchs of people and not of land. Cohesion was achieved with the Act of Union between England and Scotland in 1707. For the first time since Edgar the Peaceable, a Head of State, Queen Anne, was described as monarch of Britain. In 1801 empty claims to France and Aquitaine were finally dropped, when the union of kingdoms was extended to include Ireland. ¶ The growing Empire enabled Disraeli to persuade Parliament to create Queen Victoria Empress of India in 1876, a title that was dropped at India's independence in 1947. In 1927, following Ireland's division by Home Rule, imperial possessions were redefined when George V was styled king of 'the British Dominions beyond the Seas'. As the Empire dissolved, its affiliation was maintained through the formation of the Commonwealth of Nations, of which George VI was titled as Head. This family of former colonies, which ranged from independent republics, such as India and Pakistan, to the self-governing realms that held the king still as their Head of State, was oddly named. 'Commonwealth' still echoed the Civil War, when Oliver Cromwell removed both crown and head from the anointed monarch in 1649, making himself Lord Protector of the Commonwealth. ¶ When she inherited her father's crown in 1952, Elizabeth II's titles were reorganized so as to reflect that she was individually queen of many different nations: for instance, Queen of Australia, of New Zealand and of Canada, countries that no longer have any constitutional ties with the United Kingdom. Therefore, while many countries each possess their own title for her, in Britain the coins still spell out the titles of Cerdic's successor as 'Elizabeth II.DG.REG.FD.', representing *Deo Gratia Regina Fidei Defensor*, or 'By Grace of God, Queen, Defender of the Faith'. Further changes may come as a response to devolution. ¶ At the opening of Scotland's new Parliament in 1999, the Presiding Officer hinted at restoration of the traditional title, Queen of Scots. It would be just another step in the path by which the title seeks to adapt in order to

reflect changing needs. The role of the Sovereign is to serve the title and thereby to serve both the people and the constitution.

The Queen of Canada wears the insignia as Sovereign of two Canadian orders of chivalry. The Order of Canada comprises a Royal Crown hanging from the national colours of red and white in a bowed ribbon, from which is suspended a white enamel hexagonal snowflake. In the centre is the red maple leaf from the national flag. This is also at the centre of the blue enamel cross of the Order of Military Merit, which in turn hangs from a Royal Crown that is suspended from a yellow-edged dark blue ribbon.

Page of Honour
Thomas Howard was Third Page of Honour to the Queen from 1995 to 1998. The distinction of being a Page of Honour is usually granted to young sons of members of the nobility and gentry, and especially of senior members of the Royal Household. The current four Pages include two cousins, Arthur Chatto and Charles Armstrong-Jones, respectively 20th and 16th in line to the throne. The Queen is their great-aunt. M C

Chelsea In-Pensioner
Battery Sergeant Nicholas Keating MM was 101 years old when he sat for this portrait photograph in the Royal Hospital, Chelsea, where he was resident for nearly 12 years. His scarlet coat is based on the service dress from the Duke of Marlborough's time, and his hat is called a Shako. He wears, from left to right, the Military Medal, the First World War medals known as 'Pop, Dick and Harry', the Defence Medal and War Medal from the Second World War and the Long Service and Good Conduct Medal. In the 320 years of its existence the Royal Hospital has been home to over 25,000 In-Pensioners, and finally accepted its first women candidates in 2009. J C

The Sovereign
Every day when the Queen is in residence in Balmoral during the summer she attends to her duties of reading a selection of the hundreds of letters she receives daily, most of which are answered by her staff. She continues to see her Private Secretaries, who bear the red boxes containing official papers and documents that require her attention and, in some cases, approval and signature. The Queen continues the tradition of thoughtful stewardship of the Balmoral estate that has preserved Queen Victoria's 'dear paradise in the Highlands'. J C

PAGE 14
Grand Bard and Cornish Gesedd
Initiate Bards are given a bardic name by the Grand Bard when they are accepted into the College of Bards. From left to right: Gwas Towan (Christopher Uren), Grand Bard Bryallen (Ann Jenkin), Past Grand Bard Map Dyvroeth (Richard Jenkin), Past Deputy Grand Bard Cummow (Reverend Brian Coombes). Since the first Gorsedd in 1928 over 1,000 men and women have been invited to become Bards, and the current roll stands at 496. The crown worn by the Grand Bard, with its motif of oak leaves, was made by Tan Dyvarow (Francis Cargeeg) at his workshop between Hayle and Lelant. The bright yellow headdress of the Former

Grand Bard bears the Celtic symbol of the awen, a Welsh word meaning 'inspiration', to represent the attributes of Justice, Truth and Love. *Present holder* Steren Mor (Maureen Fuller). J C

PAGE 16
Baron of the Bachuil
Alastair Livingstone, the previous Baron of the Bachuil, is descended from An Gorm Mòr, renowned for his great strength. His people lived in fear of a mighty bull that lived across from Loch Linnhe, so An Gorm Mòr decided to fight the creature in a day-long struggle. On his weathered gravestone is the figure of a man holding a long staff, probably the staff of St Moluag. The Bachuil is once more in the safekeeping of the Livingstone family, having been 'temporarily' lent to the Duke of Argyll in the late 1800s upon his request to show it to a friend. It was finally returned by the 12th Duke of Argyll before his death in 2001. *Present holder* Niall Livingstone. J C

PAGE 19
Speaker of Tynwald
Tony Brown held office as Speaker of Tynwald from 2001 to 2006, before becoming Chief Minister of the Isle of Man for nearly five years. Tynwald is over 1,000 years old, and is thus the oldest parliament in the world with an unbroken existence. Each July on Tynwald Day, the members of Tynwald

process to Tynwald Hill for proceedings presided over by the Lieutenant-Governor. The year's legislation is read out by the Deemsters, and if any Act is not read out it lapses immediately. Tynwald Day was first codified by the Manx parliament on the hill in 1417, and new laws are declared in both English and Gaelic. *Present holder* The Honourable Stephen Rodan MHK. J C

PAGE 20
Hereditary High Steward of the Liberty of St Edmund
Frederick Hervey, 8th Marquess of Bristol, is the Hereditary High Steward of the Liberty of St Edmund. The impressive ruins of the Norman abbey church of St Edmund, which replaced an earlier Saxon church, suggest that it was one of the largest in the country at the time of its construction. The abbey has played its part in English history, being the site of a meeting between King John and his dissatisfied earls and barons in 1214 that led to the signing of Magna Carta a year later. J C

PAGE 23
Lord Archbishop of Canterbury
In 2012 the 104th Lord Archbishop of Canterbury the Most Reverend and Right Honourable Dr Rowan Williams announced his retirement after ten years in the role. He declared that his successor 'will need the constitution of an ox and

the skin of a rhinoceros' as he negotiates a role for the Church in the second decade of the 21st century. *Present holder* The Most Reverend and Right Honourable Justin Welby. J C

PAGE 24
Lord Paramount of Holderness
Rodrica Straker, pictured with her son Jack, became the 47th Lord Paramount of Holderness on the death of her father, John Chichester-Constable, in 2011. He had spent many years restoring the Elizabethan family home of Burton Constable, which still contains the bones of a 58-foot sperm whale. The title holds the right to 'royal fish' stranded on the nearby shore, and when a whale was stranded in 1825 it was claimed for the Lord Paramount. David Peaks, Captain, Graham Stark, Deputy Warden, and Colin Gibson, Bowman, have been members of the Burton Constable Company of Bowmen for a total of 40 years. J C

PAGE 26
Lord High Chancellor
Serving as Lord High Chancellor from May 2010 to September 2012, the Right Honourable Kenneth Clarke MP is a political veteran of several Conservative governments and has been the Member of Parliament for Rushcliffe since 1970, making him one of the longest-serving MPs currently elected. The Salisbury Room,

in which this portrait was taken, is the quiet area of the House of Lords library. The library contains some 60,000 printed books and journals, available for use by any of the 400 or so members of the Lords to support their work in making laws and holding the Government to account. *Present holder* The Right Honourable Chris Grayling MP. JC

PAGE 28
Dame de Rosel and Butler to the Duke of Normandy
Emma Lemprière-Johnston was last called upon to perform her duties as Dame de Rosel and Butler to the Duke of Normandy in May 2005, when the Queen and Prince Philip toured the Channel Islands to mark the 60th anniversary of their liberation from German occupation. This was the Queen's sixth visit as monarch, having first visited as Princess Elizabeth in 1949, when memories of the occupation were still very fresh. MC

PAGE 31
Boy Bishop of Hereford
Murray Warwick-Jones was installed as Boy Bishop of Hereford in December 2000. As part of this recently revived tradition the Boy Bishop delivers a sermon on a topic of his choosing and carries out his duties for three weeks in the lead-up to Christmas, including officiating at the carol service. Salisbury and Newcastle Cathedrals have a similar tradition, as do parish churches in Claines in Worcestershire, Longparish

in Hampshire and North Walsham in Norfolk. *Present holder* Jo Moore. MC

PAGE 32
Verderers and Agisters of the New Forest
Seated on the back bench in the Verderers' Hall are, left to right, Clive Maton (National Park Verderer), Diana Westerhoff (Natural England Verderer), Pat Thorne (DEFRA Verderer), Dionis Macnair (elected Verderer), Ralph Montagu (Forestry Commission Verderer), Dominic May (Official Verderer), Anthony Pasmore (senior elected Verderer), David Readhead (elected Verderer, co-opted), Tony Gerelli (elected Verderer) and Richard Deakin (elected Verderer). On the lower bench are, left to right, Colin Draper (Higher Level Stewardship Scheme manager), Linda Ryan (assistant clerk to the Verderers), Sue Westwood (clerk to the Verderers), Kevin Penfold (Forestry Commission acting deputy surveyor), Mark Street (Forestry Commission land agent). The Agisters standing from left to right are Peter Rix, Andrew Napthine, Mike Lovell, Robert Maton and Jonathan Gerelli. JC

PAGE 34
Keepers of the Crown Lands of the New Forest
The Keepers of the Crown Lands of the New Forest have specialist skills and knowledge that they bring to their roles. From left to right: Andy Shore (fencing and

hedging), Tim Creed (bats and forest by-laws), Jonathan Cook (butterflies), Patrick Cook (deer), Graham Wilson (country crafts and heather burning), Andy Page (former head keeper, now in charge of West Country wildlife), Ian Young (now retired), Matthew Davies (shooting and gun dog training), Howard Taylor (birds, bats and river life), Alan Stride (tree felling) and Maarten Ledeboer (butterflies and wild boar). JC

PAGE 36
Lord Warden of the Cinque Ports
Queen Elizabeth, the Queen Mother was the only woman to have held the post of Lord Warden of the Cinque Ports. Until her death in 2002, she spent time each year at Walmer Castle and was keen to play her part in this photographic collection, holding strong views about where she was to be photographed. 'Between the guns pointing at France, of course,' she declared. *Present holder* Admiral the Lord Boyce KG GCB OBE DL. JC

PAGE 39
Queen's Champion, Lord of the Manor of Scrivelsby
The current and 34th Queen's Champion and 33rd Lord of the Manor of Scrivelsby is Lieutenant-Colonel John Dymoke MBE DL. He acted as Standard Bearer of the Union Flag at the coronation of the Queen in 1953. His namesake, Sir John Dymoke, was the King's Champion at Richard II's coronation in 1377, the

first Dymoke to fulfil the role after the male line of the Marmion family, the original office holders, died out. Although he only held the military rank of captain at the time, by virtue of his title of Queen's Champion Sir John took precedence over Field Marshal Montgomery during the coronation. JC

PAGE 40
Lord Bishop of Sodor and Man
Before becoming Lord Bishop of Sodor and Man in 1989 the Right Reverend Noel Jones CB had a notable ministry as a naval chaplain, rising to become Chaplain of the Fleet and Archdeacon of the Royal Navy. Although the Isle of Man is not part of England, the diocese of Sodor and Man is a diocese of the Church of England. With only 28 parishes, it is the smallest of the Church's 44 dioceses. *Present holder* Right Reverend Robert Paterson. MC

PAGE 42
Master and Brethren of St Cross
The Reverend Tony Outhwaite was Master of the Hospital of St Cross for 13 years. Like Brother Harold Kay and Brother Jim Heavens, brothers of the almshouse must be single, widowed or divorced, over 60 years old and be willing to attend daily morning prayers in the church. They are expected to wear their gowns and tend the flowerbed outside their door. The cricket ground close by St Cross and the River Itchen is believed to be the meadow in which John

Keats was inspired to compose 'Ode to Autumn'. *Present holder* Reverend Reginald Sweet. JC

PAGE 44
Sergeant at Mace and Hornblower of Ripon
Alan Oliver, as Hornblower of Ripon, had a responsibility to prevent catastrophe from striking the city. Legend has it that if the Hornblower does not sound the horn announcing the start of the nightly Watch correctly the face of Hugh Ripley, the last Wakeman and the first Mayor, who took office in 1605, will appear in a window of the Mayor's House and plague will descend upon Ripon. Patrick Webb served as Sergeant at Mace, with responsibility for the mayor's chains of office. *Present Sergeant at Mace* Jim Vauvert. *Present Hornblower* George Pickles. JC

PAGE 46
Bailie of the Abbey Court of Holyrood and Moderator of the High Constables
John Scott Moncrieff, an Edinburgh lawyer, combines his role as Bailie of the Abbey Court of Holyrood with that of Consul of Monaco in Scotland. Geoffrey Ballantine, Moderator of the High Constables, wears the uniform of blue cloth with silver buttons and hat worn up at one side, proposed by George V in 1910. MC

PAGE 49
Lady Marcher of Cemaes and Mayor of Newport
Hyacinthe Hawkesworth was Lady Marcher of Cemaes until her death in 2011. She appointed Jeremy George as Mayor of Newport, and one of his duties was to beat the bounds on horseback every August. *Present Lord Marcher of Cemaes* Alexander Hawkesworth. *Present Mayor of Newport* John Edwards. M C

PAGE 50
Master Treasurer of the Honourable Society of the Inner Temple
During his year in office as Master Treasurer of the Inner Temple in 1996, Edward Nugee TD QC presided over not only the members, but also the Inner Temple's share of the Temples Conservation Area. This estate, combined with that of the Middle Temple, contains one of London's largest concentrations of Grade I-listed buildings. The Round Church sits at the centre of the two legal communities and their meandering boundary, which winds through the clutter of buildings marking the end of one Master Treasurer's jurisdiction and the start of another's. *Present holder* Simon Thorley QC. M C

PAGE 52
Master Treasurer and Master Reader of the Honourable Society of the Middle Temple
Michael Sherrard CBE QC was Master Treasurer of the Middle Temple in 1996, while Anthony Walton QC served as Master Reader. Middle Temple is an independent extra-parochial area, historically not governed by the City of London Corporation and falls outside the ecclesiastical jurisdiction of the Bishop of London. *Present Master Treasurer* Christopher Symons QC. *Present Master Readers* (Lent) Professor Graham Zellick CBE QC; (Autumn) The Honourable Mrs Justice Parker. M C

PAGE 54
Prime Minister and First Lord of the Treasury
When the Right Honourable David Cameron MP entered No.10 Downing Street in May 2010, after several days of tense negotiation to form a coalition government with the Liberal Democrats, he was the youngest Prime Minister for 198 years. He is the 12th Prime Minister and First Lord of the Treasury to serve under the Queen, whose reign has spanned 15 General Elections. Every Tuesday afternoon the Prime Minister of the day travels to Buckingham Palace for a short private audience with the Queen. No records are kept of what is discussed at these meetings, which give the Prime Minister a chance to draw on the wisdom and experience of the Sovereign and to offer, in return, an

insight into the pressing issues of the day. If neither the Queen nor the Prime Minister can attend in person, the discussion is conducted by telephone. M C

PAGE 59
Serjeant-at-Arms for the House of Commons
Group Captain Michael Naworynsky OBE was Deputy Serjeant-at-Arms in the House of Commons from 2008 to 2013 after a career in the RAF and the MOD. His logistics and operational training were vital in maintaining the security of Heads of State visiting Parliament. At the time of this portrait he was Acting Serjeant-at-Arms. The Serjeant, or the Deputy Serjeant, sits in the Commons chamber and is responsible for security for the duration of the sitting. *Present holder* Lawrence Ward. J C

PAGE 60
Bearer of the Dog Whipper's Rod
Anthony Turner is Bearer of the Dog Whipper's Rod at Exeter Cathedral, seen here clearing the way for Head Verger Michael Greaves, Canon Tom Honey, Deputy Head Server Malcolm Pomeroy, Head Server David Norris, Canon Carl Turner and Server John Wood. Relics of this unusual office also exist in the dog whipper's pew in St Margaret's Church in Wrenbury, Cheshire, and in Dog Acre park in Birchington-on-Sea, Kent, which was land granted to the village's dog whipper for his services. The first record of

a dog whipper, named Old Hayward, in Birchington's parish church of All Saints appears in 1622. J C

PAGE 62
Justices of the Peace and Clerk to the Justices
Sara Cator, Dick Meadows and Lisa Pank serve as Justices of the Peace (JPs) in Norfolk, assisted by Clerk to the Justices David Carrier. JPs, who come from a wide range of backgrounds and cultures, require no legal qualifications, but are carefully screened and given training. The role requires a commitment of 26 half-days a year in court, and JPs are expected to serve for at least five years. M C

PAGE 66
Heralds
The Officers of Arms, from left to right: (back row) Bluemantle Pursuivant Peter O'Donoghue, Wales Herald Extraordinary Michael Siddons, Maltravers Herald Extraordinary John Martin Robinson, Norfolk Herald Extraordinary Major David Rankin-Hunt, Arundel Herald Extraordinary Alan Dickins, Fitzalan Pursuivant Extraordinary Colonel Alastair Bruce of Crionaich; (front row) Somerset Herald David White, Lancaster Herald Robert Noel, York Herald Sir Henry Paston-Bedingfeld Bt, Clarenceaux King of Arms Hubert Chesshyre, Earl Marshal of England Duke of Norfolk, Garter King of Arms Thomas Woodcock, Norroy and Ulster King of Arms Patric Dickinson, Chester Herald Timothy

Duke, Windsor Herald William Hunt, Richmond Herald Clive Cheesman. The Robing Room, where this portrait was taken, is where the Queen puts on the Imperial State Crown and her ceremonial robes before the State Opening of Parliament. The canopy above the Chair of State is carved with the English rose, the Scottish thistle, the Irish shamrock and Queen Victoria's monogram. J C

PAGE 68
Lord Lyon King of Arms
Sir Malcolm Innes of Edingight KCVO served as Lord Lyon King of Arms for 20 years until 2001, at which time he was appointed Orkney Herald of Arms Extraordinary. In addition to being the heraldic authority for Scotland, the Lord Lyon is responsible for Scottish State ceremonies, the equivalent role to England's Earl Marshal. *Present holder* David Sellar. J C

PAGE 71
Hereditary Master of the Royal Household
Torquil Campbell, the 13th Duke of Argyll, is the latest to hold the many titles accreted over the centuries. One such title is Chief of Clan Campbell, or MacCailein Mòr, which is Gaelic for 'the Great MacColin' and refers to Cailean Mòr (Colin the Great) of Lochawe, who was killed in fighting with Alexander, Lord of Lorne, in 1296. M C

PAGE 72
Hereditary Captain of Dunstaffnage
Michael Campbell of Dunstaffnage is the Hereditary Captain of one of Scotland's oldest stone castles, which overlooks Loch Etive in Argyll and Bute. Legend tells of a ghost, known as the Ell-maid, that haunts the ruins in the form of a girl dressed in green. The four-storey gatehouse, a harled tower house, remains the property of the Captain of Dunstaffnage and is where he spends three nights each year to maintain the hereditary title. J C

PAGE 75
Master of Bruce
The Honourable James Bruce is Master of Bruce and grandson of the 11th Earl of Elgin and 15th Earl of Kincardine. His ancestor Robert the Bruce is buried in the abbey at Dunfermline, which was once the capital of Scotland. The pulpit under which the tomb rests was carved out of Scottish oak in 1890 by William Paterson of Edinburgh, as a gift to the Earl of Elgin. J C

PAGE 76
Duke
Ralph Percy, 12th Duke of Northumberland, oversees

a large business enterprise from within the walls of Alnwick Castle that extends well beyond the modern-day visitor attractions of the castle and its grounds. Farming has given way to the development and management of property as the main income stream that secures the heritage of this dukedom for future generations. It is estimated that, since the Black Prince became the first domestically appointed Duke in 1337, there have been fewer than 500 British men to have held this rank. The last non-royal dukedom was created in 1889 for the Earl of Fife in honour of his marriage to Princess Louise, Queen Victoria's granddaughter. Sir Winston Churchill was offered a dukedom upon his retirement from politics in 1955, a special honour as former British Prime Ministers retiring from the Commons are more usually offered earldoms, but he declined. M C

PAGE 78
Governor of the Company of Merchant Adventurers of York
Trevor Copley served his one-year term as Governor of the Company of Merchant Adventurers of York in 2001 while working as a director of Rowntree's. Many members of the Rowntree family have been Merchant Adventurers through the generations, as membership is passed down by patrimony as well as by nomination. Construction of the Merchant Adventurers' Hall began in 1357, and this Grade 1-listed building is a rare survivor of a structure that combines the three functions of a medieval guild. The Great Hall is where the merchants first gathered to conduct their business and to meet each other socially; the Undercroft served as an almshouse for the sick and the poor; and the Chapel offered spiritual care. *Present holder* Fred Brown. J C

PAGE 80
Lord Warden of the Stannaries
Sir Nicholas Bacon Bt OBE DL has served as Lord Warden of the Stannaries since 2006. Once the holder of this office was virtually an independent governor in the distant county of Cornwall, but today the Lord Warden still ensures that the Duke of Cornwall gets his income, albeit not from tin, which is now too costly to mine. Most of the mines are flooded or ruined, such as the Phoenix United Mine near Minions on Bodmin Moor (pictured), though several have been given a new lease of life as museums, to mine the rich seam of tourism in the South-west. M C

PAGE 82
Lord of the Manor of Alcester
Henry Seymour, the 9th Marquess of Hertford, is Lord of the Manor of Alcester. He sits surrounded by the Court Leet (left to right): Bread Weigher John Bull, Fish and Flesh Tasters Ian Taylor and Michael Jackson, Ale Tasters William Bowen and Glynn Bromwich, Marshal to the Court Jeremy Howell, Constable Ron Leek, High Bailiff David Young, Surveyor of the Highways Bob Allard, Hayward Keith Greenway, Steward of the Manor John Hill, Immediate Past High Bailiff Foster Richardson, Search and Sealer of Leather Bernard Hyde, Brook Looker Hamilton Leek, Chapelayne Reverend David Capron, Town Crier and Beadle Keith Tomlinson, Low Bailiff Rory Duff. J C

PAGE 85
Master of the Horse
Saville Crossley, 3rd Lord Somerleyton, entered public service in 1972 when he was appointed a Lord-in-Waiting to the Queen and became Master of the Horse in 1991, a post he held for seven years. Like his grandfather, the 1st Lord Somerleyton, he was created a Grand Cross of the Victorian Order. *Present holder* Samuel Vestey, 3rd Baron Vestey. M C

PAGE 86
Master of the Rolls
Lord Bingham of Cornhill's distinguished legal career included nearly four years as Master of the Rolls, followed by his appointment as Lord Chief Justice, the first Master of the Rolls to be given that position for over 350 years. His contribution to public life was recognized when he became the first judge to be made a Knight of the Garter. *Present holder* The Right Honourable Lord Dyson. M C

PAGE 88
Searcher of the Sanctuary and High Bailiff of Westminster Abbey
Sir Roy Strong, a distinctive figure in the world of the arts, has been Searcher of the Sanctuary and High Bailiff

of Westminster Abbey since 2000. Lord Luce KG GCVO succeeded Lord Hurd as High Steward in 2011. Elizabeth Woodville, consort of Edward IV, twice sought Sanctuary in the Abbey with her children during the Wars of the Roses, and in 1470 gave birth to the future Edward V while there. J C

PAGE 91
Queen's Remembrancer
During his 11-year period as the Queen's Remembrancer Master Robert Turner oversaw the annual Trial of the Pyx ceremony, dating from 1249. The Queen's Remembrancer swears in a jury of 26 goldsmiths who then count, weigh and measure a sample of 88,000 gold coins produced by the Royal Mint. 'Pyx' is the name of the box in which the coins are kept. *Present holder* Steven Whitaker. M C

PAGE 92
Lord High Admiral of the Wash
Michael le Strange Meakin holds the hereditary title of Lord High Admiral of the Wash. The former family home of Hunstanton Hall provided inspiration for P.G. Wodehouse, a regular visitor, who used to write while drifting around the moat in a punt. He would have appreciated the whimsy of a land-based admiralty. J C

PAGE 95
Lord Mayor of London
Alderman David Wootton was the 684th Lord Mayor of London from 2011 to 2012, and is a Past Master of the Worshipful Company of Fletchers. His officers were Swordbearer Lieutenant-Colonel Richard Martin MBE, Common Cryer and Serjeant-at-Arms Colonel Geoffrey Godbold OBE TD DL, and City Marshal Colonel Billy King-Harman CBE. *Present holder* Roger Gifford. JC

PAGE 97
Lord Mayor of London
Alderman Michael Oliver was Lord Mayor of London in 2001 and is a Past Master of the Worshipful Company of Ironmongers. Behind him, from left to right, stand the Drumbeater with Musketeers, the Company of Pikemen, and two officers of the Company of Pikemen and Musketeers: the Captain, Colonel Richard Burford TD, and the Lieutenant, Captain David Horn. MC

PAGE 98
City Remembrancer
The present City Remembrancer is Paul Double LVO, who took office in 2003. The Remembrancer is the only non-Member of

Parliament who is allowed to sit in Parliament, and he can also attend sittings in the House of Lords. There have been many moves to remove the City's special ability to petition Parliament, which was last invoked in its full ceremonial form in 1948 when the City ceased to be a separate parliamentary constituency. JC

PAGE 100
Livery Companies – Master of Tallow Chandlers
Brigadier Keith Prosser was the 437th Master of the Worshipful Company of Tallow Chandlers, which received its Royal Charter in 1462. The candles produced by tallow chandlers, from animal fat, were to be found in humbler surroundings than those made by wax chandlers, whose beeswax candles graced churches and fine houses. The Company was obliged to supply the City Watch with 60 men and its candles helped to light the streets. The original Tallow Chandlers' Hall, built on the buried walls of the Roman Governor's palace, was destroyed in the Great Fire of London, save for two beams that are now kept in the cellars of the current building. The 'new' Hall was completed in 1677 and survived the Blitz to remain one of the City's best-preserved livery halls. *Present holder* Sir Michael Snyder. JC

PAGE 102
Senior Grecian
When she was Senior Grecian at Christ's Hospital School, Lucy Palmer would have given an oration on

Speech Day before the Lord Mayor of London. Christ's Hospital is often referred to as Bluecoats after the distinctive uniform, known as 'Housey' in school slang. When plans were discussed to update the Tudor-style uniform, over 95 per cent of pupils voted to retain it, wishing to maintain the strong traditions that give the school its unique identity. MC

PAGE 104
King's College Choristers
For some 30 million listeners around the world Christmas only truly begins when the first notes of 'Once in Royal David's City' are broadcast from the 16th-century chapel of King's College, Cambridge. Moments before the service starts on Christmas Eve the choirmaster will tell one of the young choristers that he has been chosen to sing the first solo. The choir has now formed its own record label to distribute its recordings after many years with EMI. MC

PAGE 106
Tolly-keepers of Winchester College
Winchester College boasts one of the richest slangs of any of Britain's many public schools. Indeed, its slang even has its own name, 'notions', and 'New Men' (new pupils) are issued with a slim volume listing the most common 'notions' to aid their initiation into the complex traditions of this ancient school. MC

PAGE 110
Lord of the Isles
While Prince Charles, the Prince of Wales, became Lord of the Isles upon his mother's accession, one tiny island, Cara off Kintyre, acts as a reminder to its owners, the Macdonalds of Largie who are descendants of the original Lords of the Isles, of their once far-reaching family inheritance. JC

PAGE 112
Lady of the Isles
When in Scotland, Camilla, Duchess of Cornwall and Lady of the Isles, stays at Birkhall on the Balmoral estate. This was the former home of Queen Elizabeth, the Queen Mother, who referred to it affectionately as a 'little big house'. JC

PAGE 114
Messenger Sergeant Major and Clerk of the Cheque of the Yeomen of the Guard
Messenger Sergeant Major Alexander Dumon MVO MBE and Clerk of the Cheque and Adjutant Colonel Shaun Longsdon held their posts for eight and 13 years respectively. The Messenger Sergeant Major taps his silver-headed black baton on the ground as the left foot falls, when the Yeomen of

the Guard march. The Clerk of the Cheque, who lives in St James's Palace, must have reached the rank of lieutenant-colonel or major in the army or the marines in order to be appointed. *Present Messenger Sergeant Major* Clive Stevens. *Present Clerk of the Cheque* Brigadier David Innes OBE. MC

PAGE 116
Standard Bearer of Her Majesty's Body Guard of the Honourable Corps of Gentlemen-at-Arms
Major Michael Webster is Standard Bearer of the Honourable Corps of the Gentlemen-at-Arms, while Major Rupert Lendrum and Major Charles Macfarlane are two of the 27 Gentlemen. The uniform of the Corps is that of a Dragoon Guard's officer from the 1840s, with epaulettes to protect from sword blows to the shoulder, and swan feather plumes in their helmets. Their axes were adopted in 1526 to provide more efficient protection when fighting on foot. The three golden tassels represent the cloth that was used to soak up blood and were introduced to keep a reliable grip on the handle. *Present holder* Major General Jonathan Hall CB OBE. MC

PAGE 118
Queen's Swan Marker
David Barber was named as the Queen's Swan Marker in 1993. He is aided here by Guy and Lee Wootten, whose family firm of boat builders at Cookham Dean has existed in the same spot for over 100 years. With

the welfare of swans on the busy Thames uppermost in his responsibilities, the Swan Marker arranges the temporary removal of the birds during summer rowing regattas. JC

PAGE 121
Gentleman Usher of the Black Rod
Lieutenant-General David Leakey CMG CBE was appointed Gentleman Usher of the Black Rod in 2010. The office used to rotate among retired senior officers from the Armed Forces, but since 2002 recruitment has been opened up, although it is still a Crown appointment with responsibility for the security of the House of Lords. JC

PAGE 123
Clerk of the Closet
The Bishop of Guildford the Right Reverend Christopher Hill wears the Badge of Office of the Clerk of the Closet in the Chapel Royal. In the balcony to his left, in red, is the Deputy Clerk of the Closet, Sub-Dean of the Chapels Royal, Sub-Almoner and Domestic Chaplain to the Queen, the Reverend Prebendary William Scott, and dressed in black is Philip Chatwin, the Keeper of the Closet. In the body of the chapel is David Baldwin RVO, the Serjeant of the Vestry, who holds the silver virge made for George II in 1727. JC

PAGE 124
Lord-Lieutenant and Custos Rotulorum
Lady (Elizabeth) Gass has been Lord-Lieutenant of Somerset since 1998 and was formerly chairman of Exmoor National Park and a member of the English Heritage Commission. Her home is in West Somerset, in the historic house where her family, the Acland-Hoods and their ancestors, have lived for many generations since the manor was granted to an ancestor in the reign of Henry II. Several of Lady Gass's Hood forebears served in the Royal Navy, rising to high rank, including Captain Alexander Hood, who sailed round the world with Captain Cook. JC

PAGE 126
Master of Trinity House
Prince Philip was Master of the Corporation of Trinity House for 42 years, the longest serving Master in its nearly 500-year history. The Duke's great-great-grandfather, Prince Albert, also served as Master, and this portrait mimics an engraving in the Royal Collection that depicts Prince Albert standing in the same position in the entrance hall of Trinity House. During the Second World War some lighthouse lights were extinguished and others dimmed, so Trinity House pilots worked at night to guide ships into safe ports. During the Thames Diamond Jubilee Pageant in 2012 *Trinity House Number 1* boat, carrying the present Master, preceded the Royal Barge,

exercising its traditional role of escorting the monarch when in territorial waters. *Present holder* HRH the Princess Royal. JC

PAGE 129
Chief Yeoman Warder
Tom Sharp was proud to be the first Chief Yeoman Warder from Merseyside and worked at the Tower of London for 20 years. The Warders, who live in residences carved into the walls around the Tower, must have completed a minimum of 22 years in the Armed Forces and achieved the minimum rank of warrant officer before joining the corps. *Present holder* Alan Kingshott. JC

PAGE 130
Queen's Guide over Kent Sands
Cedric Robinson MBE has been Queen's Guide over Kent Sands for more than 50 years. In guiding the unwary over the treacherous sands of Morecambe Bay he was walked the equivalent of twice around the world. He once took Prince Philip across the sands by horse and carriage, but has yet to escort the Queen. The quixotic qualities of the terrain have influenced local vocabulary. There is a saying in these parts that 'It'll mire a cat', meaning that even a nimble cat would sink in such dangerously shifting sands. The Bay's 120 square miles have even swallowed entire cars, minus their foolhardy occupants. JC

PAGE 132
Abbot of St Benet-at-Holme
The Right Reverend Graham James took on the ancient title of Abbot of St Benet-at-Holme when he was enthroned as Bishop of Norwich in 2000. On the first Sunday of August the Abbot preaches a service at this isolated ruin, arriving along the River Bure by means of the traditional Norfolk wherry. The mill within the abbey gatehouse was originally built to crush colza seed for oil lamps but was converted into a drainage mill in the 1800s. MC

PAGE 135
Lord Clerk Register and Keeper of the Signet
David Charteris, 12th Earl of Wemyss and 8th Earl of March KT DL, served as Lord Clerk Register and Keeper of the Signet for 33 years. The office finally became purely ceremonial when Scotland's Principal Clerk of Session was granted a commission that allows the Signet to be used. *Present holder* The Right Honourable Lord Mackay of Clashfern KT PC QC. JC

PAGE 137
Poet Laureate
When Andrew Motion succeeded Ted Hughes as

Poet Laureate in 1999, he became the first poet to hold the post for a fixed term of ten years. After Alfred, Lord Tennyson's death in 1892, who had been Poet Laureate for 42 years, still the longest tenure of any laureate, the post was left vacant for four years as no one was deemed worthy to follow him. *Present holder* Carol Ann Duffy. MC

PAGE 138
Mr Houison Craufurd
Since washing the Queen's hands in 1954 Peter Houison Craufurd, 27th Laird of Craufurdland and Braehead, was not called upon to perform the service again, although he always had a silver ewer, a silver bowl and a silver salver holding a towel ready to carry out his duties. If need be he would have called upon his sons Alexander and Simon as the ceremony requires three people. *Present holder* Alexander Houison Craufurd. JC

PAGE 141
Hereditary Royal Falconer
John Borthwick, 24th Lord Borthwick, holds the title of Hereditary Royal Falconer, following the death of his father, who successfully established his family's claim to the Borthwick title in 1986. Vital documents to support the claim were discovered in an old cardboard box under the billiard table in a house on the Borthwick estate, near Edinburgh. The peregrine falcon is one of the fastest creatures on the planet, capable of reaching speeds of over 200 miles per hour in a stoop, or head-first dive. JC

[245]

PAGE 142
Lord Mallard of All Souls
At the last 'hunting the Mallard' ceremony at Oxford's All Souls College in 2001, Dr Martin West, as Lord Mallard, sang the Mallard Song. The first verse and chorus are as follows: '*The Griffine, Bustard, Turkey & Capon | Lett other hungry Mortalls gape on | And on theire bones with Stomacks fall hard, | But lett All Souls' Men have ye Mallard. | Hough the bloud of King Edward, | By ye bloud of King Edward, | It was a swapping, swapping mallard!*' Since 2010 candidates for All Souls' coveted Examination Fellowships have no longer had to answer the notorious one-word exam question. Candidates for the two annual seven-year fellowships must still sit 12 hours of rigorous exams in four papers, however. JC

PAGE 144
Chancellor of Cambridge University
Lord Salisbury of Turville was elected the 108th Chancellor of Cambridge University in 2011, and joked in his installation address that seven of his predecessors ended their terms of office on the executioner's block. The Chancellor is elected for life, although his predecessor, the Duke of Edinburgh, retired at the age of 90, and serves as the constitutional head of the university with 'power to see that all officers of the university duly perform their duties'. With roles to play in university ceremonies, Carl Hodson is the University

Marshal, Fergus Todd is the Chancellor's Train-Bearer, and Nicola Hardy and Sheila Scarlett are the Senior and Junior Esquire Bedells respectively. MC

PAGE 146
Bodley's Librarian
David Vaisey CBE was Bodley's Librarian for ten years until 1996. Oxford University's Bodleian Library is a constantly growing resource, with currently 11 million volumes in storage and 50,000 e-books. Latest acquisitions include 10,000 boxes of material from the Oxfam archive, the worldwide charity founded in Oxford in 1942, which will join such cultural treasures as four engrossments of Magna Carta and a copy of Shakespeare's First Folio, which is currently being digitized to allow universal access. *Present holder* Sarah Thomas. MC

PAGE 148
Senior Constable of Oxford University
George Davis was Senior Constable of the Oxford University Police, a position that is now known as Principal Proctors' Officer since the Constabulary was disbanded and re-formed to carry out the same duties of disciplinary investigations, crowd control and assisting at ceremonies, but without police powers. Bowler hats are still worn for ceremonial occasions by the two full-time and 12 part-time officers. *Present holder* Tim Pearson. MC

PAGE 154
Queen of Scots
While the Queen is a frequent visitor to her beloved Scotland, during her Diamond Jubilee celebrations in 2012 she made a special celebratory tour, and was welcomed to her 'ancient and hereditary kingdom of Scotland' by the Lord Provost in the Ceremony of the Keys in Edinburgh. To commemorate the history of the Most Ancient and Most Noble Order of the Thistle, which honours Scots who have contributed to public life, she attended a service with its Knights. JC

PAGE 155
Knight of the Thistle
George Younger, 4th Viscount Younger of Leckie KT KCVO, was made a Knight of the Most Ancient and Noble Order of the Thistle in 1995. In 2012 the Queen made Prince William an 'Extra Knight', in common with his grandfather, father and aunt, the Princess Royal. 'Extra Knights' do not count towards the 16-member limit of the order. JC

PAGE 156
Chief of Clan Cameron
The 28th Chief of Clan Cameron, Donald Cameron,

served with the Queen's Own Cameron Highlanders (TA). This regiment was the last to wear the kilt in battle, earning themselves the soubriquet 'Ladies from Hell'. The Lord Lyon Court has registered 149 clans with clan chiefs. JC

PAGE 158
Captain General of the Queen's Body Guard
The Royal Company of Archers have many duties during visits to Scotland by the Queen. They attend the annual garden party at the Palace of Holyroodhouse, and the service of installation of Knights of the Thistle at St Giles' Cathedral in Edinburgh. The Company provided a guard on vigil during Queen Elizabeth, the Queen Mother's lying-in-state. Members of the Royal Company of Archers, from far left to right: Major General Mark Strudwick CBE; Colonel A.K. Miller OBE; Officer: Thomas Watt; Captain General and Gold Stick: Major Sir Hew Hamilton-Dalrymple Bt GCVO; Ensign: Captain George Burnet LVO; Brigadier: Colonel Bill Bewsher LVO OBE. *Present holder* David Ogilvy, 13th Earl of Airlie KT GCVO. MC

PAGE 160
Sisters of the Hospital of the Most Holy and Undivided Trinity
Anne Staley, Heather Scott and Dorothy Moon are three of the 12 Sisters of the Hospital of the Most Holy and Undivided Trinity, who, according to the rules of the 17th-century foundation,

are expected to 'live lovingly together, as Sisters ought to do, and... help and cherish one another in sickness and in health'. MC

PAGE 162
Gold Stick in Waiting
The office of Gold Stick in Waiting is shared between the Colonel of the Life Guards, currently Field Marshal the Lord Guthrie of Craigiebank GCB LVO OBE DL, and the Colonel of the Blues and Royals, currently the Princess Royal, who is the first woman to hold the appointment. In addition to attending State occasions Gold Stick in Waiting takes part in the processions for the coronation and the State Opening of Parliament. JC

PAGE 164
Governor of the Royal Hospital
General Sir Redmond Watt KCB KCVO CBE is Governor of the Royal Hospital in Chelsea. He stands with In-Pensioners David Griffin of the Royal Marines and Warwickshire Regiment, Dorothy Hughes of the Royal Artillery, Douglas Clarke of the London Scottish and Tom Metcalf of the Parachute Regiment. The statue of founder Charles II was regilded to commemorate the Golden Jubilee in 2002. JC

PAGE 166
Grand Master
Field Marshal HRH the Duke
of Kent KG GCMG GCVO
ADC(P) has been Grand
Master of the United Lodge of
England since 1967. To raise
funds to build Freemasons'
Hall, one of England's finest
art deco buildings, a lunch
was held in 1925 at London's
Olympia for some 7,250
Freemasons, which is believed
to be the largest ever catered
meal served in Europe. The
Grand Master is always a
member of the British Royal
Family, thus he may appoint a
Pro Grand Master to act as his
principal adviser and to take
his place on occasions when
royal duties prevent him from
attending. JC

PAGE 168
Queen's Bargemaster
Robert Crouch MVO became
a Queen's Waterman in
1981 and Bargemaster in
1989, before retiring in 2003.
He was apprenticed to his
father as a third-generation
Thames waterman at the
age of 17. There are 24
Royal Watermen under the
command of the Queen's
Bargemaster. The original
number of 48 was halved by
Edward VII. At the State
Opening of Parliament the
Queen's Bargemaster and
four Royal Watermen travel
as boxmen on coaches in
order to guard the regalia as
it travels from Buckingham
Palace to the Palace of
Westminster and back. *Present
holder* Paul Ludwig. MC

PAGE 170
Lord Great Chamberlain
David Cholmondeley, 7th
Marquess of Cholmondeley
KCVO, is Lord Great
Chamberlain. Since 1902
this hereditary title has
been jointly vested in the
families of the marquessate
of Cholmondeley, the
earldom of Ancaster and the
marquessate of Lincolnshire,
and is held in turn for the
duration of a monarch's
reign. JC

PAGE 173
Member of Privy Council
Lord Steel of Aikwood KBE
PC was appointed a Privy
Counsellor in 1977, after his
election to the leadership
of the Liberal Party. He
wears the uniform of the
Privy Council given to him
by the family of Sir Henry
Campbell-Bannerman, the
Liberal Prime Minister from
1905 to 1908. According to
a custom believed to have
been introduced by Queen
Victoria after the death of
Prince Albert, Privy Council
meetings are held standing up,
and even the Queen remains
standing. JC

PAGE 174
*Knight Grand Cross of Order
of Bath*
Air Chief Marshal Sir Michael

Alcock GCB KBE, like many
other Knights Grand Cross
of the Order of the Bath, had
a distinguished career in the
Armed Forces before retiring
from the air force in 2006.
The order consists of the
Sovereign, the Great Master
(currently the Prince of Wales)
and three classes of members:
120 Knights and Dames Grand
Cross (GCB), 295 Knights and
Dames Commander (KCB and
DCB) and 1,455 Companions
(CB). JC

PAGE 178
*Governor and Commander-in-
Chief of Gibraltar*
Admiral Sir Hugo White
GCB served as Governor
and Commander-in-Chief
of Gibraltar from 1995
to 1997. The Governor's
residence since 1728 was
originally a Franciscan
convent, completed in 1531.
Its dining room is believed to
contain the most extensive
display of heraldry in the
Commonwealth. *Present
holder* Vice Admiral Sir Adrian
Johns KCB CBE KStJ ADC. JC

PAGE 181
*Hereditary Banner Bearer of
Scotland*
Alexander Scrymgeour,
12th Earl of Dundee, is
Hereditary Banner Bearer of
Scotland. Prior to the official
restoration of the earldom
of Dundee in 1953, the 7th
de jure Earl was presented
as Banner Bearer at George
IV's levee in Edinburgh in
1822, and the 9th de jure Earl
was commanded by Queen
Victoria to attend as Banner
Bearer when a statue of the
Prince Consort was unveiled
in Edinburgh in 1876. JC

PAGE 182
*Bearer of the National Flag of
Scotland*
Ian Maitland, 18th Earl of
Lauderdale, is the Hereditary
Bearer of the National Flag
of Scotland. The Saltire,
the oldest flag in the Union,
the Commonwealth and
Europe (Denmark's is the
oldest state flag, dating to
1219), is commemorated at
Athelstanford, the village 20
miles east of Edinburgh that
was the site of Angus's vision
of St Andrew in 832. JC

PAGE 185
*Perpetual Warden of the
Woodmen of the Forest of Arden*
Charles Finch-Knightley,
12th Earl of Aylesford, is
Perpetual Warden of the
Woodmen of the Forest of
Arden. The Woodmen's
shooting ground is at Forest
Hall on the Packington
Estate in Warwickshire. A
traditional song is sung to
the winner of the society's
archery tournaments by his
fellow Woodmen: '*Hail to
the hero, winner of the Bugle |
Better than the rest this morning
| What a great surprise! | Some
will thank their lassie, | Some
will call it art. | Some will be
more truthful, | Just a lucky
dart.*' The man who has made
many of the Woodmen's
bows, Alan Pritchard, was
honoured by the Worshipful
Guild of Bowyers with its
Gold Certificate in 2007 in
honour of his contribution to
the 'mistery' of bowyery. JC

PAGE 186
*Queen's Trustee of the British
Museum*
HRH Prince Richard, the
Duke of Gloucester KG GCVO,
is the Queen's Trustee on the
Board of the British Museum.
The Coins and Medals
department, for which he has
supervisory responsibility,
holds over a million objects,
including coinage from the
7th century BC. JC

PAGE 188
*Keeper of the Royal Academy
Schools*
Eileen Cooper RA was
made Keeper of the Royal
Academy Schools in 2011,
the first woman to be elected
as an officer of the Academy.
She emerged as a major
British figurative artist in the
1980s. Alex Chase White,
Coco Crampton and Alice
Theobald are studying for
the Schools' Postgraduate
Diploma in Fine Art. They
follow in the footsteps of
such illustrious alumni as
Constable, Turner, William
Blake and Sir Anthony Caro,
who studied sculpture at the
Schools before becoming
an assistant to Sir Henry
Moore. In recent years the
disciplines available for study
have broadened to include
installation and time-based
and digital media. JC

Sculptor in Ordinary in Scotland

Alexander Stoddart became the 7th Sculptor in Ordinary in Scotland in 2008, succeeding Sir Eduardo Paolozzi. He traces his beginnings as a sculptor to his early fascination with the Wallace monument at the foot of the road on which he lived as a boy in Elderslie, traditional birthplace of the Scottish hero. JC

Herb Strewer

Miss Jessica Fellowes, holder of the honorary title of Herb Strewer, has not yet been called upon to perform her services for royalty. However, in 2003 the Herb Society asked her to open the garden at Northamptonshire's Sulgrave Manor, ancestral home of George Washington, upon which she strewed fragrant herbs. MC

Superintendent of the Corps of Queen's Messengers

Major Iain Bamber was Superintendent of the Corps of Queen's Messengers, who carry classified material between the Foreign and Commonwealth Office (and other government departments) and overseas posts. There are currently 15 Queen's Messengers, reduced from a staff of 25 under Major Bamber. *Present holder* Tony Brown MC

Officers of the Most Venerable Order of the Hospital of St John of Jerusalem

Prelate Right Reverend Michael Mann KCVO, Bailiff of Egle the 3rd Lord Remnant CVO, Chancellor Professor Anthony Mellows TD and Lord Prior the 3rd Lord Vestey served as officers of the Order of St John of Jerusalem. A restructuring of the order's constitution in 1999 removed restrictions of nationality and religious belief on full membership. *Present holders* Prelate Right Reverend John Nicholls, Bailiff of Egle Robin Oake MBE QPM, Chancellor Reverend Canon Dr Paul Denby, Lord Prior Professor Anthony Mellows OBE TD. MC

President of the Methodist Conference

Reverend Dr John Taylor served his one-year term as President of the Methodist Conference in 1998. John Wesley, the founder of Methodism, was one of ten surviving children, whose mother ensured that they had six hours of daily home schooling. His family believed that the young John was marked out for special work when, aged six, he was saved from an upstairs window when the family house burnt down. *Present holder* Reverend Dr Mark Wakelin. MC

Queen's Piper and Page of the Presence

When Pipe Major Derek Potter, of the Royal Scots Dragoon Guards, became the 13th Queen's Piper in 2008, he was the first cavalry soldier to hold one of the highest honours for a piper serving in the Armed Forces. For the first time in the post's 170-year history, an Irish Guardsman rather than a Scot was appointed in 2012. *Present holder* Pipe Major David Rodgers. JC

Marshal of the Diplomatic Corps

Sir Anthony Figgis KVCO CMG, pictured here with the High Commissioner to the Court of St James's from the Republic of Zambia, His Excellency Mr Silumelume Mubukwana, served as Marshal of the Diplomatic Corps from 2001 to 2008. The Marshal accompanies Ambassadors and High Commissioners into the presence of the Queen for the handing over of Letters of Credence, in what is still a highly formal occasion. Today only the Marshal and the Queen's Equerry are required to walk backwards when they leave the Queen's presence. *Present holder* Charles Gray CMG. MC

Superior General of the Tyburn Nuns

Mother Xavier McMonagle OSB leads the Tyburn Nuns as their Superior General. This young order is expanding, with the latest nunnery to be built in the diocese of Minna in Niger State, northern Nigeria. Pilgrims arrive daily at their convent near Hyde Park to exchange the chaos of central London for the spiritual calm of the martyrs' shrine. JC

High Almoner

The Right Reverend John Taylor, Bishop of St Albans, was High Almoner from 1988 to 1997, in a succession of office holders that can be traced back to the early 12th century. The High Almoner is responsible for the Maundy Thursday service at which coins are distributed to elderly people in recognition for particular service to their communities. While the common coinage has featured three different portraits of the Queen, that on Maundy coins has remained unchanged since 1953. The coins are distributed in white and red purses: the white purse contains Maundy coins equivalent to the Queen's age, in denominations of 1, 2, 3 and 4 pence, and the red purse contains common coinage. Historically, the service was always held in London, until the Queen chose, early in her reign, to rotate the service among churches in England and Wales. In 2008 the service was held for the first time

in Northern Ireland, at St Patrick's Church of Ireland Cathedral in Armagh. *Present holder* The Right Reverend Dr John Inge, Bishop of Worcester. MC

Counsellors of State

The Duke of York and the Earl of Essex were both Counsellors of State before Prince William and Prince Harry reached the age of 21, thereby displacing Prince Edward. The Counsellors are appointed from among the Duke of Edinburgh and the four adults next in succession aged 21 or over. JC

Lieutenant-Governor and Commander-in-Chief of Jersey

General Sir John McColl KCB CBE DSO took up the five-year post of Lieutenant-Governor and Commander-in-Chief of Jersey in 2011. He retired as Deputy Supreme Allied Commander Europe. He is the first office holder to be selected by a panel made up of the island's Bailiff, a senior Jurat and a member of the appointments commission. JC

Knight Commander of the Most Noble Order of Garter

The Queen appointed Prince William Knight Commander

of the Most Noble Order of the Garter in 2008. New appointments to the order are always announced on St George's Day, while investitures are often held on the first day of Royal Ascot week, in June, when the court is at Windsor Castle. J C

PAGE 216
Keeper of the Great Clock
Mike McCann is Keeper of the Great Clock, responsible for the smooth running of possibly the world's most celebrated clock, known to millions by the name of the bell by which it is heard, Big Ben. He and his small team must, twice a year, change the time on each of Parliament's 2,000 clocks, including the Great Clock itself. J C

PAGE 218
Master Gunner of St James's Park
General Sir Timothy Granville-Chapman GBE KCB is Master Gunner of St James's Park. After 65 years in St John's Wood, the King's Troop has returned to its spiritual home of Woolwich and a state-of-the-art new garrison. The Troop's six First World War-era 13-pounder field guns have come full circle, as they were originally made in the Royal Arsenal in Woolwich. The 1913 George Gun is only used for State funerals, when it is pulled by six black Irish Draught horses from F Sub Section. The new facilities contain stabling for 140 horses and the army's largest blacksmith's forge, which shoes over 70 horses a week. J C

PAGE 221
Garrison Sergeant Major
Garrison Sergeant Major London District William Mott OBE MVO was appointed in 2002. He is in charge of the drill for all State ceremonials, such as the State Opening of Parliament and royal weddings. In recognition of such work done by Garrison Sergeant Majors, the Queen approved the revival of the original badge made for Sergeant Majors appointed to the court of William IV. Warrant Officer Class 1 'Bill' Mott served in the Falklands and was aboard HMS *Sir Galahad* with fellow Welsh Guards when it was bombed by the Argentine air force, causing the death of 48 soldiers and seamen. He is one of the last serving soldiers to have been awarded a Falklands medal. J C

PAGE 223
First Sea Lord and Chief of the Naval Staff
Admiral Sir Jock Slater GCB LVO ADC served as First Sea Lord and Chief of the Naval Staff from 1995 to 1998. The body of Admiral Lord Horatio Nelson was brought to the Old Admiralty Building, now used by the Foreign and Commonwealth Office, the night before his funeral on 9 January 1806. M C

PAGE 225
First Sea Lord and Chief of the Naval Staff
Admiral Sir Mark Stanhope KCB OBE ADC was First Sea Lord from 2009 to 2013. *Present holder* Admiral Sir George Zambellas KCB DSC. J C

PAGE 226
Order of Merit
Nathaniel Rothschild, 4th Baron Rothschild, OM GBE FBE was made a Member of the Order of Merit in recognition for his philanthropy in the arts. As a private project, he restored Spencer House, one of London's finest surviving 18th-century townhouses, and has been a major benefactor in the restoration of Waddesdon Manor. J C

PAGE 228
Chief Butler of England
Dr Siegfried Youssineau bought the Lordship of the Manor of Kenninghall in the 1990s, and with it a claim to the office of Chief Butler of England. Manorial lordships are frequently available for sale, and there are three distinct elements that comprise a manor: the title (which is most commonly bought and sold), the remaining land and any manorial rights. J C

PAGE 230
High Sheriff of Norfolk
Francis Cator served his one-year term as High Sheriff of Norfolk from April 1994. The origin of 'pricking' the name of the High Sheriff stems from the difficulty of removing a hole in vellum, compared to erasing a pen mark, thereby making it harder to tamper with the result. It was a costly honour to be chosen, and one not always willingly undertaken. *Present holder* Countess of Leicester. M C

PAGE 232
Member of Parliament
Lady Sylvia Hermon is Member of Parliament for North Down, which she first represented as an Ulster Unionist, before being elected as an independent at the 2010 General Election. Female Members of Parliament today number 146 out of a total of 650. M C

PAGE 234
President of the Supreme Court of England
The Right Honourable the Lord Phillips of Worth Matravers KG was the first President of the Supreme Court of England upon its creation in 2009. The Supreme Court is housed in the 1913 neo-Gothic Middlesex Guildhall, one of over 200 existing buildings within a mile's radius of Charing Cross that were considered as a suitable home for the final court of appeal. *Present holder* The Right Honourable the Lord Neuberger of Abbotsbury. M C

PAGE 236
The Sovereign
The Sovereign wears the 18-foot-long Robe of State, made for her coronation, and the Diamond Diadem, created for George IV to wear before his crowning in 1821 and familiar to millions from its appearance on British coins and stamps. Around her neck she wears a necklace given to Queen Victoria during her Golden Jubilee from 'the Women of the British Empire', and the Collar of the Order of the Garter. J C

PAGE 239
The Sovereign
In Canada, the Queen's official title is Her Majesty Elizabeth the Second, by the Grace of God of the United Kingdom, Canada and Her other Realms and Territories, Queen, Head of the Commonwealth, Defender of the Faith. Since her coronation the Queen has visited Canada 22 times, most recently in 2010. In 1976 she opened the Montreal Olympic Games, in which Princess Anne competed in the British Equestrian team. The Burmese tiara that the Queen wears in this portrait was made in 1973 with rubies given to her as a wedding present by the Burmese people. J C

INDEX

[252]

THE MAKING OF THE BOOK

Alastair Bruce: This book is a manifestation of both a childhood fascination and a lifetime of enquiry. My parents watched as their son, dressed as a bishop or an admiral, wandered about the garden props that served as cathedrals and warship-filled dockyards in my imagination. They witnessed coronations with crowns made of clay and saw troops reviewed by a child adorned in insignia fashioned from Cornflakes packets and silver foil. ¶ Encouraged to mature this instinctive interest by clever schools, I applied the question 'why?' to all the traditions, rituals and uniforms I encountered with every passing year. Gradually the tapestry of Britain's cultural inheritance revealed itself because in the provenance of every detail can be discovered something new and surprising about this nation's story. It really is incredible what is stored in the semiology of a painting, the trappings of a church or the impact of an ancient title. ¶ Fed up with the popular indifference to Britain's vulnerable culture that prevailed during the last two decades, often juxtaposed with a fervent desire to laud and protect the endangered detritus of foreign cultures, it was logical for me to find a way of recording and unwrapping the stories behind what Britain can boast as its own. ¶ Working with two friends who both wrestle with competing creative enthusiasm has been a tonic. Julian and Mark feel the same way about all this as I do and we are encouraged by the humour and interest that stories of our collective discoveries engender. Hopefully, our book will be a catalyst for others to look more closely at what still survives in their surroundings. Let there be no mistake, this stuff is vulnerable. The unknowing are conditioned to take the easy route and laugh at men in silk stockings. This misses a key point. ¶ Of course, Britain must modernize and evolve every element of its institutions with reinvention, but it does not need to destroy the past in this process. History proves that a confident nation can walk comfortably with its past. *Keepers* is our proclamation, with joy, of this option.

Julian Calder: The idea for *Keepers* was germinated when I read an obituary of Hamon le Strange, Lord Admiral of the Wash. I could see there was a picture here so I phoned his nephew Michael le Strange Meakin, and set in train the pursuit of offices and their holders that became this book. The aim of the photography in *Keepers* is to capture the title not the person. As a portrait photographer I am guaranteed to get a likeness, but a portrait should be more than this. I have found that to reinforce the portrait I like to include the relevant location, symbols, uniform and, if possible, history in the photograph. The portraits have involved a discussion with the subject and a location recce before the shoot itself. I asked Buckingham Palace if I could take a photograph of the Queen to commemorate the Diamond Jubilee, and the result is a portrait of the Sovereign working at her desk, in the warm autumnal afternoon light of Balmoral. I wanted to illustrate that the Queen is still fulfilling the commitments to 'service and duty' that she undertook at her coronation 60 years ago.

Mark Cator: Sheathed in ubiquitous conformity, the essence of modernity is liable to morph into utilitarian banality. Take, for example, the Superintendent of the Queen's Messengers, whom I photographed in 1996 and who is now referred to as a Secure Logistics Expert, a sort of hybrid of dictate, style and digital élan. ¶ And that was the beauty of working on *Keepers*. It documented a little bit of magic, a little bit of left field, a little bit of eccentricity, went its own way, and all along I was this small boy peering through the upstairs bannisters at the peculiarities and performances of an adult world below. Then, for a brief period, I moved from bemused observer to active photographer and became a participant in the pantheon of history that this book encapsulates. ¶ I pay tribute to the influence of Eugène Atget and Benjamin Stone, two extraordinary pioneers of photography, and am indebted to their vision and passion to document a passing world. But if *Keepers* was to mark the end of an age, then it too will serve as a small record for an evolving society.

Julian Calder and Alastair Bruce photograph the Queen in the Thistle robes by the Gelder Burn, assisted by Andy Bate. Photo Paul Whybrew.

Watched by parliamentary researcher Stephen Knott, Julian Calder photographs Lieutenant-General David Leakey, Gentleman Usher of the Black Rod, in Westminster Hall.

Mark Cator discusses the shoot with members of the Honourable Corps of the Gentlemen-at-Arms in the courtyard of St James's Palace.

Mark Cator sets up the shot for the Queen's Body Guard for Scotland outside the Palace of Holyroodhouse.

Alastair Bruce and Mark Cator arrive at No. 10 Downing Street to photograph Prime Minister David Cameron, First Lord of the Treasury.

Julian Calder and Alastair Bruce line up the shot for the Searcher of the Sanctuary and the High Steward in the cloisters of Westminster Abbey.

ACKNOWLEDGEMENTS

The authors wish to thank Her Majesty the Queen and all Members of the Royal Family for giving their time to this project. Our gratitude extends to everyone who appears in this book for giving their time, patience, support and enthusiasm, and also to all those who do not appear but who were responsible for setting up each portrait, often putting up with endless letters, emails and months of badgering. Finally, we thank Professor Phil Cleaver, Jenny Penny, Tamsin Shelton, Joe Thomas, Stephen Knott, Clare and Isabel. We certainly enjoyed travelling around the country and meeting so many different people in the making of this Diamond Jubilee Edition.

A CIP catalogue record for this book is available from the British Library

ISBN 978-0-9553253-3-5

Designed and typeset by Prof. Phil Cleaver and Jenny Penny of
et al design consultants (www.etal-design.com)
Typeset in Monotype Bembo Book
Printed and bound in Great Britain by Butler Tanner & Dennis,
(www.butlertanneranddennis.com)
Printed on 170gsm Finesse Silk

Edited by Tamsin Shelton (www.tamsinshelton.com)
Picture preparation by Joe Thomas (www.joe-digital.com)

Text copyright © Alastair Bruce, 2013 (www.alastairbruce.com)
Photographs copyright © Julian Calder 2013 (www.juliancalder.com) and
© Mark Cator 2013 (www.markcator.co.uk)

Design and layout copyright © Julian Calder Publishing 2013